Daoism and Chinese Culture

To my uncle, Ernst-August Roloff,
whose sharp mind, humor, and art of living
have been a constant source of inspiration

Daoism
and
Chinese Culture

Livia Kohn

Three Pines Press

Three Pines Press
PO Box 207
Magdalena, NM 87825
www.threepinespress.com

9   8 7 6 5 4

Second Edition, 2004
Printed in the United States of America
⊗ This edition is printed on acid-free paper that meets
the American National Standard Institute Z39.48 Standard.
Distributed in the United States by Three Pines Press.

Cover art: *Empress Chang Blessed by Daoist Deities*, San Diego Mu-
seum of Art (Gift of Mr. and Mrs. John Jeffers). Used by permission.

Library of Congress Cataloging-in-Publication Data

Kohn, Livia, 1956-
 Daoism and Chinese culture / Livia Kohn. —1st ed.
     p. cm.
Includes bibliographical references and index.
 ISBN 1-931483-00-0 (alk. paper)
1. Taoism. 2.China — Civilization. I. Title.
  BL 1920 .K64 2001
  299'.514 — dc2   2001001409
                    CIP

Contents

List of Illustrations

Part One, title. Laozi riding on his ox. Source: Contemporary poster, from Qingyang gong, Chengdu, Sichuan.

Part Two, title. The Lingbao talisman of the north. Source: *Lingbao wufuxu*.

Part Three, title. The immortal embryo exits the practitioner's body. Source: *Jinhua zongzhi*.

Part Four, title. Sinners are being punished in the second hell. Source: *Yuli zhibao chao*.

Fig. 1. The "Gymnastics Chart" from the tomb at Mawangdui. Source: *Daoyin tu*.

Fig. 2. Zhang Daoling, the first Celestial Master. Source: *Zengxiang liexian zhuan*.

Fig. 3. The layout of a Daoist monastery. Source: *Huayin xianzhi*.

Fig. 4. The gods of the Dipper in celestial procession. Source: *Doumu jing*.

Acknowledgments

This book is the result of fifteen years of teaching Daoism using a variety of different models, including historical surveys, textual readings, thematic arrangements, and theoretical, comparative analyses. In the course of my work I have compiled an anthology (*The Taoist Experience*, 1993) to make original sources accessible to students. That work has a thematic focus, presenting the mythology of the Dao, the understanding and practices of the body, various methods of meditation, and the visions of ultimate attainment, all as reflected in texts from different schools and different periods.

Now, to balance and supplement that selection of original sources, and to offer an introduction that can also be used in courses on world religions and Chinese history, I have prepared a textbook. Although formatted as a chronological survey, the text is thematically divided into four parts: Ancient Thought, Religious Communities, Spiritual Practices, and Modernity. This division serves to create a more integrated vision of the characteristics of the Daoist tradition in their historical context, and to enhance students' awareness of broader theoretical and comparative issues. These include different forms of religious organization, differences between ritual and meditation, and the role of religion in a contemporary environment.

The division also helps establish connections with relevant information on Chinese history and religion, such as Confucianism, popular religion, and the role of foreign dynasties and political measures in religious developments. This division, however, does not mean or even imply that Daoist thought occurred only in ancient times, that religious communities appeared only in the early middle ages, or that spiritual practices were the prerogatives of the Tang and Song dynasties. Indeed, all the different aspects of the Daoist religion are mentioned in all chapters, but they receive a more in-depth treatment in the appropriate parts.

There are selected citations from original materials, and every chapter has a list of supplementary references both for further readings and to original sources in translation. The suggested readings are limited and represent only a very small selection from a fast growing field of excellent scholarly research. They are largely works in English and they tend to focus more on books than on articles. This, again, does not imply that other works are not important or have not influenced the presentation of Daoism in this volume. In particular, numerous scholarly studies published in French, German, Chinese, and Japanese are not listed here even though they have been essential in developing the field of Daoist studies and in shaping my own understanding of the religion. For references to additional relevant scholarly work, including works in these various languages, the reader is referred to the relevant chapters in the *Daoism Handbook*, edited by Livia Kohn (Leiden, 2000), and the *Encyclopedia of Taoism*, edited by Fabrizio Pregadio (London, 2003).

My work on this book has tremendously benefited from the experience of teaching Daoism, and I am indebted both to Boston University for supporting this teaching and to my students over the years for their eagerness to learn and the many questions they have raised. I am also grateful to the University of Michigan, Göttingen University, and Eötvös Lorand University (Budapest), for opportunities to teach selections of Daoist texts and to present specific topics or historical periods of Daoism in advanced seminars.

In the production and editing of this book, moreover, I am greatly indebted to the encouragement and suggestions of a number of friends and colleagues, most notably John Berthrong, Stephan-Peter Bumbacher, Louis Komjathy, Jeffrey Kripal, James Miller, Harold D. Roth, and Brock Silvers, as well as the two very thoughtful readers for Three Pines Press. I also wish to thank Stephen Little for his help in obtaining the cover illustration and David Akin for his thorough copy-editing of the volume. The second edition has benefited greatly from the support of Shawn Arthur and Louis Komjathy.

Note on Transliteration

The transliteration used in this book is Pinyin, the official form of transcribing Chinese used in mainland China. Although Pinyin is most commonly used today, older works and some recent studies still make use of the traditional Wade-Giles system. Generally, vowels are very close in both systems, with the one exception that Wade-Giles uses the "ü" with umlaut while Pinyin for the most part does not, especially after the vowels "j" and "ch." The pronunciation is "ü" in either case.

Consonants differ more significantly. Whereas Pinyin conforms to standard English usage, in Wade-Giles all aspirated consonants (written with an apostrophe) are pronounced as original (T' = T, P' = P), while nonaspirated ones are pronounced softly (T = D, P = B). Thus the traditional transliteration "Taoism" and the more modern "Daoism." In addition, "J" in Wade-Giles is "R" in Pinyin, and pronounced like a deep, growling "R." Finally, the various "tch" and "dse" sounds differ:

PY	WG	Engl.	Example
x	hs	soft sh	Xu = Hsü = Shü
j	ch	soft dch	Juan = chüan = dchüen
q	ch'	sharp tch	Qi = ch'i = tchee
zh	ch	soft dch	Zhang = Chang = Dchang
ch	ch'	sharp tch	Cheng = Ch'eng = Tcheng
zhi	chih	soft dch-rr	
chi	ch'ih	sharp tch-rr	
zi	tzu	soft dse	Laozi = Lao-tzu = Laodse
ci	tz'u	sharp tse	
si	ssu	hissing sse	

Map of China

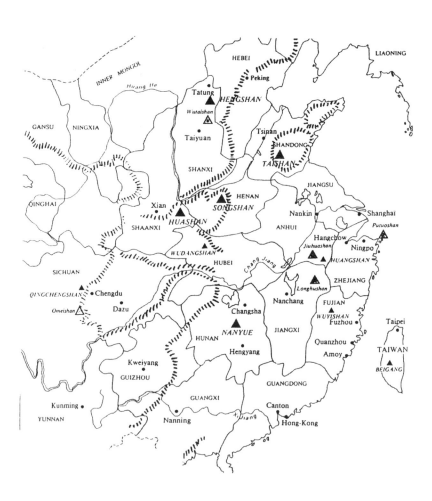

INTRODUCTION

Daoism is the indigenous organized religion of traditional China. It is best known in the West as "Taoism" — using an older mode of transliterating Chinese — and as such for its philosophy and health practices. Its philosophy is mainly associated with the notion of "Dao" or "Way," and involves ideas of naturalness and ease, nonaction and going along with the flow. Its health practices are seen in the context of Taiji quan and Qigong, and involve techniques of deep breathing, slow motion, and gentle stretches. While both philosophy and health practices form an intricate part of Daoism and play an important role in the religion, they are only partial aspects of a larger picture, which also includes a social and political vision, elaborate rituals and priestly hierarchies, protective talismans and exorcistic spells, as well as advanced spiritual meditations and ecstatic soul travels to the stars.

This multifaceted, complex nature of Daoism has only been recognized recently. Nineteeth-century missionaries, the first Westerners to come in contact with materials considered Daoist, did not see Daoism in this light at all. Rather, when confronted with the ancient texts associated with Laozi and Zhuangzi that expressed the philosophy of Dao, they could not reconcile their being part of the same tradition as religious practitioners performing rituals and self-cultivation exercises.

Instead, they were fascinated by the texts and disgusted by the practices. The philosophical works they found subtle and of a high inspirational value. Latinizing the names of Chinese thinkers (Kongfuzi into Confucius, Mengzi into Mencius), they created Laocius out of Laozi and integrated his ideas into a Western frame of thought. "Dao" became another expression for God, and the teachings of nonaction and going along with the flow were understood as a way to achieve mystical union. A notion of transcendence was attached to Dao, and a Christian sense of meekness and turning the other cheek was seen in descriptions of its weakness and softness.

2 / Daoism and Chinese Culture
2 / Daoism and Chinese Culture

The works of the ancient Daoist "thinkers" were thus rendered accept-able to a Christian perspective and treated with reverence and polite-ness. Not so the religious practices. Any ritual or cultivation activities, associated with organized communities or lineages, were considered nonsensical and superstitious, a danger to the Christian mission that had to be extirpated or at least ignored.

This initial interaction pattern of Westerners with Daoist materials is re-sponsible for the problematic distinction of "philosophical" and "reli-gious" Daoism, and the one-sided positive evaluation of the former and rigid condemnation of the latter. It is clear today that the ancient Daoist texts have very little in common with Christian values and are not "phi-losophy" in our sense at all. Rather, the ancient "thinkers" represent the first instance of a literati tradition of Daoist thought which continued throughout Chinese history. Also, even they, it seems, undertook spiri-tual excercises transmitted from master to disciple, thus setting a first model for later self-cultivation groups. Then again, looking at the tradi-tion from the perspective of practice, many ritual and longevity tech-niques of later centuries were also highly sophisticated and made impor-tant contributions to Daoist thought and Chinese culture.

A more subtle understanding of Daoism in its full complexity began with the reprint of the Daoist canon (*Daozang*) in Shanghai in 1923-25. The canon is a collection of about 1,500 texts which contains scriptures, commentaries, hagiographies, cultivation manuals, and liturgies. Com-pleted in 1445, it was the result of an intense compilation effort over sev-eral decades and continued earlier compilations of Daoist materials that went back as far as the fifth century C.E., but had been lost, burned, or otherwise destroyed. Even this canon was hidden away in the depth of monasteries and almost forgotten, so that in the early twentieth century, only two sets of woodblocks survived.

The blocks were collated and reprinted in Shanghai, and the canon be-came accessible outside of Daoist institutions for the first time. It was then picked up by local scholars as well as by academics from France and Japan, whose governments had colonial interests in East Asia. To facilitate their political ambitions, the French and Japanese encouraged their scholars to collect information on Chinese indigenous beliefs and practices and made the acquisition of texts easy. As a result, most aca-demic studies of Daoism beyond the ancient texts were first created in China, France, and Japan, whose learned scholars produced many semi-nal works in the field.

A wider spread of the study of Daoism occurred in the 1960s, after the Daoist canon was reprinted in Taiwan in a reduced, sixty-volume edition. Both affordable and transportable for the first time, it made its way not only into more libraries but also into the homes of many academics and interested students. A new generation of scholars arose who opened many new venues and aspects of the religion, and whose students are the leading scholars of today — not only in China, Japan, and France, but in many different countries all over the world. Through their work, Daoism for the first time is now being seen in a wider comparative context and evaluated in the light of abstract religious phenomena, such as shamanism, mysticism, monasticism, ritual, and meditation. Also, for the first time today a set of comprehensive and powerful reference works has been created, that standardize terminology and classifications and make the religion accessible to all.

As revealed by sources in the canon and uncovered by international scholars, the Daoist religion is highly complex. It has a long history that began with the works of Laozi and Zhuangzi around 400 B.C.E., underwent several stages of organization and development, is still evolving in China today, and has, most recently, begun to make inroads in the West. Throughout its development, it has always been closely linked with Chinese history and culture, and many of its features cannot be understood unless seen in a larger context.

For example, the thought of naturalness and nonaction of the early thinkers is but one reaction to the social and politIcal instability China underwent at the beginning of the iron age; the integrated vision of the various Daoist teachings in the sixth century was predicated by the political urge for unification at the time; and the importance of oracles and direct communication with Daoist gods today can be directly linked to the popular rise of spirit-writing in the seventeenth and eighteenth centuries. Embedded in Chinese history and culture, Daoism also grew under the strong influence of Buddhism, from which it adopted aspects of worldview, such as ideas of karma, rebirth, and hell; ethics, including precepts and monastic vows; and philosophical speculation, such as notions of emptiness and the logic of enlightened states. Daoism also fruitfully interacted with popular religion, from which it integrated numerous ritual and protective practices as well as local and martial deities.

Despite all these connections and influences, Daoism is a highly unique religious tradition with characteristics and practices clearly distinct from those of Buddhism, Confucianism, and popular religion. It has its own

specific cosmology centered on Dao as the underlying power and consti-
tuting pattern of the universe. Dao may be described as unfathomable
and ineffable or represented by celestial powers, but it is always seen as
lying at the root of creation yet manifest in all that exists on the mundane
and visible plane. Dao is subtle and soft and essentially benevolent. Me-
diated through *qi* or cosmic, vital energy — also a key concept in Chinese
medicine and general cosmology — Dao is essential and accessible to human beings in their everyday life. Aligning oneself with Dao, creating
harmony and a sense of participation in it, will bring out the best in people and create a state of overall goodness and wellbeing — in cosmos, nature, society, and the human body. Unlike in Confucianism, this state of
goodness is not primarily achieved through a moral effort; unlike in
Buddhism, worldly harmony is not ultimately unsatisfactory because it
is impermanent and conditioned by the senses; unlike in popular religion, it does not depend on ghosts, gods, and ancestors to be found. The
terminology of all these cultural strands is similar and the differences to
Daoism are often subtle, but there is a definite distinction to be made.

The same can be said about transmission patterns and the practices of
self-cultivation and ritual. Daoist transmission always involves some
form of direct contact with Dao as the underlying power of the cosmos.
It can be achieved through semi-mystical intuition that is sometimes me-
diated by a scripture, through a trance-like vision of a Daoist god or immortal, or through the offices of an ordination master and the oral
transmission of lineage secrets. Daoist self-cultivation, although it applies practices also found in Chinese medicine and the longevity tradition, is distinct from the latter because its first and foremost aim is not
the attainment of good health, more money, and a better sex-life (nothing
wrong with those, either), but a greater sense of belonging to Dao, of in-
teracting with the underlying force of the larger universe, a transformation of self and body into a more cosmic, Dao-focused entity.

Ritual, moreover, in Daoism is distinct because it takes the form of an
audience with the celestial forces and representatives of the Dao. The
Daoist priest becomes a celestial officer with all the rights and powers
this entails. His empowerment and interaction with the gods, moreover,
take place through written documents, making ritual essentially a bureaucratic act and therefore binding for both parties. This is different
from Confucian and popular rites, which are essentially sacrifices, offerings of food and prayers to the forces of nature and the ancestors. Confucian and popular ritualists remain human throughout, and the interac

tion with the gods is oral. While food and drink offerings afford a certain leverage to engage the deities in reciprocally supportive actions, the sacrifices are not as binding as the bureaucratic Daoist petitions and celestial orders. The again, Daoist ritual is also different from its Buddhist counterpart, which is an adaptation of Indian *puja* and therefore consists essentially of the formalities of a host receiving an honored guest. This, too, lacks the typical Daoist features of celestial empowerment and written communication with the divine.

In all these respects, therefore, Daoism has clear characteristics that delimitate it effectively from the other traditions of China and the various features of Chinese culture. Within the Daoist tradition, then, one can distinguish three types of organization and practice: literati, communal, and self-cultivation.

Literati Daoists are members of the educated elite who focus on Daoist ideas as expressed by the ancient thinkers, commonly known as *daojia* or "Daoist school" after an early bibliographical classification. They use these concepts to create meaning in their world and hope to exert some influence on the political and social situation of their time, contributing to greater universal harmony, known as the state of Great Peace (*taiping*). The lineage and legitimation of such literati Daoists comes from the devotion and dedication to the classical texts, which they interpret in commentaries and essays, and whose metaphors they employ in stories and poetry. They may live a life of leisure or be active in society as local officials, poets and writers, or teachers at academies, but in all cases their self-identity derives from ideas centered on Dao. Literati Daoists have been part of the tradition since its inception, and the ancient thinkers Laozi and Zhuangzi may well be considered their first example. But they also appear among commentators to the texts, patriarchs of religious schools, thinkers of Confucian or Buddhist background, and academics today.

Communal Daoists, too, are found in many different positions and come from all levels of society. They are members of organized Daoist groups that follow *daojiao* or the "Daoist teaching." They have priestly hierarchies, formal initiations, regular rituals, and prayers to the gods. Some communal Daoists organizations are tightly controlled fraternities with secret rites and limited contact to the outside world. Others are part of ordinary society, centered on neighborhood temples and concerned with the affairs of ordinary life—weddings and funerals, protection and exorcism. Their expression tends to be in liturgies, prayer hymns, and moral rules. Historically, they have been documented from the second century C.E. onward and shown a high degree of continuity over the millennia. While specific rites and organizational patterns changed, there is a distinct line from the early millenarian movements to the Celestial Masters today, and one can see a clear link between the ritual of medieval China and contemporary liturgies, both lay and monastic.

The third group of Daoists focus on self-cultivation and are known as practitioners of *yangsheng* or "nurturning life." They, too, come from all walks of life, but rather than communal rites, their main concern is the attainment of personal health, longevity, peace of mind, and spiritual immortality—either in mystical oneness with Dao or through visions of and interaction with the gods. They tend to pay little attention to political involvement, and their organization depends strongly on the master-disciple relationship. Their groups can be small and esoteric, with only a few active followers (as certain Taiji lineages), large and extensive with leanings toward organized religion (as the contemporary Falun dafa), or vague and diffuse with numerous people practicing a variety of different techniques (as in modern Qigong). Again, historical continuity is strong. The earliest examples of self-cultivation groups are found before the Common Era, tentatively among the followers of Laozi and Zhuangzi and quite evidently among the magical-practitioners and their lineages. These groups, moreover, gave rise to religious schools, beginning with a few dedicated immortality seekers and growing into leading Daoist organizations.

Interconnected from the beginning, these three types of Daoism—literati, communal, and self-cultivation—although distinct in their abstract description, are not mutually exclusive in practice. On the contrary, as contemporary practitioners often emphasize, to be a complete Daoist one must follow all three paths: studying worldview and being socially responsible, performing rituals and praying to the gods, and undertaking self-cultivation for health and spiritual advancement.

Historically, too, the tendency was to integrate all forms, so that certain literati Daoists were also ordained priest and masters of meditation, followers of organized groups studied the classics and engaged in gymnastics, and self-cultivation practitioners wrote poetry and prayed to the gods. But there is no norm, and one cannot categorically state that *only* those people are Daoists who exhibit the clear presence of *all* three kinds of religious activity. Even someone dedicated to only one aspect, a marginal or informal member of the religion, might still consider himself a Daoist and may well have an important contribution to make. To do justice to the Daoist tradition, we must therefore examine its different aspects on all the different levels and under careful consideration of their historical and cultural contexts.

Reference Works

Kohn, Livia, ed. 2000. *Daoism Handbook*. Leiden: E. Brill.

Pregadio, Fabrizio, ed. 2003. *Encyclopedia of Taoism*. London: Curzon Press.

Further Readings

Kirkland, J. Russell. 1997. "The Historical Contours of Taoism in China: Thoughts on Issues of Classification and Terminology." *Journal of Chinese Religions* 25: 57-82.

Kohn, Livia, and Harold D. Roth, eds. 2002. *Daoist Identity: History, Lineage, and Ritual.* Honolulu: University of Hawaii Press

Robinet, Isabelle. 1997. *Taoism: Growth of A Religion*. Translated by Phyllis Brooks. Stanford: Stanford University Press.

Schipper, Kristofer. 1994. *The Taoist Body*. Translated by Karen C. Duval. Berkeley: University of California Press.

Seidel, Anna. 1990. "Chronicle of Taoist Studies in the West 1950-1990." *Cahiers d'Extrême-Asie* 5: 223-347.

Sivin, Nathan. 1978. "On the Word 'Taoist' as a Source of Perplexity." *History of Religions* 17: 303-30.

Part One

Ancient Thought

CHAPTER ONE

LAOZI AND THE DAODE JING

The earliest thinker venerated in the Daoist religion, and the best known of all Daoist texts are known by the name of Laozi, which literally means "Old Master" or "Old Child." Both the person and the text arose around 500 B.C.E. in a period of great change not only in China but the world over. Indeed, the German philosopher Karl Jaspers called this period the "axial age" in his seminal work *The Origin and Goal of History* (1953). The term refers to the fact that at this time in many different cultures new thinkers and religious leaders arose who, for the first time, placed great emphasis on the individual as opposed to the community of the clan or tribe. Examples include the Buddha in India, Zoroaster in Persia, Socrates in ancient Greece, and Confucius in China. The ideas proposed by these thinkers and religious leaders had a strong and pervasive impact on the thinking of humanity in general, contributing significantly to our thinking even today.

China at this time was undergoing tremendous economic and political changes. The arrival of iron-age technology, and with it better plough-shares, wagon axles, and weapons, had caused an increase in food pro-duction and massive population growth, as well as greater mobility and wealth among the people. This in turn led to a heightened hunger for power among local lords, who began to wage wars in order to expand their lands and increase their influence, setting large infantry armies against each other. While the central king of the Zhou dynasty (1122–221 B.C.E.) was still officially in charge of the entire country, there were in fact many independent states in a more-or-less constant state of conflict. The period is thus appropriately named the Warring States (*zhanguo*). It was a time of unrest and transition which left many people yearning for the peace and stability of old, and ended only with the violent conquest of all other states and establishment of the Chinese empire by the Qin dynasty in 221 B.C.E.

Most Chinese philosophers of the Warring States, in accordance with the situation they faced, were concerned with the proper "way" or "method" (*dao*) leading to the recovery of the harmony and social manageability of an earlier, golden age. Their works tend to be characterized by a strong backward focus and feudalistic vision. Although Western scholars usually characterize them as "philosophers," they always placed a strong emphasis on the practical dimensions of their teachings, both in regard to the individual's social behavior and to his or her personal self-cultivation. In fact, at the core of most ancient Chinese thought are practices of social discipline and the transformation of individuals and communities. Followers often congregated in small, almost sectarian groups rather than in what we think of as "philosophical schools."

The earliest text later to be revered in Daoism, and by extension its entire "philosophical" tradition, is no exception to this. It must always be considered as just one expression of a tradition that in essence focused on practical and social transformation, and can therefore be best understood within the wider context of the thought at the time. Later historians writing about the Warring States period after the fact, around 100 B.C.E., distinguished six major philosophical schools, each of which proposed one particular area as being most responsible for the state of social and cosmic disharmony, and offered remedies accordingly: the Confucians focused on social etiquette and proper ritual; the Daoists emphasized the natural flow of things; the Mohists (named after the philosopher Mozi) saw the solution to all problems in universal love; the Legalists thought that a set of strict laws and punishments was necessary to return order to the world; the Logicians found the key flaw in the inaccurate use of language and the resulting confusion in people's minds; and the Yin-Yang cosmologists understood social and personal harmony to depend on the cycles of the seasons, the movements of the stars, and other macrocosmic phenomena. Of these six schools the most important to understanding Daoism are the Confucians, who will be discussed first, and the Yin-Yang Cosmologists, who will be examined in Chapter 3.

Early Confucianism

Confucianism goes back to the thinker Confucius, Kongfuzi or "Master Kong" (551–479 B.C.E.), the illegitimate son of the ruler of Lu, a small state in eastern China (modern Shandong). Trained in elementary feudal arts as well as to read and write, he became a minor functionary in the state's administration, then developed certain ideas of his own as to the causes of his country's problems and their remedy. In an effort to see his ideas put into practice, he left his employment and traveled through China, presenting himself as a potential prime minister to many local rulers — as did numerous lesser nobles at the time who had either technical skills, military expertise, or advice on government. However, no ruler decided to employ Confucius, and so he returned home and began to teach interested disciples in private, soon establishing a name for himself and his ideas. The disciples later collected his sayings into a volume known as the *Lunyu* (Analects), which today has twenty chapters, of which the first nine are believed to be historically closer to Confucius himself.

The main concept of early Confucianism as presented in this text is the idea of ritual formality or etiquette (*li*). The character represents the image of a ritual vessel — an object claimed to have been Confucius's favorite toy as a child — and indicates the proper behavior in all social situations. It can be interpreted on three levels: in society, government, and religious ritual. Socially, *li* means proper behavior among people of different rank and status, defined through the five relationships: ruler-minister, father-son, husband-wife, elder-younger brother, friend-friend. In each case, there is a senior and a junior, and each has obligations toward the other, expressed in the so-called Confucian virtues.

Among these, "mutuality" (*shu*) is most important. This means that the senior partner always should treat the junior with care and concern, while the junior owes the senior obedience and respect. One should never inflict on others what one is not willing to receive oneself, or as the text says: "Do not impose on others what you yourself do not desire" (12.2; 14.15). Other, more specific virtues include benevolence or humaneness (*ren*) toward one's fellow human beings, righteousness or social responsibility (*yi*) toward social organizations and groups of people, especially if one is in a senior position, as well as, if a junior, filial piety or obedience (*xiao*) toward one's parents, and loyalty (*zhong*) toward the ruler or state. Naturally nobody, not even the ruler of the country, is ever always in a senior or junior position, but different social contexts require different forms of behavior, degrees of formality, and structures of command. According to Confucius and his followers, if everyone knew his or her standing at any given moment and acted fully in accordance with it, society would be fully harmonious. This will not be achieved by laws or force. As the *Lunyu* says:

> The Master said: Guide them by edicts, keep them in line with punishments, and the common people will stay out of trouble but will have no sense of shame. Guide them by virtue, keep them in line with *li*, and they will, besides having a sense of shame, reform themselves. (2.3)

The same idea also applies to government organizations, which should act in proper accordance with their specific duties and not infringe upon or compete with each other; and also to religious rituals, where it is important to honor the ancestors and the local and cosmic deities with proper formalities, offering sacrifices of food and drink. One should spare no expense or trouble to create harmony with the otherworldly spheres and always attain the right state of mind. As the text has it:

> When the Master offered sacrifice to his ancestors, he felt as if the ancestral spirits were actually present. When he offered sacrifice to other spirits, he felt as if they were really there. (3.12)
>
> Zigong [a disciple] wanted to do away with the sacrifice of a lamb at the ceremony in which the beginning of each month is reported to the ancestors. Confucius said: "You love the lamb, but I love the ceremony." (3.17)

Everybody in society should participate in this ideal Confucian world of *li* to their best ability, and while some may have a stronger natural inclination toward it than others, everyone can learn. In fact, learning in Confucianism is the key method of attaining the proper feeling for *li* in all given situations, and good behavior that creates social harmony is at first a learned response, which becomes natural after many years of training. Methods of training include the traditional arts of the nobility (poetry, calligraphy, numerology, music, archery, and charioteering), together with the study of history and the important books of old. Confucius himself is credited with compiling the Confucian canon, a collection of six ancient works or classics that became the standard source of knowledge and formal education in traditional China. They are the *Shujing* (Book of Documents), *Shijing* (Book of Songs), *Yijing* (Book of Changes), *Chunqiu* (Spring and Autumn Annals), *Liji* (Book of Rites), and one not extant today, the *Yuejing* (Book of Music).

Learning here is considered not a burden but a pleasure, an exciting adventure of becoming increasingly aware of oneself and the social intricacies in one's surroundings. Thus the very first line of the *Lunyu*: "The Master said: is it not a pleasure to learn and to practice from time to time what one has learned?" (1.1). Learning will eventually make one the ideal Confucian, a superior person or gentleman (*junzi*) who follows his parents and leaders in all respects and honors the social conventions to the best of his ability. A gentleman then creates further goodness by radiating friendliness and harmony throughout, from his family to his neighborhood, village, county, state, and into the greater universe at large. Society and the state will be well ordered and benefits will reach to all.

Laozi

In contrast to this vision of a completely organized and well-oiled social system, the proponents of the cosmic "Way" proposed a return to naturalness and the spontaneity of organic so-being. Their ideas were first represented by the thinker Laozi, who unlike Confucius is an historically elusive figure. Frequently called Lao Dan or "Old Dan" in the early texts, he was allegedly a learned and somewhat reclusive official at the royal Zhou court, where he served as an archivist. That is to say, the story goes that he was literate and of lesser aristocratic standing, and worked in one of the many offices of the ruling dynasty as a copyist and administrator of written documents. The *Zhuangzi* tells that his call to fame came when Confucius, eager to expand his knowledge of the ancient rites, went to the Zhou capital to consult him. Lao Dan, instead of imparting his knowledge, rebuked Confucius, advising him to forget all about things to cram into his head and instead let go of everything and follow the natural Way. Confucius, stunned for several days, finally emerged with the verdict that he had met many impressive people in his day but none like Lao Dan who was "truly like a dragon," free from all constraints and powerfully soaring in the sky.

This is all that is known about Laozi before the Han dynasty, when his first official biography appears in the *Shiji* (Record of the Historian, dat. 104 B.C.E.) by Sima Qian, a collection of facts and hearsay. Scholars today are divided concerning Laozi's historicity. Many accept the ancient information and take him to be a historical person who served as a minor official under the Zhou dynasty and wrote the book named after him. Others see him more as a legendary figure who may or may not have existed at any one time, but who certainly did not do all the things told about him, and who was not the sole author of the *Laozi*, which they see as a conglomerate of sayings that grew over the centuries. Devout religious Daoists of later centuries and today, in contrast, have a completely different understanding. They see Laozi as a historial manifestation of the divinity of the Dao and the book associated with him as a revealed text of celestial origins.

The most radical modern, scholarly reading of Laozi's biography is by A. C. Graham (repr. in Kohn and LaFargue 1998). According to him, even the earliest story about his meeting with Confucius was not based on historical fact but was originally a legend concocted by the Confucians who wished to document their leader's intense search for knowledge. The tale duly became common knowledge, and around 300 B.C.E. was adopted into the *Zhuangzi* and became part of the lore of "Daoists." At this time they did not yet exist under this name, but they can be described as a group of people who practiced self-cultivation and longevity, advised the return to a natural way of life and government, and were loosely connected by a set of sayings that documented their ideas and practices. As China moved closer to unification under the Qin dynasty, all philosophical schools geared up to make their pitch for political influence, and the "Daoists" too got a bit better organized and arranged their inherited sayings into a set text. This text they then linked with the alleged teacher of Confucius, the "Old Master," and called it the *Laozi*.

To enhance their claim for longevity, Graham claims, they not only insisted that Laozi was a contemporary of Confucius, who died in 479 B.C.E., but that he was also identical with a historiographer by the name of Dan (a different Chinese character), who predicted the rise of the Qin in 374 B.C.E. This made Lao Dan a man who lived for about two centuries and laid the foundation of an important feature of later beliefs, the so-called transformations of Laozi. According to this, he was of supernatural stature, resided originally in the heavens, and appeared at regular intervals in the world to advise rulers and give revelations to deserving seekers. Having set up this claim of Laozi's longevity, the "Daoists" were a bit stymied when the Qin ruler, very impressed and full of concern for his own immortality, asked them why this wondrous personage was no longer there to advise him in person. In response, they created a further story which too became the root of many later legends. They said that

> after some time Laozi realized that the [Zhou] dynasty was de-
> clining and decided to leave. When [riding a gray ox] he
> reached the western frontier, Yin Xi, the guardian of the pass,
> said: "You want to withdraw forever. Please write down your
> ideas for me." Thereupon Laozi wrote a book in two sections
> dealing with Dao and Virtue. It had more than five thousand
> words. Then he left, and nobody knows what became of him.
> (*Shiji* 63)

This explained, in one swoop, why Laozi was no longer there and how the text *Laozi* came into existence. It also set the stage for the two other main appellations of the text, *Wuqian wen* (Text in Five Thousand Words) and *Daode jing* (Book of the Dao and Its Virtue). In later developments of the story, Laozi is further said to have crossed into Central Asia and even reached India, where he continued to spread his teachings and became the teacher of the western people, known to the Chinese as *hu* or "bar-barians." They in turn called him "buddha" and made his teaching known as "Buddhism." This story of the "conversion of the barbarians" appears first in the second century C.E. to explain the growing influx of Buddhism into China, and was later—with further mythical develop-ments and alterations—turned into a highly polemical and anti-Buddhist story, which claimed that all the basic rules of Buddhism (celibacy, shaved head, vegetarianism) were imposed by Laozi only to curb the violent, beastly, and filthy tendencies of the "barbarians."

In the early stages, however, the "Daoists" with their story succeeded in attracting the attention of several rulers and, in the early Han dynasty, Laozi became a highly venerated figure, while his text grew into a semi-sacred book widely recited and venerated among the upper classes. His fame in turn led an up-and-coming family named Li to claim him as their ancestor. In this they were following common practice at the time, when many local clans reached for success at the central court. They also gave him a formal first name, Er, and set him up with a birthplace—a village called Bozhou near the city of Luyi in modern Henan, located (not sur-prisingly) rather close to the district where the Han rulers themselves came from. All this information is found already in the *Shiji*, showing that even in the first century B.C.E. Laozi was an honored sage with a firm place in the pantheon of the Han aristocracy. Later he would be fur-ther venerated and mythologized, and the *Daode jing* would officially be recognized as a "classic" (in 737 C.E.), to play an important role both in religion and literati culture.

The Daode jing

The *Laozi* or *Daode jing* is a short text in about five thousand characters — the actual count varies among editions — that is commonly divided into eighty-one chapters and two parts, one on Dao (1-37), and one on De (38-81). It is written in verse — not a rhyming, steady rhythmic kind of verse, but a stylized prose that has strong parallels and regular patterns — and contains sections of description contrasted with tight punchlines. The text has been transmitted in several different editions, three of which are most important today. The first is the so-called standard edition, also known as the transmitted edition. Handed down by Chinese copyists over the ages, it is at the root of almost all translations of the text. It goes back to the third century C.E., to the erudite Wang Bi (226-249) who edited the text and wrote a commentary on it that Chinese since then have considered inspired. It has shaped the reception of the text's worldview until today.

The second edition is called the Mawangdui edition, so named after a place in south China (Hunan) where a tomb was excavated in 1973 that dated from 168 B.C.E. It contained an undisturbed coffin surrounded by numerous artifacts and several manuscripts written on silk, mostly dealing with cosmology and longevity techniques, such as gymnastics and sexual practices. Among them were two copies of the *Daode jing*. The Mawangdui version differs little from the transmitted edition: there are some character variants which have helped clarify some interpretive points, and the two parts are in reversed order, i.e., the text begins with the section on De, then adds the section on Dao. The manuscripts are important because they show that the *Daode jing* existed in its complete form in the early Han dynasty, and that it was considered essential enough to be placed in someone's grave.

The third edition was discovered in 1993 in a place called Guodian (Hubei). Written on bamboo slips and dated to about 300 B.C.E., the find presents a collection of various philosophical works of the time, including fragments of Confucian and other texts. Among them are thirty-three passages that can be matched with thirty-one chapters of the *Daode jing*, but with lines in different places, and considerable variation in characters. Generally, they are concerned with self-cultivation and its application to questions of rulership and the pacification of the state. Polemical attacks against Confucian virtues, such as those describing them as useless or even harmful (chs. 18–19), are not found; instead negative attitudes and emotions are criticized. This Guodian find of this so-called "Bamboo Laozi" tells us that in the late fourth century B.C.E. the text existed in rudimentary form, and consisted of a collection of sayings not yet edited into a coherent presentation. Another text found at Guodian, the *Taiyi sheng shui* (Great Unity Creates Water), gives further insights into the growing and possibly even "Daoist" cosmology of the time, as does a contemporaneous work on self-cultivation, the "Inward Training" (*Neiye*) chapter of the *Guanzi*. It appears that, gradually, a set of ideas and practices was growing that would eventually develop into something specifically and more religiously Daoist.

Dao and Nonaction

The *Daode jing* has often been hailed as representing the core of the Daoist worldview and the root of Daoist mysticism. But it is in fact a multifaceted work that can, and has been, interpreted in many different ways, not least as a manual of strategy, a political treatise on the recovery of the golden age, a guide to underlying principles, and a metalinguistic inquiry into forms of prescriptive discourse. It can be read in two fundamentally different ways: as a document of early Chinese culture or as a scripture of universal significance.

Looked at in terms of Chinese culture, concepts of statesmanship, political principles, military strategy, and royal virtues become essential, and the focus is on understanding the text in the context of contemporaneous works and the social and political situation of the time. Seen as a scripture of universal significance, ideas of personal cultivation, freedom of mind, and the attainment of spontaneity and naturalness take center stage — the text's main appeal is its timeless characterization and alleviation of the human condition. Both approaches are equally important and have been proposed by readers and scholars over the centuries; both are also evident in numerous traditional commentaries and the uses of the text throughout Chinese history.

The basic concept in the text is Dao or "Way." It can be understood either metaphysically as the underlying source and power of the universe, practically as the way in which the world functions, or analytically as the way in which people can (or cannot) speak about reality. The text does not make its understanding easy. Rather, the first chapter of the standard edition begins by saying that Dao cannot be named or known with ordinary human senses. It may be described as lying at the root of creation and the cycles of nature, the "mother" of all that keeps nature and society in harmony.

In religious terms Dao is seen as a mystical power of universal oneness; more metaphysically, it is a fundamental ontological entity or absolute truth. Some scholars have also read it in terms of relativist thinking, as a universal way that can never be approached or described, while others see it as a supreme principle that is too deep to be properly expressed in words. The intellectual historian Benjamin Schwartz describes it as "organic order" — "organic" in the sense that it is part of the world and not a transcendent other as in Western religion, "order" because it can be felt in the rhythms of the world, in the manifestation of organized patterns.

Another way to think of Dao, which appears in later religious literature, is as two concentric circles, a smaller one in the center and a larger on the periphery. The dense, smaller circle in the center is Dao at the root of creation — tight, concentrated, intense, and ultimately unknowable, ineffable, and beyond conscious or sensory human attainment (chs. 6, 14, 25). The looser, larger circle at the periphery is Dao as it appears in the world, the patterned cycle of life and visible nature. Here we can see Dao as it comes and goes, rises and sets, rains and shines, lightens and darkens — the ever-changing yet everlasting alteration of natural patterns, yin and yang, life and death. This Dao is what people and rulers need to adapt to; they should go along with it to create harmony and be at ease with it to find fulfillment. As the text says:

> The Dao remains in spontaneous nonaction.
> If rulers and kings can maintain it,
> The myriad beings will transform by themselves.
> Once transformed, should desires arise,
> Quell them with nameless simplicity
> And teach them to know when to stop.
> Knowing when to stop creates tranquility,
> And the myriad beings will rest firmly in themselves.
> (ch. 37; Henricks, *Guodian*, A:7)

The inner, central Dao at the root of creation, on the other hand, is there as an ultimate to relate to beyond the activities of daily existence; it maintains the outer circle but does not actually do anything in itself. Finding intuitive access to this inner Dao will help in creating harmony with its outer ring and sensing universal harmony on a deeper level. Aligning oneself with the root of all will create an empowerment for oneself and a perfect society of great peace.

Dao is always good (chs. 4, 8, 34). Bad times, bad things, bad people, all forms of evil happen when things move against the flow of Dao. That does not mean that there is no room for recession, decline, or death. All these things are there, but not considered evil (ch. 5). Rather, they are a necessary part in the ongoing flux of life in which everything is relative and related to everything else. Yin and yang are interdependent and relative forces that always move together and in alteration, and neither of them is evil. Evil occurs when violent decline is forced upon nature or society at a time of growth, or when massive expansion is pushed forward at a time of rest or reduction. It is essential, therefore, to know the patterns of Dao — either personally or politically — and learn to adapt to its rhythms.

It is important to understand that although religious Daoist texts from many ages note this distinction between the ineffable, creative Dao at the center and the manifest, patterned Dao at the periphery — they also never tire of insisting that there is always only one Dao. The two are not essentially different, but are the same inherent and integrated entity. This notion of the underlying unity of existence pervades Chinese thought, so that medical texts, for example, express it in the notion of *qi*, cosmic or vital energy, which is only one at all times but can move at different speeds of vibration or oscillation. Thicker, slow moving *qi* is considered gross and appears as the body; finer, fast moving *qi* is subtle and appears as the mind. But as there is only one *qi*, body and mind are made up of the same basic material. In the same way, Dao at the root of creation is never separate or essentially different from Dao in the human and natural world, and the cultivation of the self has an immediate impact on the harmony of the cosmos.

The way to be with Dao is through nonaction (*wuwei*) and naturalness (*ziran*; chs. 16, 21, 32). This does not mean doing nothing, becoming like a vegetable, or being totally spontaneous without any planning whatsoever. Rather, it means letting go of egoistic concerns and passions and desires on the personal level, finding a sense of where life, nature, and the world are headed on the social level, and abstaining from forceful and interfering measures in the political realm. As the text says:

> Act on things and you will ruin them.
> Grasp for things and you will lose them.
> Therefore the sage acts with nonaction and has no ruin,
> Lets go of grasping and has no loss.
> (ch. 64; Henricks, *Guodian*, A:6)

In traditional China this idea was mainly applied in politics, but over the years people have also found it helpful in ordinary life. An example for a modern application is given by Liu Xiaogan in a discussion of "natural-ness" as understood in China today (in Kohn and LaFargue 1998; also Csikzentmihalyi and Ivanhoe 1999). He presents the case of a farmer who is about to modernize his farm. If the farmer looks around and finds many modern methods being applied, understands the rationale behind them and their advantages for everyone concerned, and if he has both the time to investigate the new methods and the money to make the in-vestment, then the time is right and things in all likelihood will proceed smoothly.

If, on the other hand, he works only for egoistic profit to the detriment of everyone else, or if a government or corporation forces him to change his basic methods at a time when he has neither time for exploration nor money to invest, then he is likely headed for trouble and disaster. "The principle of naturalness," Liu says, "always prefers inner dynamism to external force." Nonaction as applied naturalness accordingly means that things grow and develop in their own way and to the benefit of all, and that human beings have to find alignment with the natural patterns to fulfill themselves and avoid harming others and the world at large.

The concept of one Dao and its application in nonaction and naturalness also means that everything in the world is utterly interrelated in a vision similar to what is today called the holographic universe. Since every-thing is part of the same one Dao, all that everything does, however slight, must have an impact on everything else. The world is one inter-connected whole, where every single thing and every being moves and acts in a certain way, emitting *qi* at a certain frequency that can either harmonize with or go against the greater flow of Dao. A good metaphor to make this clearer, which is also found in Daoist texts, is that of sound. According to this, Dao brings forth a perfect tone, which is deeply em-bedded in everything and every being, yet all beings also bring forth their own sounds. The goal of practicing nonaction and naturalness, then, is to be as much "in tune" with Dao as possible. Conversely, the more "out of tune" any individual is, the more "evil" they are from the point of view of Dao, and the less they can find self-realization, being instead unhappy and unfortunate. Seen in a wider context, society and the world should ideally—as they were in the golden age of the distant past—be in complete harmony or perfect tune with Dao, and it is the task of the sage and ruler to bring about this greater harmony and ideal society.

Sage and World

The world at present, now as much as when the *Daode jing* was first conceived, is not a golden realm of happiness, bliss and total harmony with Dao. The reason for this, according to the *Daode jing*, is found in the complexity of social structures and the loss of purity in human hearts, which has led to power-seeking and war. Social complexity, the text claims, has much to do with the establishment of formal organizations and the advocacy of Confucian virtues (chs. 18–19), which bury the inherent purity of Dao under many layers of moral injunctions, social rules, and administrative procedures. Impurity of heart, at the same time, is caused by an overload of sensory experience (ch. 12), by the mass availability of luxury goods and a hankering after them, by the pursuit of higher and better positions, and by the striving for power and advancement.

The way to recovery is the practice of simplicity (ch. 19)—a message that has made the *Daode jing* very popular in alternative circles of Western societies. Simplicity is expressed in two forms, first as a physical restraint on accumulating too many things, abstention from eating rich and fancy foods, and generally a tendency to keep one's circumstances limited to what one really needs. Second, it may involve a mental exercise of tranquility and purification, which helps clear the mind and heart from the overload of sensory inputs and the cravings and desires associated with the world. This, as the *Guanzi* chapter on "Inward Training" describes, involves the alignment of body and limbs in a formal seated posture, proper ways of breathing, and the rectification of mind and *qi* in meditative contemplation. It says:

When you enlarge your mind and let go of it,
When you relax your *qi* and expand it,
When your body is calm and unmoving,
And you can maintain the One and discard the
    myriad disturbances —
Then you will see profit and not be enticed by it,
You will see harm and not be frightened by it.
Relaxed and unwound, yet acutely sensitive,
In solitude you delight in your own person.
This is called "revolving the *qi*":
Your thoughts and deeds seem heavenly.
(ch. 24; Roth, *Original Tao*, 115)

Practitioners thus reach a state of pervasive tranquility and equanimity and attain a mind that is stable, ordered, and fully concentrated in a state of "maintaining the One." Free from the distractions of the world, such a mind is eager to delve into the depths of Dao and spontaneously reaches naturalness and nonaction.

The *Daode jing* does not spell out any meditative or self-cultivation techniques and contains no claim about physical immortality. But it portrays the sage (*shengren*) as one who has realized this mind and transformed into a person of Dao: socially responsible, unassuming and nondescript in his person, yet entirely benevolent and helpful in all situations (chs. 2, 27). He does not speak or preach but acts appropriately at all times; he may have a high position in society — and ideally is even the ruler (and thus, in ancient China, usually male) — but he will not think of himself as "possessing" anything, nor will he insist on his position, his way, or his personal wishes (chs. 3, 64). On the contrary, his mind will be full of Dao, seeing the inherent patterns of nature and the world and thinking of the greater good of all (chs. 22, 80). He is a representative of universal virtue, embracing all beings and developing peace within and goodness without. The text has:

The more taboos and prohibitions there are in the world,
the poorer the people will be.
The more sharp weapons the people have,
the more troubled the state will be.
The more cunning and skill man possesses,
the more vicious things will appear.
The more laws and rules are made prominent,
the more thieves and robbers there will be.
Therefore the sage says:

I take no action, and the people transform naturally.
I love tranquility, and the people become naturally upright.
I engage in no activity, and the people prosper naturally.
I have no desires, and the people become naturally simple. (ch. 57)

Thus, more than just a good person in himself, the sage is a catalyst of goodness in the society around him. He filters the benevolent and creative powers of Dao into the world and by his very being makes the world a better place, one where Dao is heard more fully and can aid in the realization of universal goodness. The sage in the *Daode jing* is accordingly also a master of military strategy, because he will know at all times how the pattern of the world is moving and which military action will be most successful at what times — successful in the sense of creating peace and stability and putting an end to hostilities. The ideal Daoist, in this early stage of the tradition, is thus far from a world-denying hermit. Rather, he has a great deal of social responsibility, intuiting Dao not merely for himself but for everyone, and giving maximum help and support to all beings, society, and the cosmos. Following this tradition, certain strands of later Daoism have exhibited a strong social dimension, focusing on the creation of an ideal society as their central concern. They support periods of withdrawal for the sake of practicing simplicity and attaining an attunement with Dao. But ultimately Daoists of such strands are socially responsible and encourage their followers to work actively and even politically for the greater goodness of all.

The contrast with Confucianism diminishes at this point, and the old juxtaposition of Confucians as socially active and Daoists as withdrawing and focused on self-cultivation turns out to be a fallacy in the common Western conception of Daoism. Confucians differ from Daoists, but the disagreement is not about whether or not to be socially active and whether or not to give in to personal greed and passions. Rather, the dividing issue is how to achieve social harmony and how to behave in society. *Daode jing*-type Daoists reject the establishment of formal administrative structures, complex hierarchies, social rituals, and sophisticated systems of morals and virtues. They prefer to be simple and unassuming, unencumbered by high positions and heavy administrative duties; they rely on cultivating the inherent goodness in people, their sense of rightness that comes forth through nonaction and naturalness, to create a harmonious world. The sage, then, is the master of this pure social behavior, one who will never assume or possess but who aids the world in creating itself in its most harmonious form.

Further Readings

Csikzentmihalyi, Marc, and Philip J. Ivanhoe, eds. 1999. *Religious and Philosophical Aspects of the Laozi*. Albany: State University of New York Press.

Graham, A. C. 1989. *Disputers of the Tao: Philosophical Argument in Ancient China*. La Salle, Ill.: Open Court Publishing Company.

Ivanhoe, Philip J. 1993. *Confucian Moral Self-Cultivation*. New York: Peter Lang.

Kohn, Livia. 1998. *God of the Dao: Lord Lao in History and Myth*. Ann Arbor: University of Michigan, Center for Chinese Studies.

Kohn, Livia, and Michael LaFargue, eds. 1998. *Lao-tzu and the Tao-te-ching*. Albany: State University of New York Press.

LaFargue, Michael. 1992. *The Tao of the Tao-te-ching*. Albany: State University of New York Press.

Schwartz, Benjamin. 1985. *The World of Thought in Ancient China*. Cambridge, Mass.: Harvard University Press.

Original Sources in Translation

Henricks, Robert. 1989. *Lao-Tzu: Te-Tao ching*. New York: Ballantine.

Henricks, Robert. 2000. *Lao Tzu's Tao Te Ching: A Translation of the Startling New Documents Found at Guodian*. New York: Columbia University Press.

Kohn, Livia. 1993. *The Taoist Experience*. Albany: State University of New York Press. Chs. 1, 2, 10, 38.

Lau, D. C. 1979. *Confucius*. Baltimore: Penguin Books.

Lin, Paul J. 1977. *A Translation of Lao-tzu's Tao-te-ching and Wang Pi's Commentary*. Ann Arbor: University of Michigan, Center for Chinese Studies.

Roth, Harold D. 1999. *Original Tao: Inward Training and the Foundations of Taoist Mysticism*. New York: Columbia University Press.

Daode jing, standard edition, appears in numerous translations; for guidance, see the article by LaFargue and Pas in Kohn and LaFargue 1998.

CHAPTER TWO

THE ZHUANGZI

The question of the goodness in people and of their original, natural mind rises to the forefront in succeeding generations. The two major leaders of Confucianism and Daoism after the hoary masters, Mencius (c. 371–289 B.C.E.) and Zhuangzi (c. 370–290 B.C.E.), both place the mind at the center of their speculations, moving towards an internalization in their understanding of the world. This can be seen as the logical next step following the overall tendencies of the axial age, or again as a general tendency in the development of the world's religions. As Paul Ricoeur has found in a study of Western religions called *The Symbolism of Evil* (1967), humanity has tended to see the world first in cosmic, then social, and finally in personal or psychological terms. Evil accordingly was understood first as defilement, incurred through the violation of a taboo, then as social infringement or shame (sin), and eventually located in the individual and experienced as guilt. This transition is most visible in Western religions, but it also applies to China—although the latter never developed a guilt culture to the same degree as the West, since it always placed a higher emphasis on the community than on the individual.

Ancient Chinese thought of the third century B.C.E. can in this overall context be seen as an effort to grapple with the mind, or consciousness, as the key factor in shaping human society and the world. The need to find remedies for the social tensions of the time is never ignored, but the emphasis shifts markedly to an even more internal, psychological understanding. Before, then, examining the vision of the Daoist thinker Zhuangzi, let us look briefly at the ideas of his Confucian contemporary.

Mencius

Mencius, Mengzi or "Master Meng," like Confucius, came from eastern China and was both a government official and a professional teacher and thinker who spent many years traveling to local rulers to offer his advice. He inherited Confucius's thought through the lineage of the latter's grandson and followed him in the effort to find ways of restoring the idealized golden age of the mythical sage rulers. But Mencius's focus was different in that he located the key to social harmony less in rites and etiquette than in the human mind, which he declared to be originally good. Confucius had not made any statements regarding the nature of the mind, but only emphasized that learning was at the center of the enterprise and that people had different inherent capabilities for it.

Mencius now categorically states that the human mind is essentially good and has certain universal, natural qualities which lie at the root of all virtues, including those proposed by Confucius. He pinpoints four, which are appropriately called the "four beginnings":

> The feeling of commiseration is found in all men; the feeling of shame and dislike is found in all men; the feeling of respect and reverence is found in all men; and the feeling of right and wrong is found in all men. The feeling of commiseration is the beginning of benevolence; the feeling of shame and dislike is the beginning of righteousness; the feeling of respect and reverence is the beginning of etiquette; and the feeling of right and wrong is the beginning of wisdom. These four are not instilled in us from the outside. We originally have them within us. (6A6; 2A6; Chan, *Source Book*, 54, 65)

His main argument for these four qualities is that in certain situations all people would instinctively do the right thing and not hesitate even to think. For example, when "one sees a child about to fall into a well," one would reach out a hand and try to grab him no matter what. For Mencius, therefore, all people possess instinctual or innate knowledge of the good, and have the ability to do good in all social situations. And when their naturally good mind is developed to the fullest, everyone can live the ideal life in perfect harmony. Evil consequentially is no longer part of social circumstances or interaction but rather is the result of people's failure to acknowledge and develop their innate goodness.

Learning then becomes the search for the "lost mind," an effort to re-cover what is already there naturally. This mind can be accessed through words, but on a deeper level lies with the *qi*, the vital energy or life force of the person, which can be controlled by will and thought or obscured by outside, sensory data (2A2; 6A15). Once people have found access to their original mind, they can begin to spread the goodness around them. Here Mencius maintains some of Confucius's social thinking by propos-ing that the expression of innate goodness has to begin with benevolence within the family and righteousness in the immediate community.

This is different from the ideal of universal love proposed by his rivals, the followers of the philosopher Mozi. From the community, moreover, as outlined in the *Daxue* (Great Learning) chapter of the *Liji*, the good must spread further until it reaches the state and leads to the ideal of humane government which is for the benefit of the people and not the profit of the ruler. He says:

> If the people have a constant livelihood, they have constant minds. Without a constant livelihood, they lack constant minds, and without those they will go astray, stopping at no depravity or nastiness. When they then turn criminal, to pur-sue and punish them is to entrap them. How can that be possi-ble under the government of a benevolent man? Therefore a good ruler will always be respectful and thrifty, courteous and self-effacing, taking from the people only according to proper regulations. (3A3; Lau, *Mencius*, 97)

This, in turn, will help to stabilize the country and enhance social har-mony, the ideal condition for people to realize their deeper mind and find true harmony in life.

Zhuangzi

Master Zhuang, originally called Zhuang Zhou, was of lower aristocratic background, highly erudite, and a minor government servant. He first worked for a local southern Chinese state, then withdrew to dedicate himself to his speculations, teaching his ideas to disciples and either writing them down himself or inspiring others to do so. The same *Shiji* chapter (ch. 63) that discusses the legendary Laozi mentions that Zhuangzi was famous for his way with words. Indeed the text associated with him is regarded as the first document of Chinese literary fiction and is famous for the high quality of its language.

The text *Zhuangzi* emerged from within the same overall political environment as the *Daode jing*, but it has a different focus in that it is more concerned with mental attitudes and condemns active political involvement. Zhuang Zhou found that the ongoing arguments among the different philosophical schools were futile and would not lead to serious improvements. He concluded that "right" and "wrong" were highly volatile categories, that all viewpoints were relative, and that the mind and its perception tended to be fallacious and one-sided. As a result, he makes a strong case for the cultivation of nondual perception and a way of life that is free from constraints—mental, personal, and social—and flows along smoothly with the course of Dao.

Unlike the *Laozi*, the *Zhuangzi* is written in prose and is a rather long text. It contains many episodes, fables, and fictional dialogues, and represents not only the teachings of Zhuang Zhou himself but also those of several other emerging "Daoist" trends. Also unlike the *Daode jing*, which was interpreted in a strong commentary tradition while exerting a diffuse influence on Chinese society in general, the *Zhuangzi* has received few commentaries but its worldview and language have inspired literary works throughout the centuries. They have aided the formulation of religious visions of various traditions, not only Daoist but also poetic and Buddhist (especially the Chan or Zen school). The ideas expressed in the text, moreover, can readily be interpreted within a framework of mysticism, and compared in that respect both to the *Daode jing* and to Western religious concepts.

The *Zhuangzi* consists of thirty-three chapters and is divided into three parts: Inner Chapters (1-7), Outer Chapters (8-22), and Miscellaneous Chapters (23-33). This division was established by the main commentator of the text, Guo Xiang (252-312), who lived in the same period as Wang Bi, the principal editor of and commentator on the *Daode jing*. Both men were part of an intellectual movement known as Xuanxue or "Profound Learning" (sometimes inappropriately called "Neo-Daoism"). This arose after the end of the Han in reaction to the strong control of intellectual life by officials of this dynasty. It focused on a search for a more spiritual dimension of life through the recovery and reinterpretation of less political classics, including Daoist works and the *Yijing* (Book of Changes). According to Guo Xiang's postface to his edition, the *Zhuangzi* he received consisted of fifty-two chapters, many of which had extraneous materials and stories he found unworthy of Zhuang Zhou. He duly proceeded to eliminate these parts, which dealt with magic, exorcism, dream interpretation, ecstatic journeys, medical lore, and natural transformations. He then set out to streamline the rest into a division he found suitable. Both our current edition of the text and the main orientation of its worldview are therefore received through Guo Xiang, and his ideas of what the *Zhuangzi* was all about.

Early Daoist Trends

Within the existing text, then, which scholars believe still contains materials from the third and second centuries B.C.E., four distinct strands of Daoist worldview and practice can be found. There is first the school of Zhuang Zhou himself, which is documented in the Inner Chapters (also considered the oldest) and in chapters 16–27 and 32 of the later parts of the book. Then, as analyzed by A. C. Graham, there are the strands of the so-called primitivists (chs. 8–10), the syncretists (chs. 11–15, 33), and the hedonists (chs. 28–31). We will look at these latter strands first, and then focus on the worldview associated with Zhuangzi proper.

The primitivist chapters express a worldview very similar to that of the *Daode jing*, but one more radical in its proposition of simplicity and the return to an uncomplicated life. They condemn all forms of culture as evil and destructive, and see the ideal society strictly in terms of the *Daode jing*:

> Let there be a small country with few people —
> They might have plenty of utensils, but nobody would use them,
> They would be concerned with death and never travel far.
> They might have boats and carriages, yet nobody would ride
> in them;
> They might have shields and spears, yet nobody would
> line up with them.
> The people there would again knot cords to communicate,
> They would sweeten their meals, adorn their robes,
> enjoy their homes, and take pleasure in their customs.
> Two neighboring villages of this kind might be visible to
> each other,
> They might even hear each other's dogs and roosters,
> Yet the people in either would grow old and never go back
> and forth. (ch. 80)

The idea is, then, to keep people living in small communities where they eschew all technology and revert to homemade utensils, never leave their villages and, although able to see and hear the next village, feel no curiosity about it and do not even visit it. The idea is to keep people in one place as much as possible, to have them maintain a simple outlook on life and strong inner contentment by limiting their horizons of experience, and generally to establish political and social stability by holding the populace under tight control—physical, social, and intellectual.

The primitivists, sometimes also called anarchists, hate all government and idealize the time before the arrival of iron-age technology, before the invention of the plow, the iron axle, and the sword. They suggest that when there were fewer people, no communications, no governments, and no infantry-fought wars, life was simple, easy, and good. They are, in one word, the proponents of a movement back to the stone age and away from everything "modern" society has to offer. Their vision is not the same as that of the *Daode jing*, which still advises ways of working with the present rather than rejecting it altogether, but it is built on the same fundamental ideas of simplicity, nonaction, and small, controlled social units. Later this primitivist strand in Daoism was continued in the ideal of the anti-social hermit who preferred his lonely hut and simple food to a comfortable and well-appointed life in society. This figure has appeared variously throughout Chinese history and is still present today, as Bill Porter has demonstrated in his book *The Road to Heaven* (1993).

The syncretist sections of the *Zhuangzi*, next, demonstrate the integration of more formalized forms of cosmology and worldview into the basic understanding of Dao. Already, the *Daode jing* made a rudimentary distinction between Dao as the creative and ineffable center and its manifestation in the visible world. Now the latter aspect of Dao is formulated in more technical detail and outlined in organized and recognizable patterns. The rhythm of yin and yang, already present in the *Daode jing*, is further subdivided into subtler phases that also take into account observations of the structure of the natural world, the movements of the stars, and the divination signs (hexagrams) of the *Yijing*. Also, the ideas of other thinkers of the time are merged into the system, allowing for social hierarchies and enforced regulations as part of Dao. This dimension of ancient Daoist thought became dominant under the Han dynasty, when cosmology was even further formalized and adopted as a key governing tool by the new rulers. It also became the basis of much later Daoism.

The hedonist strand is the third "Daoist" tendency A. C. Graham has isolated in the *Zhuangzi*. It implies a worldview of ease and leisure, a life of no constraints and no restrictions, an attitude of giving in to desires and serving only one's own happiness and satisfaction. The underlying idea here is that "what is good for me is good for the universe." The reasoning behind it is that if the individual is part of Dao, then whatever he or she feels and wants is also part of Dao, and therefore all one's personal desires are expressions of the greater cosmic goodness and have to be satisfied without fail.

The hedonist strand, represented by a philosopher known as Yang Zhu (ca. 440–360 B.C.E.; also described in the *Liezi*, an early Daoist text that was lost then reconstituted), is like that of the primitivist in radicalizing a certain aspect of the teaching of the *Daode jing*, but it picks a completely different one: the idea that all and everything belongs inherently and inextricably to Dao. Its representatives refuse to acknowledge the difference between inner purity and potential forms of disharmony caused by desires and a sensory overload, and they proceed to accept every aspect of life as positive and part of Dao. The result is a certain ruthlessness when it comes to making personal sacrifices—Yang Zhu would not give up even a nail on his finger if he could thereby save the world—and a freewheeling, happy-go-lucky attitude toward life in general. Hedonist ideas have continued in Daoism in the figure of the eccentric poet and social dropout (a good example is the poet Liu Ling, ca. 200 C.E.), forever drunk and in total disregard of social conventions. It is also apparent in certain later immortals, such as the famous Eight Immortals, who are well known for their ease in life, their eccentric leisure activities, and their happy laughter at everything and with everyone.

These three strands identified in various chapters of the *Zhuangzi* have their own part to play in the greater picture of Daoism through the ages. Their main expression, however, is not found primarily in the text but evolves later and comes to the fore at different times and in different forms of the religion. The dominant mode of the *Zhuangzi* is the vision associated with Zhuang Zhou himself and his immediate disciples. Its overall outlook and many of its technical terms and metaphors have pervaded both Daoism and Chinese literature ever since.

The World of Zhuang Zhou

The worldview associated immediately with Zhuangzi himself can be best described by examining the text's Inner Chapters, which begin with "Xiaoyao you" (Free and Easy Wandering, ch. 1). Its first story describes the freedom experienced by the huge Peng bird when it soars into the sky, then points out how the little quail looking at the giant above it has no clue as to what it might feel to be like this. Over a number of episodes the chapter continues to make the same point: people and beings have a certain quality within themselves which determines the way they are (their personal Dao). They can realize this inner core to the fullest and attain "perfect happiness," but this realization is limited by who they are and where they stand in the greater scheme of things. There is no point in trying to be something else, they cannot even begin to comprehend what life is like for beings of a totally different size and dimension. Freedom and ease in life do not come from wishing to attain one single goal that is the same for all—a high social position or scholarly erudition, for example—but from realizing who one is and where one stands in the world and doing what one knows best to the fullest of one's ability.

This basic idea of the *Zhuangzi* can be and has been interpreted in different ways. Some scholars (and many later Daoists) consider it a form of mysticism, where one attains a state beyond ordinary consciousness and becomes one with Dao. Others (and some later poets and ecstatics) find in it a philosophy of life that praises eccentricity, self-indulgence, and an anti-social attitude. Then again, it has been read (notably by the commentator Guo Xiang) as a form of social thought that emphasizes stratification and limitation, discouraging people from trying to go beyond their niche and urging them to find contentment and happiness in whatever qualities and status they have. And some scholars, inspired by later poetry and fiction that makes heavy use of *Zhuangzi* metaphors, have seen in the text an early and beautiful manifestation of the Chinese literary genius, the first appearance of fiction in traditional China.

The second chapter is called "Qiwu lun" (Seeing Things As Equal). It discusses the mental and intellectual attitude necessary to attain free and easy wandering. Its main point is that people in their ordinary lives accumulate knowledge and are subject to emotions, which are inevitably dualistic. "The me and what I said make two, and two and the original one make three," as the text states. It also says:

> Joy and anger, sadness and delight, worry and regret, fickleness and stiffness, fascination and idleness, imperiousness and consideration—they arise in us like music from hollows or fungi from dampness [out of nowhere]. Day and night they alternate before us, yet nobody knows where they sprout from. . . . Yet without them, there would be no I. And without an I, there would be no place for them to go.

Instability on both the intellectual and emotional levels thus causes people to remain caught in a delusory self and an imaginary world full of tensions. Making comparisons and evaluations, they are always thrown back and forth and never experience life immediately and to the fullest, or gain even the least bit of security. Everything is open to doubt:

> How can I know that what I call knowing is not really not knowing? . . .

> How do I know that loving life is not a delusion? That in hating death I am not like a man who has gone from home and does not find his way back?

The way the *Zhuangzi* deals with the problem in this chapter is to fight the mind with the mind. It emphasizes the futility of making distinctions, points out the impossibility of knowing anything for certain, and stresses the difference in perspectives among different species. This part of the text has often been considered a fine example of traditional Chinese philosophy, notably as an expression of skepticism and relativism.

In addition, several famous stories in this chapter have become the source of metaphors in later literature and religion. One of them is "Three in the Morning":

> An owner of a troop of monkeys was distributing nuts to them, saying: "You'll get three in morning and four in the evening." The entire troop was upset and got very angry. So he said: "Well, if that's the case, you'll get four in the morning and three in the evening." The monkeys were delighted.

Another is the "Butterfly Dream," which has inspired poems, essays, and dramas alike:

> Once Zhuang Zhou dreamed that he was a butterfly, flying and floating happily around, content with himself and doing what he liked. He did not know that he was Zhuang Zhou.

> Then he woke up, and there he was, firm and clearly Zhuang
> Zhou. But he did not know whether he was in fact Zhuang
> Zhou who had just dreamt he was a butterfly, or a butterfly
> who was now dreaming it was Zhuang Zhou.

Later chapters take up the same issue of the relativity of all understanding and the inadequacy of one viewpoint to convey truth. For example,
in the story on "Zhuangzi and the Skull" (ch. 18), Zhuang Zhou sees an
old bleached skull at the roadside and starts talking to him, expressing
his empathy for the sorry state of the skull's owner. At night the dead
man appears to him in a dream to assure him that being dead was the
best thing that ever happened to him and that he would not exchange a
kingdom among the living for the happiness and freedom he had now.
Another famous story in the same chapter is "The Happiness of Fish":
Zhuang Zhou and his friend and philosophical opponent, the sophist
Hui Shi, cross a bridge over a stream and look at the many fish swim-
ming in the water. When Zhuang Zhou comments on how happy these
fish are, Hui Shi questions him as to how he knows the happiness of fish,
which Zhuangzi counters by asking: "How do you know I don't know
the happiness of fish?"

The "Inner Chapters" then move on to show how one can realize life as a
continuous flow of experience and live in an immediate, nondual way.
One story (in ch. 3) tells of Cook Ding who is so skilled at cutting meat
that he never has to sharpen his knife, knowing exactly where and how
to cut and going along perfectly with the natural pattern. Another describes a funeral: A friend of the deceased arrives, wails once briefly, and
walks away with a grin. When asked why, he explains that life and death
are part of the same natural flow and that there is no reason to cry and
wail.

In a more detailed account of methods, chapter 4 notes that to attain a
state of inner freedom one must most definitely stay away from politics
or any aspirations for high rank and fame, because they will lead to
nothing but exile or execution. Instead, people should practice something called the "fasting of the mind" (xinzhai) to activate their qi over
and above their sensory perception.

> Firmly concentrate your will, and you will no longer hear with
> your ears, and instead come to use your mind to perceive
> sound. Then you go beyond this and use your qi for hearing.
> Plain, ordinary hearing stops with the ears, the mind stops
> with representations, but the qi is utterly empty and so it can

> match all things. In pure emptiness of *qi*, the Dao can assemble,
> and the attainment of this emptiness is what we mean by "fast-
> ing of the mind."

This, as well as some other passages in the text, closely reflects the meditative methods outlined in the "Inward Training" chapter of the *Guanzi*,
and attests again to the practical dimension of Chinese thought at the
time.

The last portion of the "Inner Chapters" focuses on the state of perfection
to be attained. First (in ch. 5), it emphasizes that people's inner core does
not depend on the integrity and proper functioning of their bodies. Even
if a body is flawed, this does not mean the inner power is gone. Rather,
virtue can still be intact, as exemplified in a sage who has lost a foot but
is still a great person, or in the man who is terribly ugly yet attracts
women, children, and rulers to crowd around him. This view contrasts
sharply with Confucian doctrine, which places a high emphasis on bodily integrity, and is different from the views expressed in the *Daode jing*,
where virtue is seen mainly in political or social terms as the manifest
power of Dao. It is also at variance with later Daoist thinking, which favors the ideals of longevity and immortality.

Without condemning physical cultivation and long life, the *Zhuangzi*
here makes the point that the completeness of inner virtue primarily
means the realization of mental serenity and the ability to accept one's
fate with good cheer and a positive spirit. It is a state beyond ordinary
feelings and emotions, realized in the ideal "man without feelings" who
is free from the dualistic interaction with the world and goes along with
the heavenly patterns in free and easy wandering.

Next, the Inner Chapters (in ch. 6) present the realized one or perfected
(*zhenren*), sometimes also referred to as the great man (*daren*). This person, like the sage in the *Daode jing*, does not possess anything, does not
put himself forward, and does not have any willful intentions in his
mind. Furthermore, the perfected is beyond feelings and emotions, free
from dreams and worry. He easily deals with heat, cold, water, and fire,
and handles all social situations with calmness and aplomb. He is expert
in longevity practices, breathing not only with his lungs but all the way
down into his heels, and he is free from social constraints of all sorts. He
does not bemoan poverty or ill fate, but accepts all as it comes along.
Death to him is merely another transformation, as is documented in one

story of Zhuang Zhou beating the drum and singing soon after the death of his wife, and in another of four masters who happily look forward to their imminent passing which to them is a "marvelous transformation." In addition, chapter 6 has the classical description of the unified and un-trammeled mind in a state it calls *zuowang* or "sitting in oblivion," which plays an important role in later Daoist meditation: "I smash up my limbs and body, drive out perception and intellect, cast off form, do away with understanding, and completely join the Great Thoroughfare." The chapter also presents a seven-stage progress toward the ideal mind:

> Practice concentration for three days, and you can put the world out of your mind. Then go on for seven days, and you abandon all things. Once all things are gone from your perception, keep on practicing and after nine more days you can put all life out of your mind. Once you have reached this, you attain a level of clarity like the early morning sun.

> After that you move on to see your singularity in the cosmos, and once you get there, you can reach a state where for you there is neither past nor present. Eventually you transcend even this and attain the utmost freedom of going beyond life and death. Now, the end of life is no longer death for you, and the beginning of life is no longer life. (ch. 6)

In this sequence of overcoming mental assumptions and ideas, then, the state of "perfect happiness," of "free and easy wandering" is attained, a sense of utter freedom and mystical oneness with Dao, a kind of selfless and cosmic perception that lies at the core of Zhuangzi's teaching.

Both Zhuangzi and Mencius in this phase of the development of Chinese thought focus their attention on the mind of the individual and strive to find ways to create harmony in the world. But where Mencius still concentrates on the ruler as his key subject and aims for harmony to occur on the social and political plane, Zhuangzi offers happiness to everyone in any walk of life and rejects all political involvement. Again, there is a famous parable illustrating the two positions, life in honor and politics versus life as really lived:

> Once there was a sacred turtle in the state of Chu. It had been dead for over 3,000 years, and the ruler kept it wrapped in silk and contained in a precious box, honoring it in his ancestral hall. Now, this turtle—would it rather be dead and dried bones

and the object of veneration in the ancestral hall, or would it
rather be alive and drag its tail in the mud? (ch. 17)

Zhuangzi vigorously confirms that he would much rather "drag his tail
in the mud" than be venerated in some stifling position or the other. For
him, the trappings of officialdom are nothing but a form of living death,
while true happiness and fulfillment can be found in a life without obligations and worries, in a free mind and through the perfect harmony of
one's inner core with Dao.

Mysticism

This selfless perception of a mind completely merged into and pervaded
by Dao is also at the heart of the classification of the ancient Daoist
works as mystical texts. Comparing them to the modern Western concept, grown from Christian and Jewish studies, certain adjustments have
to be made. There are notably two key points of Western mysticism that
have to be put aside in favor of a more process-oriented approach: the
notion of an utterly transcendent, completely other power that resides
beyond the world yet creates and rules it (and its correlate, the idea of an
eternal and indestructible pure soul that is caught in the body); and the
focus on a mind-shattering, once-in-a-lifetime experience of union with
this divine other. Leaving these two concepts aside, there are several areas in which classical Daoist texts formulate mystical ideas.

First, there is the notion of an underlying pure force, called the "ground"
by perennialists, which is immanent rather than transcendent and pervades all, even to the most minute object, yet lies at the deepest root of
everything and cannot be comprehended or grasped with the help of the
senses. In order to attain and intuit this force, the mind has to turn away
from its involvement with sensory pleasures and outside activities to
develop an inner tranquility and openness. Second, there is the extended
process of attaining the perception of Dao. To begin, as described in the
Daode jing, practitioners should embrace simplicity, both physically and
mentally, and, as outlined in the *Zhuangzi* and the *Guanzi*, leave the
senses behind and attain a state of "seeing things as equal" and "having
no feelings." This involves a withdrawal from ordinary sensory experience and a refocusing of one's goals, a tendency to "diminish and again

diminish" (*Daode jing* 48) as opposed to the urge to accumulate things and grow bigger and better all the time.

Once the mind is emptied of worldly concerns, it is opened up to perceive the intricacies of Dao, filled anew with a more cosmic, flowing, and universal perspective. It comes to accept all things equally, to see its aloneness, to stand alone among the multitude and appear stupid and simple where everyone else is bright and complex (*Daode jing* 20). This new vision then leads to a complete letting-go of all personality, to a merging with the "Great Thoroughfare," the attainment of nonaction in all aspects of life and thought, the realization of perfect happiness and free and easy wandering. These three stages of withdrawal, openness, and merging with Dao, in turn, can be compared to three stages outlined on the basis of Christian mysticism in Evelyn Underhill's *Mysticism* (1911) the purgative, where one eliminates old ideas and attachments; the illuminative, where one is filled with a new vision and complete focus on God; and the unitive, where one finds mystical union with the deity and enters a completely new life.

In both cases, Western and Daoist, the process involves leaving the ordinary world of perception behind and learning a completely new, spiritually focused way of being in the world by undergoing a permanent transformation, which can be described in a set of phases and which is accompanied by certain breakthrough moments. The main difference — aside from the Western emphasis on transcendence and the mystical experience — is found in the understanding of the body, which is considered part of Dao and therefore healed and nurtured in the Daoist process, while it is seen as the prison and tempter of the soul in the West and as such has to be demolished and suppressed. Another difference is found in the political and social dimension, especially emphasized in the *Daode jing*, where the sage has the duty and the power to change the world into a greater realm of Dao, making all beings perfect in an increasingly perfect world. The *Zhuangzi*, too, shares some of this vision. Although the text itself rejects all involvement in politics and disregards history and social development as irrelevant, the commentary by Guo Xiang makes it clear that the attainment of perfect happiness can and should be reached by everyone, which in turn will cause the world at large to be a perfectly happy and harmonious place, a universe that as a whole is at one with Dao.

This mystical dimension of Daoism found in the selfless perception of the *Zhuangzi*, and in the ideal of nonaction and naturalness of the *Daode jing*, has continued to inspire not only practicing and initiated Daoists of the later tradition, but also thinkers, scholars, poets, and religious seekers from all levels of society and a variety of religious traditions. The two texts, while used formally in Daoist ritual and self-cultivation, have never been the sole property of Daoists. Rather, they were important to many others—poets, Buddhists, Neo-Confucians, and popular practitioners—who in turn have offered their own readings and interpretations of them and have shaped their worldview under the texts' influence. Active users of ancient Daoist texts may or may not be considered "Daoist," depending on their own self-identity, the impact of their interpretations on the tradition, and their religious affiliation and spiritual practice. But that does not diminish the Daoist tradition, rather, it documents its strength and pervasiveness and shows just how multifaceted and flexible it has been.

The veneration of the *Daode jing* and the *Zhuangzi* alone does not make a Daoist, yet it forms an expression of the Daoist tradition, a "literati" or "intellectual" form of Daoism that has, from antiquity to the present day, coexisted with and greatly enriched its more organized aspects. We cannot, therefore, divide Daoism into a "philosophical" and "religious" tradition, with the dividing line in the second century B.C.E. and a positive or negative evaluation attached to either. Instead, we have to think of the veneration of the ancient texts as one, if rather intellectual, expression of the essentially practical Daoist quest for the transformation of self and society that has been parallel to and coexistent with Daoism as religious organization, self-cultivation, and ritual. They all, moreover, are still active today and equally deserve our respect and consideration.

Further Readings

Allinson, Robert E. 1990. *Chuang-Tzu for Spiritual Transformation*. Albany: State University of New York Press.

Ames, Roger, ed. 1998. *Wandering at Ease in the Zhuangzi*. Albany: State University of New York Press.

Kjellberg, Paul, and Philip J. Ivanhoe, eds. 1996. *Essays on Skepticism, Relativism, and Ethics in the Zhuangzi*. Albany: State University of New York Press.

Kohn, Livia. 1992. *Early Chinese Mysticism: Philosophy and Soteriology in the Taoist Tradition*. Princeton: Princeton University Press.

Liu, Xiaogan. 1994. *Classifying the Zhuangzi Chapters*. Ann Arbor: University of Michigan, Center for Chinese Studies.

Mair, Victor H., ed. 1983. *Experimental Essays on Chuang-tzu*. Honolulu: University of Hawaii Press.

Wu, Kuang-ming. 1990. *The Butterfly as Companion: Meditations on the First Three Chapters of the Chuang-tzu*. New York: Crossroads Publications.

Yearley, Lee. 1990. *Mencius and Aquinas: Theories of Virtue and Conceptions of Courage*. Albany: State University of New York Press.

Original Sources in Translation

Chan, Wing-tsit. 1963. *A Source Book in Chinese Philosophy*. Princeton: Princeton University Press.

Graham, A. C. 1960. *The Book of Lieh-tzu*. London: A. Murray.

Graham, A. C. 1981. *Chuang-tzu: The Seven Inner Chapters and Other Writings from the Book of Chuang-tzu*. London: Allan & Unwin.

Kohn, Livia. 1993. *The Taoist Experience*. Albany: State University of New York Press. Chs. 4, 32, 37.

Lau, D. C. 1970. *Mencius*. Baltimore: Penguin Books.

Mair, Victor H. 1994. *Chuang Tzu*. New York: Bantam.

Watson, Burton. 1968. *The Complete Works of Chuang-tzu*. New York: Columbia University Press.

CHAPTER THREE

HAN COSMOLOGY AND IMMORTALITY

The Han dynasty (206 B.C.E.–220 C.E.) saw cataclysmic changes in the development of early Chinese thought and religion. First, Yin-Yang cosmology rose to the forefront of all intellectual and political systems, expressed in the analysis of the movements of yin and yang in a rhythm of the so-called five phases (*wuxing*). The phases are often called "elements," but this is incorrect because the word implies a static solidity rather than the dynamic process that is really intended. These five phases were then matched with different aspects of life and the universe in an intricate system of correspondences. They were also applied to the seasons, so that calendrical study and seasonal regulations became of central importance in Han thought and social life. The further application of Yin-Yang cosmology to the human body, moreover, led to a new vision of life and health in the budding field of Chinese medicine.

Daoism adopted these new forms of thought. It connected the cosmological understanding of the universe and newly emerging legal procedures of government (associated with Huangdi, the Yellow Emperor) with the vision of Dao in the *Laozi*, and formulated its own guidelines for government in a school known as Huang-Lao, which was adopted briefly as the leading political doctrine. Daoism also took seasonal regulations to heart and integrated them into its practice and adopted new medical and health methods into its self-cultivation techniques. In addition, Daoism transformed under the influence of popular shamanistic techniques of ecstasy and interaction with the spirits. It linked these with Zhuangzi's ideal of untrammeled freedom in the ideal of immortality or transcendence. As a religious ideal this meant to leave the world behind in ecstasy and survive, in an ethereal yet concrete body, in paradises and among the stars. Last, but not least, new millenarian cults emerged that paved the way for the development of Daoism as an organized religion—these will be examined in the following chapter.

43

Yin-Yang Cosmology and Huang-Lao

Yin-Yang cosmology rests on the basic premise that everything in the world consists of one underlying cosmic energy, known as *qi*, which manifests itself in one of two alternating phases, known as yin and yang. The two terms indicate originally the shady and sunny side of a hill, and just as shade increases as one descends into the valley, while sun increases as one goes up the hill, so yin and yang move into each other continuously and can be subdivided into five continuous phases: lesser yang, greater yang, yin-yang, lesser yin, and greater yin. These five energetic phases were then symbolized by five material objects and associated with numerous aspects of ordinary life; their pattern became the blueprint for all later Chinese cosmological speculation and also played a key role also in Daoism. They are:

yin/yang	phase	direct.	color	season	organ1	organ2	emotion	sense
lesser yang	wood	east	green	spring	liver	gall	anger	eyes
greater yang	fire	south	red	summer	heart	sm. int.	exc. joy	tongue
yin-yang	earth	center	yellow		spleen	stomach	worry	lips
lesser yin	metal	west	white	fall	lungs	lg. int.	sadness	nose
greater yin	water	north	black	winter	kidneys	bladder	fear	ears

The interaction of the phases was then described as occurring either in a productive or in a destructive (overcoming) cycle. That is to say, as Dong Zhongshu (c. 179–104 B.C.E.), the leading thinker of this system, has it:

> Wood produces fire, fire produces earth, earth produces metal, metal produces water, and water again produces wood. Such is their father-and-son relationship. Wood occupies the left, metal occupies the right, fire occupies the front, water occupies the rear, and earth occupies the center. Such is their order, just as that of father and son, and the way in which they receive from each other and spread out. . . .
>
> Therefore, when wood is produced, fire should nourish it, and after metal perishes, water should store it. Fire enjoys wood and nourishes it with yang, but water overcomes metal and buries it with yin. Earth serves Heaven with utmost loyalty. For this reason, the five phases are representative of the actions of filial sons and loyal ministers. (*Chunqiu fanlu* 42; Chan, *Source Book*, 279)

This is reversed in the destructive sequence. Here wood is cut by metal, metal melted by fire, fire extinguished by water, water dammed by earth, and earth ploughed by wood, thus again creating a continuous sequence of phases and their related activities. The system was applied to natural cycles and also to political measures. For example, no sharp cutting or executions, associated with metal, took place in the spring, the season of growth and of wood. It was also applied to various dynastic and political interactions, defining relationships and giving rise to predictions of future rulers.

The Daoist thought of Huang-Lao represents an increasing adoption of this cosmology in the wake of the syncretist view expressed in the *Zhuangzi*. Here, the five phases become the tangible evidence for the concept of the holographic universe, which already appears in the *Daode jing*. It is now formulated in the doctrine of "impulse and response" (*ganying*), which means that nothing ever happens without an impact on or a connection to everything else. All is closely interrelated not only by causes but also synchronously, i.e., events are not just seen following each other in the same place at different times but also as occurring in different places at the same time. In other words, according to this view, whenever something happens on one plane of existence, there is a more or less immediate echo on all the others. Earthquakes, for example, or changes in the course of the planets, have their matching events in human society and in people's bodies. And, conversely, political events are mirrored in natural and planetary movements or disasters.

In Huang-Lao Daoism this idea of impulse and response, as expressed in the movements of yin and yang, is used to give structure to the annual cycle of life, nature, and society. It is then also applied to explain why inner cultivation has a profound and lasting impact on the development and wellbeing of the world. If one's own inner organs are in proper shape, the argument goes, one's life will be well nurtured and in good order, and this—in analogy to the sage's impact on the world in the *Daode jing*—will bring forth greater harmony and peace. Especially the ruler is encouraged to pursue longevity techniques and self-cultivation, so that the world at large will benefit.

Several manuscripts from Mawangdui present this view at this time. Later Daoist texts also express it, notably the commentary to the *Daode jing* by Heshang gong (Master on the River), a legendary sage who allegedly appeared to the Han emperor Wen (r. 179–156 B.C.E.) and taught him his interpretation of the *Daode jing*. Although of uncertain date, the commentary contains many ideas associated with Huang-Lao thought. Thus it reads the *Daode jing* in terms of longevity techniques, breathing exercises, and the parallel cultivation of body and state. For example, it says:

> The Dao of heaven is the same as the Dao of humanity. Heaven and humanity pervade each other, essence and energy [*qi*] continue each other. When the ruler of humanity is clear and tranquil, the energy of Heaven will naturally be upright. When the ruler is full of desires, the *qi* of Heaven will be troubled and turbid. Thus all good and bad fortune, profit and harm issue from one's own self. (ch. 47)

> The country is the self. Dao is its mother. When one can preserve Dao within the self, keeping the essence and energy from being labored and the five spirits from suffering hardship, then one can live forever. (ch. 60)

Another work of Huang-Lao background is the *Huainanzi*, a compilation in twenty chapters sponsored around 145 B.C.E. by Liu An, the Prince of Huainan. The work comprises treatises on the workings of Dao, the realities of the skies, the earth, and the seasons, as well as discussions of state craft, military strategy, and human affairs. It contains origin myths of Dao, discussions of impulse and response, discourses on the importance of astronomy, guidelines and instructions on correct rulership, and seasonal instructions. For example, on the appropriate activities for the summer, it suggests:

> Summer occupies the south; its corresponding stems are *bing* and *ding*. It manifests the fullness of the phase fire and its matching sound is the *zhi* note, while its pitchpipe is the Median Regulator. Its number is seven, its flavor is bitter, its smell is burnt. Its sacrifices are made to the stove god, and from the sacrificial animal, the lungs are offered first. Crickets and tree-frogs sing on the hillsides, and earthworms emerge. The large melons ripen, while bitter herbs flourish. The ruler wears red clothes and mounts a carriage drawn by black-maned reddish horses, flying a red banner. (ch. 5)

Matching items in this season, therefore, include concrete, natural events (animals and plants), health and body phenomena (tastes, smells), sacrificial activities (gods, offerings), the proper attire and equipment of the ruler, as well as general cosmological entities such as the number, pitch-pipe, and musical note.

To activate the new cosmology properly, seasonal awareness had to increase greatly. This in turn made the calendar an essentially important tool in both Chinese culture and Daoism, and without it many rites and cosmological concepts cannot be understood fully.

The Chinese Calendar

The traditional Chinese calendar, like ours, distinguishes four seasons—with sometimes, to match the five phases, a fifth, a kind of Indian summer, added between summer and fall. For the most part, however, it works with four seasons which are marked by the solstices and the equinoxes. Unlike in our calendar, however, solstices and equinoxes are not considered the seasons' beginnings. Instead, they are the high points of the seasons, which begin about six weeks prior to them. This system of having eight major cadences in the year—two solstices, two equinoxes, and four seasons' beginnings—is known as the Eight Nodes (bajie), and roughly matches the festivals of Western pagan or Wiccan religion: Candlemas (New Year, Feb. 2), Ostera (Spring Equinox, March 21), Beltane (May 1), Summer Solstice (June 21), Lammas (Aug. 2), Fall Equinox (Sept. 21), Samhain (Halloween, Oct. 31), and Winter Solstice (Dec. 21). In addition, the Chinese divide their year into twenty-four solar periods of about two weeks each, which are named after weather patterns such as "great heat," "slight cold," "great rain," and "slight snow," but also include the solstices and equinoxes.

The Chinese calendar is not only based on solar calculation; it is also lunar in that it measures the months according to the phases of the moon. The first of the month is, therefore, always on the new moon, and the fifteenth on the full moon. Because the lunar year has only 354 days as opposed to the 365¼ days of the solar year, the New Year shifts backward every year. To correct for this and keep the beginning of the year in the spring, the Chinese add one month to their calendar, the so-called intercalary month, once every three years—a total of seven additional months in nineteen years. This keeps their time calculation on the correct level and maintains the continuity of always having the winter solstice in the 11th lunar month, the spring equinox in the 2nd, the summer solstice in the 5th, and the fall equinox in the 8th.

For a larger count of years, the Chinese depend on Jupiter, which revolves around the sun once in twelve years. They assign a specific zodiac animal (e.g., rat, ox, hare) to each year, as well as a so-called cyclical character or "branch" (e.g., *zi, chou, yin*). They also — in high antiquity — used to have a ten-day week, in which they numbered the days with another set of nominal characters, known as "stems" (e.g., *jia, yi, bing*). Combining the ten stems with the twelve branches in all possible permutations, a set of sixty combinations evolved, which was then used to count the years — the so-called sixty-year cycle. It looks like this

year 1 = *jiazi* (1-rat)
year 2 = *yichou* (2-ox)
year 3 = *bingyin* (3-tiger)
year 4 = *dingmao* (4-hare)
year 5 = *mouchen* (5-dragon)
year 6 = *yisi* (6-snake)
year 7 = *gengwu* (7-horse)
year 8 = *xinwei* (8-sheep)
year 9 = *renshen* (9-monkey)

year 10 = *guiyou* (10-rooster)
year 11 = *jiaxu* (1-dog)
year 12 = *yihai* (2-pig)
year 13 = *bingzi* (3-rat)
year 14 = *dingchou* (4-ox)
etc., until
year 59 = *renxu* (9-dog)
year 60 = *guihai* (10-pig)
year 61 = *jiazi* (1-rat) = year 1

This cycle was formally established in the Han dynasty and the first *jiazi* (1-rat) year known is the year 4 C.E., so that from then onward all dates can be calculated. Each new cycle was seen as a new beginning, based on the idea that human life lasted for approximately sixty years and that, once it was over, a complete renewal occurred. The set of sixty was further applied to designate months, days, and hours, and is at the root of Chinese fate calculation even today — especially important in the planning of suitable marriages. Religious rituals of all traditions are scheduled according to the auspicious or inauspicious nature of the signs, and many of the most important Daoist rites occur once every sixty years to mark the renewal of the cosmos. In addition, Daoist and other millenarian movements have focused on certain years, such as *jiazi*, the first year of the cycle, as the starting point of the new world.

Immortality

At the same time and in a different strand of development, the ideal of personal freedom and inner perfection of the *Zhuangzi* was linked with ecstatic techniques developed in southern Chinese shamanism. These techniques are documented in a collection of shamanic songs known as the *Chuci* (Songs of Chu) associated with the southern poet Qu Yuan (340–278) and dated to around 200 B.C.E. They contain songs and dances to entice the deities to descend, and relate to trance techniques and ecstatic flights that would allow practitioners to join the gods in their own realm. One poem in particular, known as *Yuanyou* or "The Far-off Journey," outlines the growing confidence of the ecstatic traveler in the otherworld and describes how he communicates with various divine beings and takes control of entire trains of spirit followers. He eventually reaches the cosmic center of all, the inner clarity of the cosmos at the Great Beginning in a state of total sensory oblivion, openness and vastness. As the text says:

> Asking the Xiang [river] goddesses to play their zithers
> for me,
> I bid the Sea God dance with the River God.
> They pull up water monsters to step forward with them,
> Their bodies coiling and writhing in ever swaying motion!
> Gracefully the Lady Rainbow circles all around them,
> The phoenixes soar up, stay hovering above--
> The music swells ever higher, into infinity.
> At this point I leave to wander yet again
> With my entourage, I gallop far away.
> (Kohn, *Taoist Experience*, 256)

Growing from this combination of Zhuangzi's mental freedom and shamanic techniques of ecstasy, the belief in a new state of spiritual attainment arose, which came to be known as immortality or transcendence. The Chinese term, *xian*, denotes a person who attains this state and shows a human figure on a mountain or, in a variant graph, someone dancing with flying sleeves. Immortals are first mentioned vaguely in the *Zhuangzi* as spirit beings who live on a distant mountain in the Eastern Sea, nourish on pure *qi*, and have magical powers such as flying through air. By the early Han dynasty, a mythology had developed around them, and they were located in either of two paradises, both depicted as mountains covered in lush greenery and with glittering palaces and surrounded by water.

The first paradise is a group of islands in the Eastern Sea known as Peng-lai and carried on the backs of giant turtles; the other is a high mountain in the Central Asia called Kunlun, layered in terraces of hanging gardens and surrounded by a "weakwater stream" (*ruoshui*). Just as Dao cannot be grasped with the senses, neither of these paradises can be reached by ordinary means—the turtles will pick up and move Penglai as soon as they spot an intruder, and the weakwater will not float even a feather. Immortals there live in palaces made from indestructible substances such as gold and gems; they hold court and have banquets where they eat the fruits of immortality, the peaches of Mount Kunlun that only ripen once in three thousand years. Their ruler is Xiwang mu, the Queen Mother of the West, a beautiful goddess with a square headdress who rules over a large staff of ladies and other immortals. She represents the deeper, yin part of the immortal realm and shares her powers with her yang counterpart, Dongwang gong, the Lord King of the East.

Contact with the immortals was sporadic and unpredictable, and ways to attain their state were many and difficult. One was to obtain a magical substance from the isles of Penglai, ingest it and be instantaneously transformed. Several rulers, notably the First Emperor of the Qin (r. 221–209 B.C.E.) and Emperor Wu of the Han (r. 140–86 B.C.E.), subscribed to this method and sent out various embassies with the goal of finding the isles and bringing back the magical food or at least a recipe. The embassies, staffed with hundreds of young lads and maidens, never found the blessed realm but some discovered land to the east anyway and landed in Japan, where even today a number of places are called "Penglai" (Hôrai) and the embassy leader Xu Fu is still venerated.

Not trusting only one method to the desired state, the same emperors also hired several so-called magical practitioners (*fangshi*), people who claimed to have either mastered the secret of immortality themselves or to be able to contact the immortals and concoct a suitable elixir. Many of these practitioners were found fraudulent and were executed, and the two emperors died anyway. They were buried with much pomp, especially the First Emperor whose tomb was surrounded by a huge army of terracotta soldiers and many wondrous gadgets.

The *fangshi*, however, were not all frauds; for the most part they were serious practitioners of immortality and longevity. They have been described as the forerunners of organized Daoists and certainly have many ties to later Daoist practice. Like the ancient thinkers, they tended to come from the lower strata of the aristocracy, were thus able to read and write, and had elementary training in various practices. Their professions were at the fringes of society, engaging them in the sciences of the day. These included astrology, dream interpretation, casting of the *Yijing*, physiognomy, and other methods of fortune-telling, as well as semi-medical arts such as gymnastics, herbs, and massages. They earned their living during the day, and at night studied the classics to develop their own exegeses. One *Daode jing* commentary (by Yan Zun, fl. 83 B.C.E.–10 C.E.) goes back to a *fangshi*, and there are many fragments of prophetic and cosmological interpretations of various Confucian texts by them, collected today under the rubric of *chenwei* (apocrypha).

In terms of practices, the magical practitioners experimented with various diets and longevity techniques, engaged in meditations and ecstatic trances, and came to be known as shamanic figures among the general populace. *Fangshi* healed diseases, exorcised demons, prayed for rain, communicated with the gods, conjured up the dead, aided the transition of souls to the otherworld, and generally helped people with charms and spells to gain protection and good fortune. Certain more eccentric figures among them, such as Chisongzi (Master Redpine), were stylized as extensively long-lived (reaching several centuries in age) or even as immortals, with magical powers, a light, often feathery body, power over nature, and the ability to fly off to Penglai at a moment's notice. The first collection of immortals' biographies, the *Liexian zhuan*, is associated with Liu Xiang (77–6 B.C.E.) and originally consisted of a set of pictures with descriptions. It contains not only biographies of wondrous immortals of old, but also immortal-style hagiographies of Laozi, the Yellow Emperor, and other mythical figures.

Longevity Techniques

The belief in immortality and its attainability is at the root of many later Daoist ideas and practices, but in the Han dynasty it was most notably supported by a general increase in organized health and medical practices. The same cosmology at the root of Han political thought and of Huang-Lao also gave shape to a new vision of the human body, which now became a close replica of the greater universe. The *Huainanzi* describes it as follows:

> The roundness of the head is an image of heaven, the square-ness of the feet matches the pattern of earth. Heaven has four

> seasons, five phases, nine directions, and 360 days. Human be-
> ings have accordingly four limbs, five inner organs, nine ori-
> fices, and 360 joints. Heaven has wind, rain, cold, and heat.
> Human beings have accordingly the actions of giving, taking,
> joy, and anger. The gall bladder corresponds to the clouds, the
> lungs to the breath, the liver to the wind, the kidneys to the
> rain, and the spleen to the thunder. (*Huainanzi* 7)

A similarly integrated understanding of the body also emerged in Chinese medicine, where it was expressed most cogently in the *Huangdi neijing* (Inner Classic of the Yellow Emperor) and applied in the newly
emerging technique of acupuncture. Here the human body was divided
into five key storage centers of *qi*—the five yin-organs (*zang*) associated
with the five phases and defined as the liver, heart, spleen, lungs, and
kidneys. These five were assisted by six yang-organs (*fu*) which would
process rather than store *qi*—the gall bladder, small intestine, stomach,
large intestine, bladder, and triple heater (an organ with no match in
Western biomedicine). A sixth yin-organ, the pericardium, was later
added to even the numbers. Each of these was then associated with a
specific energy channel or meridian (*mai*), which directed its *qi* through
the body and into the extremities. Along these one could access the *qi*
through a needle or by massage. They interacted in continuous energetic
exchange, in all cases matching the seasons and the overall rhythm of yin
and yang. As the *Huangdi neijing* says:

> The three months of fall are called the period of tranquility in
> conduct. The atmosphere of Heaven is quick and that of Earth
> is clear. People should retire early at night and rise early at
> cock crow. They should keep their minds at peace to lessen the
> harshness of fall, collect their spirit to keep the *qi* tranquil, and
> maintain the purity of their lungs [the organ associated with
> fall] in purity by not giving in to desires. This is in harmony
> with the *qi* of fall and helps to protect the harvest. (1.2; Veith,
> *Yellow Emperor*, 103)

In addition to the basic twelve meridians, two further ones connect the
center of the body: the "Governing Vessel" (*dumai*) runs along the spine,
while the "Conception Vessel" (*renmai*) is located along the front of the
torso. They are central both in medical and religious practice, because
many acupuncture points located here are also spiritually important and

serve not only in healing but also in the attainment of longevity and even immortality.

Healing, longevity, and immortality can be seen as three different stages along the same continuum of the human body. The body consists of *qi*, which is only one but comes in two forms: a basic primordial or prenatal *qi* that connects it to the cosmos and Dao in general; and a secondary, earthly or postnatal *qi* that is replenished by breathing and food and helps the body survive in everyday life. Both forms of *qi* are necessary and interact constantly with each other, so that primordial *qi* is lost as and when earthly *qi* is insufficient, and earthly *qi* becomes superfluous as and when primordial *qi* is complete (as in the case of the embryo in the womb). People, once born, start this interchange of the two dimensions of *qi* and soon begin to lose their primordial *qi*, especially through inter-action with the world on the basis of passions and desires, sensory ex-changes, and intellectual distinctions — the very same features considered most harmful for cosmic interaction in the classical texts.

Once people have lost a certain amount of primordial *qi*, they get sick and eventually die. Healing, then, is the replenishing of *qi* with medical means such as drugs, herbs, acupuncture, rest, and so on. Longevity, next, comes in as and when people have become aware of their situation and decide to heal themselves. Attaining a basic state of good health, they then proceed to increase their primordial *qi* to and even above the level they had at birth. To do so, they must follow specific diets and un-dertake breathing exercises, gymnastics, massages, sexual practices, and meditations — all still practiced today under the name of Qigong. They ensure not only the realization of their natural life expectancy but may even result in increased old age and vigor.

Immortality, third, raises the practices to a yet higher level. To attain it, people have to transform all their *qi* into primordial *qi* and proceed to increasingly refine it to ever subtler levels. This finer *qi* will eventually turn into pure spirit, with which practitioners increasingly identify to become spirit-people and transcendents. The practice that leads there involves intensive meditation and trance training as well as more radical forms of diet and other longevity practices. Immortality implies the overcoming of the natural tendencies of the body and its transformation into a different kind of energy constellation. The result is a bypassing of death (the end of the body has no impact on the continuation of the spirit-person), the attainment of magical powers, and residence in the paradises of Penglai or Kunlun.

Longevity practices, as found in a variety of Han-dynasty manuscripts as well as many later texts, therefore, occupy a middle ground between healing and immortality and can be usefully applied on either level. They represent a separate tradition. Although they are used most essentially as medical techniques and for health improvement, they also play an important role in Daoism, but they should not be considered originally or even essentially Daoist. Rather, the same practices are applied slightly differently on the different levels. For example, diets on the medical and health levels involve abstention from heavy foods such as meat and fat, as well as from strong substances such as alcohol, garlic, and onions. Instead, practitioners are encouraged to eat lightly and in small portions. As their *qi* increases, they will need ever less food, until — in immortality practice — all main staples can be cut out and food is replaced by the conscious intake of *qi* through breath. This technique is called *bigu* or "avoiding grain" and is still undertaken today.

Similarly, gymnastics, massages, and breathing exercises, first depicted in a manuscript from Mawangdui (see Fig. 1), serve to stretch and loosen muscles, stimulate the circulation, and aid the smooth flow of *qi* in the body. They are never strenuous, but change in nature as people proceed from the longevity to the immortality levels, becoming more cosmic in pattern and more counter-intuitive. Breathing for health and long life involves acordingly inhaling all the way to the diaphragm, which expands as one inhales. Breathing for immortality, on the other hand, is called "reversed breathing," and uses the diaphragm the opposite way, contracting it on inhalation.

Sexual techniques, too, are used on all levels, first with a partner, later celibately and within the practitioner. In all cases, sexual stimulation is experienced but then the rising *qi* of arousal, commonly called *jing* (essence), is reverted upward along the spine with the help of meditation and massages instead of being lost through orgasm. This is called "reverting the semen to nourish the brain" and is supposed to have strong life-extending effects. In more technical Daoist practice of later centuries, it might even lead to the gestation of an immortal embryo.

Fig. 1. The "Gymnastics Chart" from the tomb at Mawangdui. Source: *Daoyin tu*.

Post-Mortem Immortality

Why, then, would we find texts on nourishing and extending life in tombs, of all places? Why would there be not only texts but also images of feathery immortals, murals of the Queen Mother of the West, mirrors with cosmic designs and inscriptions that contain wishes for long life? Somehow this seems to contradict the whole idea of living for a long time and attaining a state that bypasses death and opens up eternal existence in paradise. Scholars have argued variously about this question, and a satisfactory solution has yet to be found. What we know so far is that death in China has since antiquity been understood as the separation of two essential souls that form the nucleus of primordial *qi* and make up the living person: the *hun* or spirit soul of celestial origin, and the *po* or material soul that belongs to earth.

As the embryo forms in the womb, the two souls join together to give it life and consciousness; as the person dies, the two souls separate again, the *hun* to return to heaven in the form of an ancestral spirit (*shen*), the *po* to return to earth as the decaying body and its ghost (*gui*). Both gradually, over five to seven generations, merge back into their original element but for at least the first several years are thought to maintain close contact with the living and to still require human-style sustenance. For this reason, corpses are buried with extensive grave goods—the real thing in the old days, paper replicas today—and regular offerings of food, drink, and incense are made at ancestral altars.

Taking these ideas together with the fact that longevity texts are found buried in tombs, we might speculate that in Han understanding—as in later Daoist views (for example, the *Xiang'er* commentary to the *Daode jing* of the third century)—the newly buried person was still thought to be present. At this stage, with the two souls just starting to separate, the *qi* would still be active in the body, and people might have thought it possible that in this new state, removed from the sensory involvements and passions of the world, the person could actually still undertake the refinement of *qi* and transformation necessary to make themselves into an immortal. As such, instead of serving as an ancestor for several generations and gradually dissolving into the greater atmosphere, the person would retain some sense of personality, attain residence in one of the paradises, and find the freedom of immortality. The highest form of this, moreover, was understood to involve the dissolution and vanishing of the body at the time of transformation, a feature known as "ascending to heaven in broad daylight," which would render both burial and tombs superfluous.

This explanation enhances the understanding of immortality as a form of spirit or *qi* transformation, a spiritual endeavor with a strong physical base. It is not bodily "immortality" in our strict sense of the word. The translation of *xian* as immortality, then, must be taken with this specification in mind; there is, as Michel Strickmann rightly pointed out, no avoiding the death that practitioners first had to die on their way to the celestial realm. The new state, on the other hand, is not one of complete transcendence either, since this would imply a Western worldview of utter otherness and a transition to a completely different dimension, which is not the case in China. "Transformation" probably comes closest, but as a technical term it is already used to translate another Chinese expression, nor does it fully express the degree of change and attainment involved. For our purposes, we will, in alignment with French and German usage, continue to speak of "immortality" in describing the key Daoist goal, but while doing so we should always keep in mind its spiritual dimension and post-mortem potentials.

The cosmology and immortality beliefs of the Han dynasty create a major change in Daoism, and yet there is also a strong continuity in the tradition in that the ideals of Laozi and Zhuangzi are transformed but not lost. Indeed, it is at this point that we can see for the first time what it means to be a Daoist, not only in thought and vaguely defined practice but as a whole-life enterprise, in personal, social, and transcendent dimensions. Practicing Daoists, in their personal goals, would then retain the ancient ideals of nonaction, tranquility, and freedom of mind, but would also undertake health and longevity practices to extend harmony to their bodies, now seen as direct manifestations of the cosmos and the basis of all spiritual attainments.

Socially speaking, they would still be committed to social harmony as in the *Daode jing* and to the worship of deities as practiced in the larger culture, but they would also follow the seasonal commandments and natural cycles of yin and yang to establish an integrated pattern of social and personal life, and contribute to the greater wellbeing of all. In terms of transcendence, they now for the first time had a more "religious" goal in the potential attainment of immortality, achieved through the transformation of the body into pure *qi* and ascension into the paradises or heavens above. The multilayered and complex nature of the Daoist tradition comes to the fore at this time, integrating new strands of Chinese thought and contributing new ways of understanding to the world of ancient China.

Further Readings

Chan, Alan. 1991. *Two Visions of the Way: A Study of the Wang Pi and the Ho-shang-kung Commentaries on the Laozi*. Albany: State University of New York Press.

Eskildsen, Stephen. 1998. *Asceticism in Early Taoist Religion*. Albany: State University of New York Press.

Graham, A. C. 1986. *Yin-Yang and the Nature of Correlative Thinking*. Singapore: The Institute for East Asian Philosophies.

Kaptchuk, Ted J. 1983. *The Web That Has No Weaver: Understanding Chinese Medicine*. New York: Congdon & Weed.

Kohn, Livia, ed. 1989. *Taoist Meditation and Longevity Techniques*. Ann Arbor: University of Michigan, Center for Chinese Studies.

Loewe, Michael. 1979. *Ways to Paradise: The Chinese Quest for Immortality*. London: George Allan and Unwin.

Seidel, Anna. 1987a. "Post-Mortem Immortality: The Taoist Resurrection of the Body." In *Gilgul*, edited by S. Shaked, D. Shulman, G. G. Stroumsa, 223–37. Leiden: E. Brill.

Original Sources in Translation

DeWoskin, Kenneth J. 1983. *Doctors, Diviners, and Magicians of Ancient China*. New York: Columbia University Press.

Harper, Donald. 1999. *Early Chinese Medical Manuscripts: The Mawangdui Medical Manuscripts*. London: Wellcome Asian Medical Monographs.

Hawkes, David. 1959. *Ch'u Tz'u: The Songs of the South*. Oxford: Clarendon Press.

Kohn, Livia. 1993. *The Taoist Experience*. Albany: State University of New York Press. Chs. 17–20, 21, 33, 39, 47.

Major, John S. 1993. *Heaven and Earth in Early Han Thought: Chapters Three, Four, and Five of the Huainanzi*. Albany: State University of New York Press.

Veith, Ilza. 1966. *The Yellow Emperor's Classic of Internal Medicine*. Berkeley: University of California Press.

Yates, Robin D. S. 1997. *Five Lost Classics: Tao, Huang-Lao, and Yin-Yang in Han China*. New York: Ballentine Books.

Part Two

Religious Communities

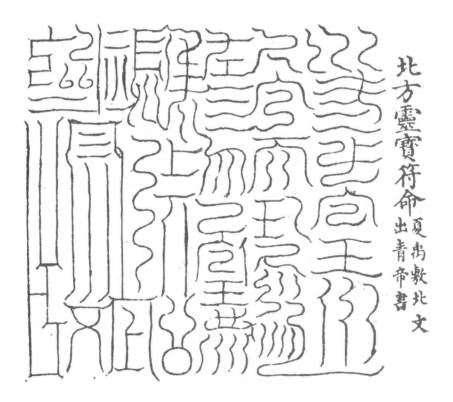

北方靈寶符命出青帝書夏禹敕北文

CHAPTER FOUR

COMMUNAL ORGANIZATIONS

Prior to the beginning of the Common Era, notable Daoist features appear in materials associated with the (lower) aristocracy and formulated largely in a political context and as philosophical speculation. This changes in the Later Han dynasty (23–220 C.E.), when the first organized religious communities are described in the texts. These communities incorporate not only social and political ideals into their worldview and practices, but also a heavy dose of popular religion. Popular religion by its very nature is a phenomenon that pervades culture, present from the earliest beginnings of time, yet it is poorly documented because it is practiced predominantly by people who are not literate, while its literate followers take it too much for granted to write about. Popular religion in ancient China involved the veneration of ancestors and gods, the performance of rites, sacrifices, and divinations, as well as the expulsion of demons and participation in shamanic séances.

The early Daoist communities of the second century C.E. consisted largely of commoners and peasants rather than aristocrats. They adopted many of these features while rejecting others, merging popular communal practices in a mass-religious movement with political visions of a world of complete harmony along the lines of Han cosmology and Huang-Lao. A major impulse for their rise came from the disastrous circumstances of the time — a succession of floods, droughts, locust plagues, famines, epidemics, and corrupt government — and they saw the resolution of all problems in the rise of a completely new world, dated with the help of five-phases cosmology and the calendar to the year 184 C.E.

There were many revolutionary and visionary movements at this time, some more identifiably Daoist than others, but we know mainly of two major organizations: Great Peace (Taiping), and the Celestial Masters (Tianshi), also known as the Way of Orthodox Unity (Zhengyi dao). The two had much in common, but were located in different regions—in the east (Shandong) and in the southwest (Sichuan), respectively—and each saw its role differently. Great Peace followers believed that they should replace the ruling dynasty and, in 184, rose in rebellion, were defeated, and became extinct as a Daoist school. The Celestial Masters saw themselves as advisers to whatever new ruler would arise, submitted to a local warlord, spread throughout China, and became a leading school of the religion which is still present and active today.

Popular Religion

Chinese popular religion, in ancient times as much as today, consists of the belief in a multitude of divine beings and the practice of rites and ceremonies to keep in good standing with them. Divine entities can be divided into three groups: nature gods, ancestors and gods derived from ancestors, and ghosts and demons.

Nature gods, to begin, are the deities of Heaven and Earth, stars and planets, rivers and lakes, mountains and fields, rain and wind, lightning and thunder, and so on. They are seen as semi-anthropomorphic or semi-beastly (water-related deities tend to be dragons, for example) and believed to be ranked in a hierarchical system of command, with Heaven at the top and the various other gods below. So, for example, the deities of the five sacred mountains would outrank those of lesser peaks, and the dragon king of the Eastern Sea would be higher in status that his counterpart in a mere lake or river. Nature gods have a great impact on human life in that they determine the fertility of the land, the amounts of rain and sunshine, the occurrence of disasters (floods, earthquakes, landslides), as well as the harmony of society and the selection of the ruler. They are propitiated through regular seasonal sacrifices offered at special nature altars and performed by all, from the king and high nobility on down to the common peasant—each according to his station. Heaven and Earth, for example, should be worshiped particularly by the central king or emperor, while the various gods of mountains, fields, and waterways have to be taken care of by the local people.

In addition to this basic nature pantheon, Han cosmologists added several new figures. Most important among them were the Five Emperors (*wudi*) as representatives of the cosmic powers of the five phases, each worshiped in their respective season and with their matching colors, numbers, tones, and so on. They also established a central deity known as the Great One (Taiyi) to hold a position in their center and rank slightly above them in a higher form of the Yellow Emperor. This Great One was associated closely with Dao, which too became a deity in the Han dynasty and was worshiped in the figure of the saintly Laozi, now equipped with supernatural and cosmic powers. There was, therefore, a tendency in popular and official religion to add human-form representations of abstract cosmic entities to the basic pantheon of nature-based gods.

Another major group of deities were the ancestors, defined as deceased immediate relatives in the male line plus their spouses, usually venerated up to five generations. Their worship was central in ancient China, and especially prominent in the Shang, the earliest Chinese dynasty (1766–1122 B.C.E.), whose people believed that most events in life were caused by either the goodwill or the curse of an ancestor and whose calendar (the ten-day week) was set up to allow regular sacrifices to all of them.

Since the Warring States period, ancestors have been understood to exist in two parts, their *hun* and *po* souls, which would separate at death and go different ways. The *hun* or spiritual part would move on into an ancestral heaven and could be accessed through worship of the ancestral tablet at home. The *po* or material part went into the grave where it had to be supplied with a legal contract to the land of the grave as well as with goods and proper care to prevent it from coming back as a ghost. Grave contracts have been found in tombs from the early centuries C.E., when grave goods consisted of meals, gifts, texts, and personal belongings. Today, grave goods are mostly paper replicas of desirable items. Ancestors were and are believed to be conscious and knowledgeable of their descendants' affairs. They require regular supplies of food, wine, incense, and incantations, and will in due return send good fortune and provide protection. The relationship is strictly reciprocal, and disasters and illnesses in life are often attributed to neglect of one's ancestral duties.

While most ancestors in their concern and influence are strictly limited to their own family, some people are considered too meritorious and too beneficial for society to be limited to serving one family only. By popular consent, and ratified in a lengthy process of official recognition, such ancestors are made into popular gods who serve one specific community or grow to become national deities. Well-known examples include the city god of Shanghai, a meritorious local official of the fourteenth century who was promoted to his supernatural position upon popular petition; and the wealth god Guandi, originally a military general of the third century, who was first locally and then nationally worshiped and whose temple is found in most major Chinese cities.

The popular gods who grew from ancestors, too, are ranked in an organized hierarchy and divided into separate departments under the rulership of the central Jade Emperor (Yuhuang), the personification of Heaven. One department is of particular importance to people since it supervises humanity, keeping track of people's good and bad deeds and adding or subtracting time from the life span. This so-called Department of Destiny is run by the Ruler of Fates (Siming), a deity first documented in manuscripts from the fourth century B.C.E. and still important today. Proper behavior on earth and regular worship of these deities will ensure good fortune and prosperity for generations to come.

A third group of supernatural entities prominent in popular religion are ghosts and demons, for the most part defined as the unhappy or discontented dead. Some are people who died violently and who have come back to wreak vengeance; others are ancestors who have been neglected by their families and are hungry and in search of sustenance; yet others are mutant animals, creatures that have somehow gained the power to change their shape and cause trouble. To deal with these, people take basic precautions such as hanging demon-dispelling branches (preferably peach wood) or talismans over their doors, muttering spells against ghosts whenever they enter an unknown area, or performing a divination before venturing out. Once a demon or ghost has made itself known, more active measures are taken, such as throwing a slipper at it, holding up a mirror which will reveal its true, hideous shape, or calling it by its name. Normally, it can stand none of these acts and will vanish forthwith. Sometimes, however, more extensive rites of exorcism are necessary, or perhaps a shamanic séance in which the demon is called out, identified, and properly vanquished.

All these deities, therefore, have been part of Chinese popular religion since antiquity and have required various forms of care through worship and veneration or preventative rites and exorcisms. The early Daoist communities, too, participated in this popular religious culture and adopted its key features — with two differences. First, they added a different type of deity to the pantheon, one that was not based on nature or a dead person, and whose key characteristic was to be utterly beyond the relationship of common mutuality. This type of divinity is represented by the immortals, who were originally humans but whose transformation into spirit beings did not involve the separation of the two souls and thus not "death" as commonly understood. These divinities also included personifications of major cosmic forces, such as Lord Lao (Laojun) as the personification of Dao, the Queen Mother of the West (Xiwang mu) as the representative of cosmic yin (and the queen of immortals), and the Lord King of the East, who stood for cosmic yang. They were considered to be of higher purity and thus greatly superior to the gods derived from dead people.

The second difference that emerged among early Daoists was that they rejected shamanic trances, blood sacrifices, and orgiastic fertility rites, and replaced them with written communications to the gods. Expressing their prayers and wishes in petitions, memoranda, and announcements, they established a formal line of communication with the otherworld, in which the master functioned as an otherworldly official himself, carrying the seals and powers of divine appointment. All this, moreover, they placed into the larger social agenda of transforming the world to a new level.

Dynastic Change

In ancient China dynasties came to power by obtaining the so-called Mandate of Heaven (*tianming*). The idea was that Heaven (*tian*), a quasi-personified divine agent, manifested itself in the movements of the planets, the patterns of nature, and high moral principles, and directed the course of mundane events by appointing or ordering (*ming*) a certain ruler to take specific actions. Usually it picked a morally upright person to begin a dynasty, and the new ruler tried his best to live up to the charge. But over time complacency would set in and later rulers became increasingly dissipated, steeped in luxury, and morally reprehensible. In due accordance with the law of impulse and response, the world was in perfect harmony or "great peace" as long as the ruler was morally upright and strove for his own and the world's proper cultivation. It fell out of order and was subject to increasingly violent calamities as the ruler became lax and depraved, and the government as a whole gave in to corruption.

Heaven communicated its choices and displeasures by sending certain signs or omens. In the beginning of a dynasty, these tended to be positive, such as the spotting of unusual animals (a unicorn or phoenix), the auspicious constellation of the planets, and the discovery of wondrous objects (marvelous stones, precious gems, or fabulous jades). As the dynasty progressed into decline, the signs became more negative, beginning with the birth of deformed children or animals and continuing into large-scale natural disasters. At the same time, new auspicious signs appeared in the vicinity of potential new rulers, morally upright individuals born at the right time in the right place and catapulted to power with a force thought to come from Heaven itself. Eventually, often after decades of civil war, the good would win and the bad would die, and the cycle repeated itself all over again under a new dynasty and a new cosmic phase.

Auspicious signs were a key step to legitimizing a new rule and in Daoism they became symbols of cosmic power and major religious implements. An early example of such signs was the so-called "River Chart" (*Hetu*; later a sacred Daoist text), apparently first a precious stone that served as part of the regalia of the Zhou ruling house. Not only a wondrous stone, it was also said to have borne unusual markings, interpreted as a chart or map presented by Heaven to the ruler. Such divine maps or cosmic diagrams (*tu*) were believed to contain the essence of the land in symbolic form, and thus provided the king (and later the Daoist) with celestial control over his realm. A different development of the sacred diagram was the talisman (*fu*), which consisted of a piece of paper with a divine sign or message in celestial script that served as a direct empowerment of its owner. Divine diagrams and messages also evolved into complete sacred texts, which often arose in their explanation, similarly containing the powers of rulership and divine control.

In the Han dynasty after the beginning of the Common Era (the Later or Eastern Han), many such divine signs appeared in various forms, including entire scriptures that were sent down from Heaven and revealed by Dao itself in its personification as Lord Lao. These divine scriptures were the first revelations of Dao and thus the first religious texts of Daoism.

Great Peace

The earliest text of this kind is known as *Tianguan li baoyuan Taiping jing* (Scripture of Great Peace and the Maintenance of Primordiality as Based on the Calendar of the Celestial Officials), which was presented to several Han rulers shortly before the beginning of the Common Era (32–1 B.C.E). It is no longer extant, but it presumably claimed divine inspiration and suggested ways of governmental reform in accordance with the cosmology of Huang-Lao. Better known is another "Scripture of Great Peace" presented to the Han court in 166 C.E. This *Taiping qingling shu* (Book of Great Peace Written in Blue) allegedly went back to the 145 C.E. revelation by Dao through its personification in Lord Huanglao to Gan Ji, a religious seeker in eastern China. It, too, has been destroyed, but it was reconstituted in the sixth century in a text called *Taiping jing* (Scripture of Great Peace), parts of which remain in the Daoist canon. Scholars have analyzed the latter and identified three different layers of text and composition, dated controversially to different periods between the second and fourth centuries. Most assume that the reconstituted text expresses a worldview typical for the Great Peace movement in the Later Han.

According to this, the entire world consists of cosmic *qi* which appears on three levels: heaven, humanity, and earth. Heaven was an anthropomorphic entity who ruled everything and enforced moral principles, expressing itself in omens and planetary movements. Humanity had to fit in with the cosmic patterns and obey Heaven's rules, in all cases matching the changes of the seasons and protecting the unfolding and growth of nature. People were divided hierarchically into nine classes, ranging from divine personages at the top, through perfected, immortals, and sages to the common people and finally slaves at the bottom. Earth was the realm of nature spirits and the dead, who had to be pacified and served in the proper way. In all cases, it was essential to maintain a smooth flow of *qi* and keep communication open on all levels — spiritual, material, economic, and physiological — especially on the political and social planes, so that no corruption could grow and preventive measures could be taken in good time.

Little is known about the actual community and practices of the Great Peace followers, but it seems that they observed dietary abstentions from alcohol and meat, undertook a meditation exercise known as "guarding the One" (*shouyi*), worshiped ancestral, nature, and heavenly spirits, and generally prepared for the next phase of the cosmic cycle, which was to bring a completely new world of universal "great peace." It was expected to begin in 184, the next *jiazi* year. They believed that their leader would bring them into the new age of revitalized longevity and that the world would be recreated in the image of their movement. A proper morality would be in place, and a complete openness of communication on all levels, to the greater happiness and perfection of the entire cosmos.

They turned more militant under the leadership of Zhang Jue from Hebei, formally known as "Great Sage, Excellent Teacher" or "General of Heaven." Together with his two brothers, the Generals of Earth and Humanity, he established a tight, semi-military organization southeast of the Chinese heartland. In 175, he began to send out messengers to other provinces and within several years, inspired by the disastrous conditions of the land, he had won tens of thousands of followers. By 183, he had them organized into thirty-six "squares" of six or ten thousand members, and each led by a deputy general. They readied themselves to die for the imminent beginning of the new world, and in 184 they rose in a massive rebellion of 360,000 that engulfed almost the entire country, except for the southwestern province of Sichuan.

Their battle cry was that the "blue heaven" of the Han was dead and the "yellow heaven" of Great Peace was at hand, and they shook the Han dynasty to its foundations. Symbolizing this color change, they wore yellow kerchiefs on their heads which caused them to be called Yellow Turbans (*huangjin*). Although the three leading generals were captured and executed early on, the rebellion ravaged the land for several decades and was only put down by local gentry and landowners, one county at a time. Small pockets of non-violent followers remained at the end of the Han dynasty in 220, but eventually these too died or were absorbed into the growing organization of the Celestial Masters.

Celestial Masters

The Celestial Masters, or the Way of Orthodox Unity, was the other major Daoist movement that arose at this time. It was located in the southwestern region of Sichuan and led by Zhang Ling or Zhang Daoling, the first "celestial master" (see Fig. 2). According to hagiographies,

Fig. 2. Zhang Daoling, the first Celestial Master. Source: *Zengxiang liexian zhuan*.

which probably merge information on several people into one narrative, he was originally from Henan in the central plains and pursued the calling of a *fangshi* and alchemist. Obtaining a secret recipe in a trance, he tried to obtain the necessary (but costly) ingredients, failed, and then moved to Sichuan where things appeared to be easier. There, in 142, allegedly on the summer solstice, on a mountain known as Heming (Crane-Cry) which has been located variously to the west of Chengdu, he entered another deep trance and had a major vision of a deity who introduced himself as Lord Lao, the personified Dao. The god told Zhang that the end of the world was at hand. He was to instruct the people to repent and prepare themselves for the momentous changes by becoming morally pure so they could serve as the "seed people" (*zhongmin*) of the new age. Closing the "Covenant of Orthodox Unity" with Zhang, the god then appointed him as his representative on earth with the title "celestial master," and gave him healing powers as a sign of his empowerment.

Zhang followed the god's orders and proceeded to wake up the people and heal the sick. As a token for his efforts, he took the sum of five pecks of rice from his followers, who included large numbers of local people and ethnic non-Chinese. The tax earned the sect the nickname "Five Pecks of Rice Sect" (Wudou mi dao). Over the years Zhang assembled a sizable following, then "transformed himself into an immortal in broad daylight," passing the organization on to his son Zhang Heng and his grandson Zhang Lu.

Under the latter, the Celestial Masters rose to greater prominence, notably through merging with another local cult run by Zhang Xiu (not a relation). This cult utilized a more stringent military-type organization and practiced a formal ritual of confession and petition—both characteristics that were to become typical of the Celestial Masters in general. Zhang Lu controlled a large territory in the southwest area (known as Hanzhong) which he divided into twenty-four districts matching the twenty-four solar energies of the year. He made amicable arrangements with the local governor and proceeded to give his organization a strong inner structure and ritual system. After about thirty years of consolidation, battles ensued which surrounding the end of the Han dynasty, and the warlord Cao Cao attacked the area. In 215, Zhang Lu submitted to Cao Cao, a move criticized by followers on both sides as an act of submission and weakness. In the event, Cao Cao became a powerful leader and decided not to tolerate a separate organization in his territory. As a result, large numbers of Celestial Masters followers were forcefully evacuated and had to migrate to different parts of the empire, spreading their cult as they went and laying the foundation for the strong Daoist school they later became.

Most information on the early Celestial Masters has come down to us in official dynastic histories which give a very sketchy and rather biased account. There are several fourth-century texts on demons and some accounts of Celestial Masters history and cosmology, as well as a number of fragments of the ritual compendium *Santian zhengfa* (Orthodox Methods of the Three Heavens), which scholars are only beginning to assemble. A hagiographic, revelatory text on Lord Lao (*Laozi bianhua jing*) has survived in manuscript form and can be dated to around 180 C.E. It is located in Sichuan, but does not belong immediately to a Celestial Masters environment. Most importantly, a commentary on the *Daode jing* ascribed to Zhang Lu and known as the *Xiang'er*, is also extant (although fragmentary) and gives some insight into the worldview and moral and longevity practices of the early Daoists.

From what information we have it appears that the followers of the Celestial Masters were hierarchically ranked on the basis of ritual attainments, with the so-called libationers (*jijiu*) at the top. They served as leaders of the twenty-four districts and reported directly to the Celestial Master himself. Beneath them were the demon soldiers (*guizu*), meritorious leaders of households who represented smaller units in the organization. All leadership positions could be filled by either men or women, Han Chinese or ethnic minorities. At the bottom were the common followers, again organized and counted according to households. Each of these had to pay the rice tax or its equivalent in silk, paper, brushes, ceramics, or handicrafts. In addition, each member, from children on up, underwent formal initiations at regular intervals and was equipped with a list of spirit generals for protection against demons—75 for an unmarried person and 150 for a married couple. The list of spirit generals was called a register (*lu*) and was carried, together with protective talismans, in a piece of silk around the waist.

Doctrines and Practices

In terms of doctrines and practices, the Celestial Masters believed in Dao at the center of creation, which was represented by the personal creator god Lord Lao, who appeared to special seekers (and virtuous rulers) as the need arose. Although described in the texts as a person with special attributes and features, Lord Lao does not appear in human form in the Daoist art of the period. Rather, in accordance with the doctrine that Dao cannot be described, he is shown as an ornate canopy or an empty throne. The belief was that he created and ruled the universe, assisted in this task by a celestial administration which kept records of life and death, and consisted of the Three Bureaus (*sanguan*) of Heaven, Earth, and Water. These three were celebrated at the major festivals of the year, known as the Three Primes (*sanyuan*), held on the fifteenth day of the first, seventh, and tenth months. These were also the occasion of general assemblies and tax management: in the first month, the tax was set according to the number of people in the household; in the seventh and tenth months, it was collected as the harvest was brought in.

Throughout the year, followers practiced the recitation of Laozi's *Daode jing* and were encouraged to follow a set of three times nine precepts based on it. These survive in a later text associated with the *Xiang'er* commentary, and are:

The basic nine precepts:
Do not strongly pursue riches and honor if you happen to
be poor and humble.
Do not do evil.
Do not set yourself many taboos and avoidances.
Do not pray or sacrifice to demons or the spirits of the dead.
Do not strongly oppose anyone.
Do not consider yourself always right.
Do not quarrel with others over what is right and wrong;
if you get into a debate, be the first to concede.
Do not praise yourself as a sage of great fame.
Do not take delight in soldiering.

The middle nine precepts:
Do not study false texts.
Do not covet high glory or vigorously strive for it.
Do not pursue fame and praise.
Do not do things pleasurable to ears, eyes, or mouth.
Always remain modest and humble.

Do not engage in frivolous undertakings.
Always be devout in religious services, of respectful mind
and without confusion.
Do not indulge yourself with fancy garb or tasty food.
Do not overextend yourself.

The highest nine precepts:
Do not delight in excess, since joy is as harmful as anger.
Do not waste your essence or *qi*.
Do not harm the dominant *qi*.
Do not eat beings that contain blood to delight in their fancy taste.
Do not hanker after merit and fame.
Do not explain the teaching or name Dao to outsiders.
Do not neglect the divine law of Dao.
Do not try to set things in motion.
Do not kill or speak about killing. (*Laojun jinglü*; see also Bokenkamp, *Early Daoist Scriptures*, 50)

These precepts convey the austerity and moral discipline required of Celestial Masters followers, as well as their sense of being special and separate from ordinary folk. Some scholars suspect that both the mantric, magic recitation of the *Daode jing* and the impulse to create precepts were inspired by Buddhist monks. The monks first appeared in China around this time and may well have had contact with the new religious groups, but the issue remains unresolved.

This changes with the fourth-century code *Laojun yibai bashi jie* (The 180 Precepts of Lord Lao), which was definitely inspired by early Buddhist community rules known as the *Pratimoksa*. It provides many detailed rules on practical living and emphasizes personal honesty and community life. The text strongly prohibits theft, adultery, killing, abortion, intoxication, destruction of natural resources, and waste of food, and regulates the proper behavior toward community members and outsiders. It prohibits fraternization with brigands and soldiers, punishes cruelty to slaves and animals, and insists upon polite distance when encountering outsiders and officials. Many details of daily life are regulated, and pettiness and rudeness are discouraged as much as the accumulation of personal wealth.

While ordinary life was governed by discipline and simplicity, the Three Primes and other major community events were celebrated in style with banquets known as kitchen-feasts (*chu*). Wine would flow, animals were slaughtered, and everyone had a mighty good time, leading certain critics of the movement to condemn their practices as "orgiastic." The same criticism was made of an initiatory practice known as the "harmonization of *qi*" (*heqi*), which involved formally choreographed intercourse between selected non-married couples in an elaborate ritual. Practitioners underwent this rite when they were promoted from one level of ritual standing to another (and gained more generals in their registers), enacting the matching of yin and yang in their bodies and thus contributing to greater cosmic harmony. From the viewpoint of religious organization, such a rite that goes against the common social values and runs counterintuitive to people's sense of shame enhances cult cohesion and binds followers that much more strongly to their leader. It is a common phenomenon in restrictive and millenarian cults, among which the early Celestial Masters must be counted.

Aside from living morally and harmonizing yin and yang, the early communal Daoists joined popular believers of the time in that they were very concerned with the impact of demons on their lives. Demons were believed to be everywhere and come in every shape, from the lowly rabbit and the dirty rat to all sorts of natural and supernatural creatures. A list of such demons has been excavated from a Han tomb, and several others are found in the earliest surviving texts of the Celestial Masters. To combat them, members had to fortify their houses and bodies with talismans, learn to recognize the demons and call them by their proper names, and visualize themselves as demon-conquering heroes. This would banish the demons forthwith and relieve followers from their harm, especially when accompanied by the ritual formula "Swiftly, swiftly, in accordance with the statutes and ordinances" (*jiji ru lüling*), which concludes all ritual incantations and petitions of the Celestial Masters and is still used today. An example is found in a fourth-century text known as *Zhougui jing* (Scripture on Cursing Demons):

> The Celestial Master said:
> I am the scourge that kills all misfortunes under heaven,
> A changing body among men, I am a demon king.
> My body tall to sixteen feet, my face square and even,
> I have copper teeth, iron molars, and a tough, sharp beak.
> In my hands a grindstone and a boiling pot,
> I hurl the thunder, throw the lightning, and swing the
> lights of heaven.
> Stars and planets lose their course, the moon hides her shining,
> Whirlwinds arise, battering earth, the sun retains his brilliance.
> Grasses and ferns scorch and wither, trees lose their foliage.

> Mountains tumble, stones cleave asunder, I break all
> river bridges.
> My carriage holds an iron cage, shot with a silver lock,
> I beat it thrice in every month, sing six sacred songs.
> Thus I search out the many demons, valiant and strong,
> Succeed in killing off the numerous misfortunes.
> While I thus brandish divine spells, who would dare approach,
> Passing fast over a thousand miles, I free all from misery.
> Swiftly, swiftly, in accordance with the statutes and ordinances!

If, despite these measures, someone was attacked by a demon, they would suffer sickness and disease. Moreover, such an attack could occur only because the person had been careless and had a moral failing. As a result, all healing of the Celestial Masters was undertaken through ritual and magic; acupuncture, herbs, and other medical treatments were expressly prohibited. First the sick person was isolated in a so-called quiet chamber (*jingshi*), an adaptation of a Han institution for punishing wayward officials involving solitary confinement. There they had to think of their sins going all the way back to their birth to try and find a explanation for the illness.

Once certain sins had been identified, a senior master would come to write them down—in triplicate and together with a formal petition for their eradication from the person's divine record. The three copies would then, in a formal ceremony, be transmitted to Heaven (by burning), Earth (by burying), and Water (by casting into a river), whose officials supposedly set the record straight and restored the person's good health. Additional measures of purification involved the ingestion of "talisman water"—the ashes of a talisman dissolved in water (*fushui*)-- gymnastic exercises (*daoyin*), and meditations (*jingsi*).

Then again, members had to perform community service on a regular basis, repairing roads and bridges and maintaining so-called lodges of righteousness (*yishe*) where travelers could stay on their journeys. Overall, the community was tight and well-controlled, and in many features matched the kinds of cults we commonly associate with the phenomenon of millenarianism.

Millenarianism

Millenarianism is the belief that the world is coming to an end and that a newer and better one will take its place. The new world, a golden age of peace and prosperity, will last forever, with a first major phase of one thousand years, hence the name. In some cases, the millennium is heralded by a savior or messiah who has been sent by the central god and will lead his "chosen people" to the new age. In such cases we speak of messianism.

Both early Daoist movements share the basic characteristics of millenarian and messianic cults and arise about the same time as Jewish apocalyptic groups and early Christianity in the West. As a general common point, millenarian movements believe that salvation in the new world is collective, to be enjoyed by the faithful as a group; terrestrial, realized on this earth and not in some otherworldly heaven; imminent, to come both soon and suddenly; total, an utter transformation of life on earth leading not merely to an improvement but to perfection itself; and divinely effected, accomplished by supernatural agencies. Most commonly, such movements arise in times of crisis and difficulty, giving expression to the hope that the present hardships will be overcome. Crisis may be precipitated by natural catastrophes, such as floods and droughts, famines and plagues; political instability through corruption, social change, and civil war; and oppression, either of certain groups within a society or of the entire society by a conquering or colonizing force.

Millenarian movements are, therefore, often expressions of economic troubles, social discontent, and personal despair. These are remedied in the movement through the establishment of a new society that considers itself "chosen" and lives according to special ethical principles and community rules revealed by the deity, setting itself actively apart from other people. Healing is often a key activity for the millenarian community not only because it symbolizes the power of the cult but also because it is the first practical step toward the wholeness and health of the new age to come.

The Daoist movements of the Later Han share all these characteristics and are very similar to their counterparts in the West. The question then arises whether these similarities are coincidental or due to historical interaction. The most commonly accepted position among scholars is that they are coincidental. The argument here is that millenarianism is a universal human phenomenon which can arise in any culture if the conditions are ripe and if there is a sense of crisis, foreboding, or impending disaster. According to this view, the belief in a new age is rooted in the inherent human faculty of hope, the need to see a better and renewed life after the end of the old. The same basic instinct that lets people time and again believe in a life after death also makes them create collective visions of world after destruction. In addition, certain traditional Chinese beliefs paved the way for an indigenous millenarian vision: the notion of dynastic cycles, the belief in the changing Mandate of Heaven, the ideal of a golden age of the past that can be recovered, and the vision of Great Peace. Millenarianism in China, then, closely resembles the Western movements, but is not entirely the same since it continues to allow for a cyclical decline and a repeated renewal at the end of cycles. Rather, it resembles most non-Western types, which are also found in tribal cultures that have little or no contact with Western concepts, thus supporting the view of independent and separate origins.

The contrary position favors the influence of Western ideas. It follows the research by Norman Cohn in his *Cosmos, Chaos, and the World to Come* (1995), which argues that millenarianism is not universal but arose very specifically and as part of an intricate cultural complex in the prophecies of Zoroaster in ancient Persia. From there it spread to be adapted by the Israelites, appeared in its classical passage in the *Book of Daniel* (165 B.C.E.), and served as a foundation for the early Christians. As a complex, it includes not only the characteristics outlined above, but also several distinct ideas: a single, monotheistic, creator deity who interacts personally with a divine seeker and gives direct instructions to his followers; time as a linear phenomenon, with a beginning through the creator god, an end at the brink of the millennium, and a complete break at the beginning of the new age; good and evil, light and darkness, as radically different forces that engage in an apocalyptic endtime battle. All these elements, Cohn argues, are part of the phenomenon of millenarianism and are much more complex than the simple feeling of hope for a better time and the various sociological commonalties. Rather, they constitute a major shift away from the old worldview of "cosmos," the regular, cyclical pattern of the universe, toward a new vision of something that had never arisen before.

Applying this understanding of millenarianism to the Chinese situation, it becomes clear that none of Cohn's characteristics of millenarian thought—monotheism, linear time, and the battle between good and evil—are found in Chinese culture before the arrival of the Daoist movements, yet play a decisive role in them. In addition, it is well known that many members of the Celestial Masters were non-Chinese, and that through the Silk Road, Han China was well connected with Persia, the Near East, and even Rome—ties with Persia, as known from archaeology, go back even to 800 B.C.E. Linguistics provides further indications of a relationship: the hailed new realm of Daqin may go back to a name used for "Rome," and the word Daluo for the highest Daoist heaven may be an adaptation of the ancient Iranian *garo-dmana*. While none of this constitutes solid proof for a direct connection, the possibility cannot be excluded, and the early Daoist movements may well have received a strong stimulus from non-Chinese sources. This, however, does not make their beliefs and practices any less Daoist or reduce their value and interest for the study of religion.

The Later Celestial Masters

After the dispersal of their original organization under Cao Cao in the early third century, the Celestial Masters spread to other parts of the country and, as their communities became integrated into the larger populace, transformed from a tightly organized cult into a more open organized religion, which they still are in China. They retained the hierarchy of registers and the priesthood, and their focus on submitting written petitions to the gods, and they continued to hold kitchen-feasts and give money to the religion. However, the tax was now transformed into a tithe, and the hierarchy was solely priestly and had no official or political standing (loyalty to the current emperor becoming a major virtue). The millenarian vision was downplayed, and practices labeled "orgiastic" were discontinued.

In fact, the openness of the organization was taken so far as to lead to a general laxity in membership and religious practices. This state was sorely deplored by Lu Xiujing (406–477), their best known representative of the fifth century and a prominent court Daoist and prolific compiler of scriptures and rituals. His *Daomen kelue* (Abridged Codes for the Daoist Community) is particularly instructive since it contains a long list of desirable changes to be made to the structure and practices of the organization, indicating just what dire straits it was in at the time — taxes remained uncollected, parishes were falling apart, libationers were practicing without proper ordination, and so on. Encouraged by his guidance, the Celestial Masters reorganized, and they have been a leading Daoist school ever since.

In terms of worldview, the school adjusted to the increasing popularity of Buddhism by recasting Lord Lao as an incarnation of the Buddha and by formulating a more substantial cosmogony. This is found especially in the *Santian neijie jing* (Scripture of the Inner Explanation of the Three Heavens), dated to about 420 C.E., when the Celestial Masters strove to establish themselves as loyal supporters of the newly risen Liu-Song dynasty. The text describes the creation:

> In the midst of emptiness and pervasion, great nonbeing was born. Great nonbeing transformed and changed into the three *qi*-energies, mysterious, primordial, and beginning. Intermingling in chaos, they followed each other and transformed to bring forth the Jade Maiden of Mystery and Wonder (Xuanmiao yunü).

> After the Jade Maiden had been born, the chaos energies congealed. They transformed and brought forth Laozi, born from the left armpit of the Jade Maiden. At birth he had white hair, thus he was called Laozi or Old Master — he is Lord Lao. . . .

> Then mysterious *qi*, clear and pure, rose up and became heaven. Beginning *qi*, thick and turbid, coagulated downward and became earth. Primordial *qi*, light and subtle, flowed everywhere and became water. Next, the sun and the moon, the stars and the chronograms were properly arranged, and Lord Lao proceeded to harmonize the three energies and form nine countries, placing nine people in each, three men and six women. (ch. 1)

In a next step, Lord Lao creates three separate religions, Daoism in the east, Buddhism in the west, and Yin-Yang popular religion in the south. Over many aeons he guides humanity, but despite his efforts a decline sets in, life expectancies decline, and people begin to engage in frivolous, orgiastic cults and blood sacrifices. The new dispensation offered by the deity to the Celestial Master Zhang Daoling, then, serves to recreate a primal state of purity and the renewal of cosmic harmony.

The text thus makes it clear that several religions coexist in the world, but that among them Daoism is the first and highest, the "greater vehicle." Buddhism in comparison is the "lesser vehicle," a distinction taken over from Buddhism, which this text claims was created by Lord Lao through the conversion of the barbarians and the birth of his assistant Yin Xi (the guardian of the pass and first recipient of the *Daode jing*) as the Buddha. The *Santian neijie jing* then applies—sometimes verbatim—the hagiography of the Buddha to Lord Lao, joining Daoism and Buddhism while maintaining a strong contrast with popular, shamanic, and orgiastic cults. Its worldview has continued to be representative of the later Celestial Masters, whose main focus remained ritual, including purification ceremonies, exorcisms, celebrations of births, marriages, and funerals, and rites of cosmic renewal.

Further Readings

Kaltenmark, Max. 1979. "The Ideology of the *T'ai-p'ing-ching*." In *Facets of Taoism*, edited by Holmes Welch and Anna Seidel, 19–52. New Haven: Yale University Press.

Kleeman, Terry. 1998. *Great Perfection: Religion and Ethnicity in a Chinese Millenarian Kingdom*. Honolulu: University of Hawaii Press.

Kohn, Livia. 1998. "The Beginnings and Cultural Characteristics of East Asian Millenarianism." *Japanese Religions* 23: 29–51.

Levy, Howard S. 1956. "Yellow Turban Rebellion at the End of the Han." *Journal of the American Oriental Society* 76: 214–27.

Poo, Mu-chou. 1997. *In Search of Personal Welfare: A View of Ancient Chinese Religion*. Albany: State University of New York Press.

Schipper, Kristofer. 1994. *The Taoist Body*. Translated by Karen C. Duval. Berkeley: University of California Press.

Seidel, Anna. 1984. "Taoist Messianism." *Numen* 31: 161–74.

Wu, Hung. 2000. "Mapping Early Taoist Art: The Visual Culture of Wudoumi Dao." In *Taoism and the Arts of China*, edited by Stephen Little and Shawn Eichman, 77–94. Berkeley: University of California Press.

Original Sources in Translation

Bokenkamp, Stephen R. 1997. *Early Daoist Scriptures*. Berkeley: University of California Press.

Eno, Robert. 1996. "Deities and Ancestors in Early Oracle Inscriptions." In *Religions of China in Practice*, edited by Donald S. Lopez, Jr., 41–51. Princeton: Princeton University Press.

Harper, Donald. 1996. *"Spellbinding."* In *Religions of China in Practice*, edited by Donald S. Lopez, Jr., 241–50. Princeton: Princeton University Press.

Hendrischke, Barbara, and Benjamin Penny. 1996. *"The 180 Precepts Spoken by Lord Lao*: A Translation and Textual Study." *Taoist Resources* 6.2: 17–29.

Kohn, Livia. 1993. *The Taoist Experience*. Albany: State University of New York Press. Ch. 8.

Nickerson, Peter. 1996. *"Abridged Codes of Master Lu for the Daoist Community."* In *Religions of China in Practice*, edited by Donald S. Lopez Jr., 347–59. Princeton: Princeton University Press.

Nickerson, Peter. 1997. "The Great Petition for Sepulchral Plaints." In *Early Daoist Scriptures*, by Stephen Bokenkamp, 230–74. Berkeley: University of California Press.

CHAPTER FIVE

SELF-CULTIVATION GROUPS

The Celestial Masters continued the Daoist pattern of linking political visions with popular religion in a cultic and organized religious setting, with great appeal to the masses. But there were also small aristocratic groups who created self-cultivation communities that followed the visions of the ancient thinkers, the ideals of immortality, and the practices of the *fangshi*. Rather than replacing the political structures of their day with new religious hierarchies and administrations, these groups rejected them and sought to escape from them, finding solace and peace in small groups of like-minded seekers and discovering a saner world in the heavenly spheres of the immortals.

The first such group is known as the Seven Sages of the Bamboo Grove. It consisted of seven aristocrats who found themselves barred from official careers due to their close ties with the imperial house of an overthrown dynasty, and so set out to create a harmonious society of their own. They established themselves in the landed estate of their leading member, Xi Kang (223–262), and there pursued various leisure activities and wrote beautiful poems and highly intellectual essays. Although they held a firm belief in immortality and sought contact with the higher spheres, their practice was less religious than escapist. It involved consuming wine in large quantities and taking narcotic and psychedelic drugs, notably the notorious Cold Food Powder (*hanshi san*), which caused great visions and made the body feel very hot. This in turn inspired the "sages" to remove their clothing and jump into the cooling waters of nearby ponds and rivers. It is not difficult to account for their impressive image of wild eccentricity and reckless abandon.

While under the influence, they would see wondrous sights of other-worldly paradises, find themselves greeted by lovely jade maidens, and experience utter freedom from all burdens and sorrows. After their return to earth and the discomforts of bodily existence, they felt deep despair at the fleeting nature of bliss and wrote down their feelings in exquisite poetry, making ample use of the metaphors and terms of Laozi and Zhuangzi. The most famous such poem is Ruan Ji's (210–263) *Daren fu* (Rhapsody of the Great Man), which describes the ideal immortal state as follows:

> Nothing can harm me, neither heat nor cold:
> I am tranquil, untouched by all.
> Nothing can hold me, neither pain nor sorrow:
> My pure breath flows silently.
> I float freely on the mists, jump up into the sky,
> Let myself go wherever it may take me.
> I flow back and forth in cosmic mysteries,
> My path leads me on in peace.
> All my desires, all my joys are no longer of this world —
> Why should I quarrel with it?
> All others live to die, but I alone survive.

The Seven Sages were not ordained or initiated Daoists, but have their place in the tradition as "literati Daoists" and as the active proponents of mystical visions in Daoist-inspired literature. Also, their social situation, the community they created, the otherworldly journeys they described, and their understanding of the celestial realm are echoed closely by several aristocratic Daoist self-cultivation groups of the following centuries.

There were three such communities: the lineage of alchemical seekers who rejected ordinary society and pursued immortality with longevity techniques and chemical concoctions; the community of southern nobles disenfranchised by northern émigrés who engaged in ecstatic visions and found their true home in the heavens of the immortals; and the group of magical and ritual practitioners who sought to control their world and their destiny with sacred charts, talismans, and spells, and were the first to adopt large segments of Buddhism into Daoist worldview and practice.

Alchemical Immortality

In continuation of Han-dynasty *fangshi* and individual immortality seekers, certain aristocrats, especially in south China, developed small groups and lineages of esoteric practice. Their goal was to attain individual ascent to the starry paradises with the help of various techniques including purifications, rituals, longevity practices, meditations, and alchemy. Many seekers of this type have remained unnamed due to the secrecy surrounding their activities, but one left behind a major collection of their ideals and methods: the would-be alchemist Ge Hong.

Ge Hong (287–347) came from an old aristocratic family located in the small town of Jurong near Jiankang (modern Nanjing). His great-uncle Ge Xuan (164–244) was a *fangshi* of some renown, and his father-in-law Bao Jing was another inspired seeker. Influenced by these two, Ge Hong virtually breathed longevity, magic, alchemy, and ecstatic religious practices. As he describes in his autobiography — the first of its kind in Chinese literature — he refused to take on official positions and even avoided social contacts because his one aim in life was to become immortal. This, according to him, involved several levels of practice: an initial ritual purification and magical protection, a prolonged period of longevity practice, and eventually — and most importantly — the concoction of an elixir or cinnabar (*dan*). He found himself sufficiently wealthy to have the leisure to pursue his goal full-time, but he yet lacked the vast riches needed to purchase the precious metals the elixir required. As a result, he undertook what practices he could but for the most part became a collector of written materials, wandering around the country in search for manuscripts and compiling several books.

He has two main works. The first is a collection of immortals' biographies, the *Shenxian zhuan* (Biographies of Spirit Immortals), which contains materials on some hundred-odd successful practitioners. The second work is a defense of alchemy, the *Baopuzi* (Book of the Master Who Embraces Simplicity), divided into the "Inner" and "Outer Chapters." Especially the "Inner Chapters" are a vast compendium of immortality techniques and practices, describing elementary protective measures against demons and evil spirits, proper alignment with yin and yang, ways to absorb solar and lunar energies, application of herbs and minerals, and the attainment of magical powers such as multilocation, invulnerability, invisibility, flying, and so on. Most importantly, it describes the procedures for preparing the elixir, and presents a list of the books Ge Hong succeeded in collecting — a total of 220 texts and 60 talismans. Although these materials are mostly lost today, their titles provide some insight into the sorts of texts available at the time: they range from pharmacological works through calendrical manuals to alchemical recipes and versions of the *Taiping jing*.

Ge Hong believed firmly in the transformation of the living body into that of an immortal: either an earth immortal with an extended life expectancy on earth; a celestial immortal with a spirit body in the heavens—especially in the heaven of Great Purity (Taiqing), a name sometimes used to designate the alchemical school; or an immortal by deliverance from the corpse (*shijie*). The latter indicates transformation while leaving a token corpse behind, such as a bamboo staff or sword. Immortals resided either in the paradises of Penglai and Kunlun or in the stars, and rode about the cosmic ethers together with the sun and the moon. The main way to attain immortality was by concocting an elixir, for which one had to have the right destiny ("immortals' bones"), obtain the right texts (often through revelation in trance), and undergo physical preparation through longevity techniques.

Once an elixir concoction could start, it had to be undertaken at exactly the right time and in exactly the right place. Ideally, it should begin at the height of yin—at midnight of the winter solstice—then follow a cosmic time schedule reduced to a microcosmic level. In terms of place, it could only be performed in a carefully chosen spot with the right kinds of streams, hills, and trees for the proper flow of *qi*. The place further had to be completely secluded because the slightest contact with a nonbeliever could ruin the entire process. Before even the first ingredient could be placed in the cauldron, a proper furnace, typically a three-tiered brick oven, had to be set up and several ritual purifications had to be undergone, including bathing, fasting, and avoidance of sex and blood. In addition, the seeker had to set up protective talismans, offer a sacrifice to the gods, swear an oath of secrecy, and make a formal pledge (often involving substantial gifts) to the master alchemist.

Next, the concoction process itself would commence, a lengthy and complicated procedure that involved creating a chemical reaction on the basis of highly disparate and often poisonous substances, such as pine needles and resin, mushrooms, persimmons, apricot kernels, deer antlers, mother-of-pearl, mica, aconite, realgar, sulfur, mercury, arsenic, silver, and gold. These various materials, which sometimes took years to collect, were then cooked according to the revealed, cosmic instructions, placed in a cauldron coated with various luting compounds and surrounded by magical and protective devices to ensure the proper atmosphere for the elixir to grow. Over many months or even years, the right times of firing and cooling, stirring and burying had to be observed to the minutest detail. The process was thought to imitate the growth of gold in the earth on a microcosmic scale, and accordingly followed the stages of cosmic creation as it was perceived at the time. Essentially the work of the alchemist occurred on three levels: the concrete concoction of the elixir for immortality; the creation of gold from base metals for personal wealth; and the replication of the cosmic processes of creation for insights into, and power over, the innermost secrets of the universe. Alchemy was, therefore, both a chemical and a mystical endeavor which led not only to chemically induced trances and visions but also to the high spiritual states necessary for immortal transformation.

If and when the elixir had been created successfully, the operating alchemist had to perform a thanksgiving sacrifice and give away large portions of his newly created gold to the gods and, anonymously, to the crowds. This practice echoes the understanding in other cultures, as described for example in Parker Shipton's *Bitter Money* (1989), that when wealth is obtained magically it can be dangerous to its owner unless it is resocialized by being given away, at least in part. Once the gods were thanked and the danger banned, the alchemist could take varying doses of the elixir, a gray-brown mud that was ingested either rolled into a pill or dissolved in liquid. Depending on the dose, he would attain various levels of magical powers, gain extensive divine protection (crowds of divine generals and supporters hovering over his every step), find a new level of lightness and radiance in body and mind, and have the choice of either extending his sojourn on earth indefinitely or ascend to heaven in broad daylight.

The most commonly used drug was called cinnabar (*dan*), which is also the generic word for "elixir." It is a mercury-sulfite that dissolves into its parts when heated, then reconstitutes itself back into cinnabar (i.e., "reverted cinnabar"). Mercury, of course, is highly poisonous; taken in small amounts it causes delusions and brain damage and in massive doses it is fatal. That Daoists at the time were well aware of this and yet still undertook these experiments shows again the strong spiritual dimension of their belief in immortality. People set their hearts fully onto the otherworld, ready to give up their worldly goods and life.

The Shangqing Revelations

A similarly small and esoteric but less alchemical community of aristo-crats grew in the mid-fourth century in the same area near Nanjing. It was associated with Mount Mao (Maoshan) as its spiritual center, and with a new set of revelations from a superior heaven called Highest Clar-ity or Highest Purity (Shangqing). It was accordingly later referred to as the Maoshan or the Shangqing school of Daoism. The driving force be-hind this new development was the estrangement many southern fami-lies felt after a mass migration of the imperial court and northern nobles, caused by the invasion of Hunnish tribes in 317, took away much of their political clout.

The northern émigrés were not only active politically; they also brought with them the beliefs and practices of the Celestial Masters—by this time part of aristocratic culture and the chosen creed of some high-ranking clans such as the Wangs of Langye (Shandong), the family of the famous calligrapher Wang Xizhi (303–361). The relationship between old south-ern aristocrats and northern émigrés was initially uneasy because the newcomers diminished the status of the old residents and introduced new ways that were neither wanted nor comfortable. Gradually a com-promise stand-off emerged, which then gave way to a degree of integra-tion and merging. In religious terms, this meant that southern families such as the Ges of Ge Hong would be at first very suspicious, then accept certain traits of Celestial Masters teachings, and eventually develop their own brand of the religion using the alchemical and ecstatic techniques at their disposal.

One popular practice at the time was to establish communication with one's ancestors with the help of a shaman or spirit-medium, mainly to find causes for unexplained illnesses and misfortunes, but also to learn of their fate in the otherworld and obtain advice on current affairs. In the 360s, two brothers of the aristocratic Xu family, Xu Mai (b. 301) and Xu Mi (303–73), hired the medium Yang Xi (330–386?) to establish contact with Xu Mi's wife Tao Kedou, who had died in 362. She appeared and told them about her status in the otherworld, explained the overall or-ganization of the heavens, and introduced the medium to various other spirit figures.

Among them were underworld rulers, divine officers of the dead, spirit masters of moral rules, denizens of the Huayang grotto on the nearby Maoshan, as well as some leaders of the Celestial Masters, notably the former libationer Lady Wei Huacun (251–334). Together they provided the medium with a detailed description of the organization and population of the otherworld, and especially of the top heaven of Shangqing. They also revealed specific methods of soul travels or ecstatic excursions, visualizations, and alchemical concoctions, gave thorough instructions on how to transmit the texts and their methods, and provided prophecies about the golden age to come with the arising of the Latter-Day Saint (Housheng), a deity known also as Lord Goldtower (Jinque dijun).

The Xu brothers wrote down everything Yang Xi transmitted from the otherworld, however disparate it may have seemed, and created a basic collection of sacred texts. They shared their new revelations with their immediate neighbors and relatives, who included the Ges of Ge Hong, the Taos of Tao Kedou, and the Wangs of Wang Xizhi. The elder Xu became a full-time practitioner and vanished into the mountains in 348, never to be heard of again. His brother continued the family affairs and passed the texts on to his son Xu Hui (b. 341), who in 370 also vanished into the mountains, where he allegedly lived for another sixty years. His son Xu Huangmin (361–429) inherited the texts but did not take them quite as seriously, transmitting them far and wide and thus allowing them to be scattered in different parts of China. There they remained until they were collected again a century later by the outstanding Daoist and Shangqing patriarch Tao Hongjing.

Tao Hongjing (456–536) was a descendant of Tao Kedou's native family and thus closely connected with the original circle of the Shangqing revelations. A learned scholar and devout seeker, he gained favor with Emperor Wu of the Liang dynasty, who saw in him the potential provider of an immorality elixir. Tao established himself on Maoshan and founded a center where practitioners could cultivate immortality, whe-ther alone and celibate or communal and married. There he pursued alchemical and pharmacological studies, working on various elixirs and editing the important manual on herbal and mineral drugs *Shennong bencao jing* (Pharmacopoeia of the Divine Farmer), which was to become essential in this field.

One day he came across an original Shangqing manuscript and was struck both by its powerful language and its high spiritual vision. He also noted the unusual quality of the calligraphy used, which he identified as the handwriting of the Xu brothers, and promptly set out on an extensive quest to recover as many original Shangqing texts as possible. It took him a number of years, but eventually he was able to piece together a close reconstruction of the original Shangqing canon and compiled a record of the revelations. This work produced his masterpiece, the *Zhen'gao* (Declarations of the Perfected) in twenty scrolls, of which only the first and nineteenth have been translated into English (Hyland 1984; Strickmann 1978). Through his efforts the Shangqing revelations became the center of a formal Daoist school, and they were in due course honored as the highest form of Daoism practiced in medieval China.

The World of Shangqing

In terms of religious worldview, the emergence of the Shangqing revelations signifies a major expansion of Daoism. Where the Celestial Masters had added the pure gods of Dao to the popular pantheon, Shangqing enlarged this to include an entirely new layer of existence between the original, creative force of Dao, represented by the creator deity Yuanshi tianwang (Heavenly King of Primordial Beginning), and the created world as we know it. This celestial layer consisted of several different regions, located both in the far reaches of the world and in the stars, and imagined along the lines of the ancient paradises Penglai and Kunlun. It was populated by various divine figures: pure gods of Dao who were emanations of original cosmic *qi*; immortals who had attained celestial status through effort and the proper elixir; demon kings, converted spirits who had risen to rank and power; and ancestors who had entered via death. These divine figures, moreover, were arranged hierarchically, transforming the Daoist otherworld into a vast celestial bureaucracy — the dead were administered in the Six Palaces of Fengdu, immortals under the rule of the Southern Palace (Nangong) beyond the Northern Dipper (Beidou), and pure gods of Dao through Highest Purity itself.

The world of the dead — Fengdu or Luofeng — was envisioned as a mountain located in the northern ocean and ruled by the Northern Emperor (Beidi). Here the dead went to be judged and punished. Upon arrival they were registered in the first palace, then divided into different groups: those who had died suddenly (second palace), the wise and sagely (third palace), and those needing special judgment (fourth palace). Once a dead person had expiated her or his sins, they could become a warden in this "earth prison" and receive the title of *gui* (demon), thereby attaining the lowest level of the immortal hierarchy. To further rise in rank, they had to accumulate hidden virtue, such as loyalty and filial piety, and receive ritual support from the living. Then they could rise to become a demon officer (*guiguan*), an underworld ruler (*dixia zhuzhe*), or even a sage (*sheng*), immortal (*xian*), or perfected (*zhen*) — higher ranks under the registration of the Southern Palace.

With this change in cosmology, the focus of immortality shifted away from the inner nature of the person and the kinds of practices he or she undertook to the quality of registration among the stars. In addition to becoming increasingly affected through direct interaction with the divine — incantations, visualizations, and ecstatic excursions — immortality became a bureaucratic act, culminating in the transfer of one's file from the administration of death in Fengdu to that of life in the Southern Palace.

Another area in which Shangqing changed the worldview of Daoism was the understanding of the human body. Based on Han cosmology and Chinese medicine, the body had been traditionally seen as a network of *qi*-storage areas and *qi*-channels, a microcosmic replica of nature and the cosmos. Now it became a veritable storehouse of divine agencies, palaces, and figures, patterned in many ways on the constellations in the stars. With this change came an entirely new nomenclature for its key parts, which are first documented in the *Huangting jing* (Yellow Court Scripture), a Shangqing meditation manual.

For example, the head was now called Mount Kunlun or the Yellow Court; it contained Nine Palaces, each the residence of a divine being who also lived — simultaneously and correspondingly — in the stars. Most important among these Nine Palaces were the Hall of Light (*mingtang*), located in the center of the eyebrows about one inch into the head, the Grotto Chamber (*dongfang*), one inch further in, and the Niwan Palace (*niwan gong*) beyond it, which is also known as the upper cinnabar or elixir field. There are altogether three such cinnabar or elixir fields (*dantian*) in the body: the upper one just mentioned; the middle one in the solar plexus or heart area, also known as the Numinous Terrace, the Scarlet Palace, and the Square Inch; and the lower one in the abdomen, an area also called Mount Kunlun, the Gate of Life, the Primordial Pass, and the Ocean of Energy. In all three, central celestial rulers reside, the so-called Three Ones (Sanyi), whose visualization will ensure a successful celestial connection.

Within the body, often several locations are given the same name, indicating their parallel positions and intimate connection within the greater cosmic scheme. For example, "Yellow Court" refers to both the head and the spleen, "Dark Towers" indicates both the kidneys and the ears, and "Flowery Canopy" (the constellation Cassiopeia) names both the eyebrows and the lungs. Other colorful names include Spirit Furnace for the nose, Flowery Pond for the mouth, Jade Fluid or Sweet Spring for saliva, Storied Tower for the throat, Great Wall for the large intestine, and Jade Stalk for the penis.

The meditation practice that went with this was mainly a technique of visualization—of the different colors associated with the organs to strengthen their *qi*, of the inner passways and palaces to learn the cosmic geography, of gods and immortals residing there to acquire familiarity with the divine figures, and of the planets and stars to merge with their power. For example,

> On the fifth of the month, at midnight, visualize the shape of the sun in your heart. Make the sun enter into the heart through your mouth and let it radiate all throughout your heart. Become one with the radiance of the sun, merge with it in harmony.
>
> Once done, you should become aware of a warm glow and brightness in your heart. Continue to practice this for an extended period, then recite the following incantation:
>
> Great Brightness, nourish my essence.
> Refine my cinnabar heart within.
> Radiant glow, merge with my light.
> Let the divine perfected come to me.
>
> Conclude by swallowing the saliva nine times. . . .
>
> After you have pursued this [thrice monthly] for fifteen years, the Great One will dispatch a heavenly chariot to receive you and you will ascend to the Great Empyrean above. (*Zhen'gao*, ch. 9)

Practitioners used meditations on their bodies to establish closer contact with the larger cosmos and align themselves with the stars and divinities above. This practice of visualization, moreover, could lead to a deep trance state, during which practitioners left their ordinary environment to go on extensive journeys into the otherworldly realm, both on the earth, exploring its far-off corners, and in the heavens, visiting the gods. Their goal was to become so familiar with the otherworldly realm that their main reality was over there, to experience—by seeing and feeling the gods and their palaces within—a cosmicization of self and world. Eventually adepts ascended to the higher heavens to take leisurely walks on the stars, a practice known as *bugang* or "pacing the [cosmic] net," aligning themselves with the rhythms of the stars and planets.

Undertaking these visualizations, Shangqing Daoists transformed themselves into cosmicized and spirit beings, their bodies becoming networks of deities and palaces, their minds in intimate relationship with heavenly divinities. Still, they continued the earlier traditions, sublimating the physiological practices of the *fangshi* and Celestial Masters and undertaking the concoction of an alchemical elixir but only upon express celestial command and as a means for the final transition into the celestial realm.

Lingbao Spells and Talismans

Toward the end of the fourth century, as Xu Huangmin began to distribute the Shangqing scriptures more widely and the original group started to lose some of its strength and cohesion, yet another aristocratic community began to grow. This was the Lingbao or Numinous Treasure school, named after its key concept of precious talisman(s) that created and maintained the world. It began in the 390s with the inspiration of Ge Chaofu, a descendant of Ge Hong who had inherited the latter's library and was also a practicing member of Shangqing. He was concerned with recovering the heritage of his own family, notably of the *fangshi* and alchemist Ge Xuan, Ge Hong's great-uncle and Daoist teachers.

To do so, he proposed an alternative worldview, one which adopted the ideas of multiple layers of heaven, celestial administration, and an extensive host of divine beings from Shangqing cosmology, but which also returned to Han-dynasty cosmology of the five phases, *fangshi* ideas and practices, and Celestial Master ritual. In his seminal first work, the *Wupian zhenwen chishu* (Perfect Text in Five Tablets, Written in Red), he emphasizes the notion of spells and talismans, cosmic sounds and signs, as being key to both creation and empowerment. The text begins:

In the east resides the First Elder of Pure Power, with the [tal-ismanic] Treasure of Peace, in the Forest of Blossoms. His spell is the deep mysterious verse of jeweled perfection. It gives life to pure spirit.

In the south resides the Perfect Elder of Cinnabar Power, with the Treasure of Brahma, in the Realm of Flaming Fire. His spell is the deep numinous verse of the southern clouds. It is a song that reaches to heaven.

In the center resides the Primordial Elder of Original Power, with the Treasure of Jade. His spell is the revelation of power of the nine heavens. It consists of words that go beyond aeons and penetrate even to the highest galaxies. . . .

The talismans and spells of the Five Elders are all created from emptiness and pure naturalness. In their original form they rest hidden above the nine heavens, on the mysterious terrace of the Seven Treasures, in the Palace of Purple Tenuity, in the Metropolis of Power. There they are guarded by the five gen-erals and their spirit officers. In accordance with the ordi-nances of deepest mystery, they are revealed only once in 40,000 aeons. (ch. 1)

While this documents the integration of five-phases cosmology, Shangqing celestial visions, and cosmic understanding of spells and tal-ismans typical for Lingbao, the magical practices of the school are docu-mented in another early text, part of which actually goes back to ancient *fangshi*, the *Lingbao wufuxu* (Explanation of the Five Lingbao Talismans). According to this, the five central talismans of Lingbao were not only powers of creation but stood at the root of all enlightened government over the millennia, and especially served the mythical ruler Yu in the control of the great flood that threatened to destroy the earth in prehis-toric times. Yu, who did not find a suitable heir for the talismans, hid them in a sacred mountain where they were found and illegitimately unearthed by King Helü of Wu around the time of Confucius. The king was duly punished and the talismans vanished again until, so Ge Chaofu claims, they were offered in legitimate revelation to his ancestor Ge Xuan, who duly made them accessible and equipped them with proper explanations, protective charms, and ritual prescriptions.

If treated correctly, the talismans would not only grant access to the otherworld and immortality for oneself and one's ancestors—the feats Shangqing practitioners spent so many hours laboring for in visualization—but even provide peace and harmony for family, village, county, and empire. The five central cosmic talismans, moreover, were only the tip of the iceberg—there were divine charts and diagrams for many geographical locations, such as the five sacred mountains and the ten great grotto heavens (underground immortal realms that connect sacred mountains), as well as for any number of personal and political designs. They were used, for example, when Daoists entered a mountain in search of the raw materials for immortality, as described in the *Lingbao wufuxu*:

> Daoists enter the mountains to collect herbs and gather the eight minerals, to find numinous mushrooms and concoct a cinnabar liquid. Hiding in the woods and caverns, they try to get rid of the multitude of obnoxious sprites. Doing any of these things, if they do not have the proper talismans, the divine herbs will be deeply hidden, the eight minerals will obscure their form, the radiant mushrooms will shade their light, all study will come to nothing, bad energies will try to harm them, and the demons will startle and upset them.

> Thus, whenever you see the nasty manifestation of a hobgoblin [in the woods], take out the numinous talismans and hold them up towards it. The goblin will naturally melt away and disappear. If a mountain sprite scares and oppresses you, similarly raise [the talismans] to urge it to leave. Even if it can appear in a thousand transformations and a myriad different forms, it will thereby have to dissipate. (ch. 1)

In addition to this individual use of the talismans, the understanding of their impact on political stability and social harmony led to their activation in communal rituals that involved formal purifications and the sending of petitions to the otherworld (as in the Celestial Masters). Over time, these rituals grew to be splendid, large-scale affairs with music, wine, and drama, led by professional masters and geared to move the cosmos in its roots. They aimed to create harmony and immortality not only for individuals but for entire clans and the society as a whole, and became highly attractive to large numbers of people.

The Buddhist Impact

As Lingbao ideas and practices became more popular, its followers conceived further scriptures which explained its cosmology in greater detail and also integrated large segments of Buddhist worldview. Buddhism had entered China already in the first century C.E. and was originally seen as the Central Asian or Indian version of Laozi's teaching, created after his emigration to the west. It met with some resistance in China, mainly because of its foreign customs and rejection of family values, yet it grew slowly and steadily, mostly supported by foreign rulers and nobles (such as the Hunnish tribes who conquered north China in 317), and carried by translations of varying quality.

Around the year 400, it began to come into its own when a group of Chinese aristocratic monks in south China, led by the famous Huiyuan (334–417), for the first time actively defied the rule of kowtowing to the Chinese emperor, thus asserting the independence of the Buddhist community (*sangha*). Around the same time, the foreign Toba-Wei dynasty (386–535) in north China greatly advanced the Buddhist cause by inviting the renowned Central Asian scholar Kumârajîva from Kucha to head a translation institute in their capital. As a result, Chinese Buddhism began to develop a greater standing of its own and was able to rely on texts that represented accurate presentations of Buddhist doctrine and worldview. Translations were moreover made of the *Vinaya* or collection of Buddhist rules, which helped standardize practice and raise the quality of monastic discipline.

Matching the success and influence of their Buddhist counterparts, Daoists of the Lingbao school rewrote their cosmology and reformed their practices. They acknowledged a new central deity, named Yuanshi tianzun (Heavenly Worthy of Primordial Beginning), who was a merging of the Shangqing creator god and the Buddha and was known as *shizun* or "World-Honored One." This deity resided on a high plane of heaven and, like the Buddha in Buddhist sutras, held court among the celestials and gave sermons in reply to learned questions. Using the divine talismans, he created the world in original perfection, then saw it decline and, like Lord Lao, descended periodically to reveal various rules and texts. However, the cycles of nature went on notwithstanding, and the world ended in destruction, to be recreated by him once again in renewed splendor. Each of these world-cycles was then called an aeon or "kalpa" (*jie*) in adaptation of Indian understanding. In one of his celestial audiences, the high god describes his activities. He says:

> "Then the [third] kalpa Opening Sovereign arrived. In its first year, the true writ of Lingbao opened the light of the three heavenly bodies. Heaven and earth were again set up properly, and the five planets shone forth brightly.
>
> "At this time I once more emerged and came to reside in the Heaven of green, beginning *qi*, known by the name Heavenly Worthy of Primordial Beginning. I spread the divine law far and wide, transforming and saving beings on all levels of heaven and earth.
>
> "When this kalpa first began, people were still pure and simple. They knotted cords for communication, thought in divine unconsciousness, and lived in perfect harmony with naturalness. Thus they all attained long life-spans of as many as thirty-six thousand years.
>
> "Then the world changed and the kalpa Highest Sovereign arose. At this time people's minds gradually declined and became more decadent. I feared things would utterly collapse, and the true teaching would no longer be complete. For this reason, I wandered from country to country and distributed heavenly scriptures everywhere. I made people join the [Daoist] teaching and develop their minds in its ways. When the kalpa was half over, I allowed for a gradual decline. People's life spans were then reduced to somewhat over eighteen thousand years." (*Zuigen pin*, ch. 1)

The creation, here described as occurring through the power of the sacred talismans, was also understood to depend on sacred sounds, as described in the earlier Lingbao text, cited above. Instead of thinking of these sounds as native Chinese spells, such as those used by the Celestial Masters to dispel demons, Lingbao Daoists now linked them with the foreign sounds of Sanskrit and identified them as "Brahma-sounds" (*fanyin*). The root power of creation, these sounds originally rested in heaven where they also manifested themselves in sacred signs, which in turn coagulated into heavenly scriptures or "perfect texts" (*zhenwen*).

These texts, written in heavenly script (as seen on talismans), were then stored in deep, holy caverns in the Mountain of Jade Capital (Yujing shan) in the Heaven of Grand Veil (Daluo tian). This was the central axis of a total of thirty-two heavens, placed in concentric circles around it. Like Buddhist heavens they were divided into three levels—the worlds of desires (six heavens), form (eighteen), and formlessness (four)—plus four Brahma-heavens for true believers. Every so often, the Heavenly Worthy would deem it appropriate—depending on the kalpa—to reveal one or the other of these pure, original texts and provide a translation into Chinese, either verbally through a spirit-medium or by magical writing on the walls of caverns. Thus the Lingbao texts were believed to have come to earth, revealed to Ge Xuan, the ancestor of Ge Chaofu.

The key revealing deity of the sacred texts was the second major god of Lingbao, the Lord of the Dao (Taishang daojun). He is typically described in scriptures as an inquisitive and compassionate deity, who would make sure the world learned all the important details regarding life, death, sins, and the proper rules to be followed. These rules, adapted from Buddhist precepts and bodhisattva vows (resolutions to work for the benefit of all living beings) involved the doctrine of karma and rebirth, which entered Daoism at this time and changed the way people looked at their lives. They were no longer only subject to the wrath and bad fortune of their ancestors; they were now also haunted by their own bad deeds of former lives, visited upon them in the particular form of rebirth they had taken or would take in the future. Rebirth could occur in any of the five Buddhist realms, among gods, humans, animals, ghosts, or hell dwellers. The latter reflected the concept that the dead, rather than being administered and punished for their sins, were condemned to long-term sentences and actively tortured with fire, ice, and weapons. Usually the punishments matched the deeds. For example,

> Anyone who curses the scriptures of the great [Daoist] law after death will pass through the eighteen hells and nine realms of darkness.

> Anyone who commits debauchery and indulges in sex will suffer from insanity. Having passed through this, he will be born among the sows and boars.

> Anyone who steals objects used for offerings or purgation ceremonies will become a slave. He will be hungry and cold and never manage to get hold of sufficient food and clothing.

> Having passed through this, he will be born among mangy dogs and poisonous snakes. (*Yinyuan jing*, ch. 2)

To prevent nasty fates such as these, serious Daoists undertook self-cultivation while also developing morally to become a kind of bodhi-sattva, who made compassion and mindfulness his first virtues and always thought of serving others. Self-cultivation changed accordingly from the standard physical and visualization techniques to also include moral practice of virtues and communal rituals for the sake of all beings. Daoists developed several new sets of precepts, as well as list of good and bad deeds. Among these, the ten precepts became dominant in the later ordination system. Daoists also began to hold large communal rituals for the sake of individuals and the cosmos, offering the opportunity of being cleansed from sins and presenting prayers and pardons to the ancestors. All this began with the Lingbao school in the fifth century and rose to great prominence later on. We will examine it in chapter 7, "Ritual and Meditation," below.

By the fifth century, then, the two main early medieval strands of Daoism, the communal organizations and self-cultivation groups transform rapidly into widespread organized religions. Where the Celestial Masters started out as a millenarian cult that combined the political vision of the *Daode jing* and Huang-Lao with popular religion, the aristocratic communities of Taiqing, Shangqing, and Lingbao began as self-cultivation groups who rejected society and based their ideas on the *fangshi* and the *Zhuangzi*. Still, both types of Daoist organizations changed as they entered the larger community of Chinese society and interacted with its new developments, most dominantly Buddhism. They became organized religions with an established priesthood, community concerns, and active rites and festivals, that nonetheless also offered opportunities for individual cultivation and attainment of immortality. Although of disparate beginnings, the two strands of early medieval Daoism thus tended to move in a similar direction, laying the foundation for the integrated Daoist system that was to become standard in the Tang dynasty.

Further Readings

Campany, Robert F. 2002. *To Live as Long as Heaven and Earth: A Translation and Study of Ge Hong's Traditions of Divine Transcendents*. Berkeley: University of California Press.

Pregadio, Fabrizio. 2000. "Elixirs and Alchemy." In *Daoism Handbook*, edited by Livia Kohn, 165–95. Leiden: E. Brill.

Robinet, Isabelle. 1993. *Taoist Meditation*. Translated by Norman Girardot and Julian Pas. Albany: State University of New York Press.

Sivin, Nathan. 1968. *Chinese Alchemy: Preliminary Studies*. Cambridge, Mass.: Harvard University Press.

Strickmann, Michel. 1978. "The Mao-shan Revelations: Taoism and the Aristocracy." *T'oung-pao* 63: 1–63.

Strickmann, Michel. 1979. "On the Alchemy of T'ao Hung-ching." In *Facets of Taoism*, edited by Holmes Welch and Anna Seidel, 123–92. New Haven, Conn.: Yale University Press.

Zürcher, Erik. 1980. "Buddhist Influence on Early Taoism." *T'oung-pao* 66: 84–147.

Original Sources in Translation

Bokenkamp, Stephen R. 1996. *"Declarations of the Perfected;"* "Answering a Summons." In *Religions of China in Practice*, edited by Donald S. Lopez, Jr., 166–79; 188–201. Princeton: Princeton University Press.

Bokenkamp, Stephen R. 1997. *Early Daoist Scriptures*. Berkeley: University of California Press.

Bumbacher, Stephan-Peter. 2000. *The Fragments of the Daoxue zhuan*. New York: Peter Lang.

Holzman, Donald. 1976. *Poetry and Politics: The Life and Works of Juan Chi (210–263)*. Cambridge: Cambridge University Press.

Kohn, Livia. 1993. *The Taoist Experience*. Albany: State University of New York Press. Chs. 6–7, 13–14, 22, 24, 26–27, 34–35, 41.

Kroll, Paul W. 1996. "Body Gods and Inner Vision: The Scripture of the Yellow Court;" "Seduction Songs of One of the Perfected." In *Religions of China in Practice*, edited by Donald S. Lopez, Jr., 149–55; 156–66. Princeton: Princeton University Press.

Ware, James R. 1966. *Alchemy, Medicine and Religion in the China of AD 320: The Nei-p'ien of Ko Hung*. Cambridge, Mass.: MIT Press.

CHAPTER SIX

DAOISM AND THE STATE

As Daoism developed more and more toward a full-grown, organized religion, it also began to have aspirations as state religion. State religion is more than just a form of worship acknowledged and supported by the state; it means that political institutions and decisions are carried by religious representatives and considered in the light of religious doctrine. As described by John W. Perry in *Lord of the Four Quarters* (1966), it typically centers on the role of the ruler as the sacred representative of a religiously viewed universe. He is seen as a father to the people, a fighter for the country, and the ritual link to the cosmos and thus to social stability and fertility. In all these roles, the ruler functions as the central axis between heaven and earth, the dead and the living, representing the divine power that metes out rewards and punishments and judges good and evil. His work, both on the mundane and the sacred planes (through the execution of seasonal and fertility rituals), serves to maintain order and keep chaos at bay, whether manifested as natural calamities, foreign invasions, or attacks by demons.

In China, the idea of a sacralized government is most commonly described as the "state cult," which means that the ruler was seen as the central axis of the cosmos, literally the "Son of Heaven," whose actions kept the universe on its track and the world in proper order. He was aided by a number of officials, first aristocrats, later successful graduates of the Confucian state examination (established in 136 B.C.E.). They had both civil and religious duties, including sacrifices to Heaven and Earth, year-end exorcisms, fertility rites, calendar determinations, and astrological observations. Reaching from the central government to every household in the empire, this state cult also supported the people's worship of ancestors, household deities like the stove god, and local gods of mountains and rivers who would guarantee fertility in every part of the country.

On the other hand, it also condemned any religious activities that were independent of official support and that did not focus primarily on the welfare of people and state. These included various shamanic cults, worship of local or indigenous ethnic gods, anything foreign such as Buddhism, and the early Daoist movements. The latter's case was exacerbated because they were associated with the Yellow Turban Rebellion of 184, and so the Daoist bid for status as state religion was neither easy nor obvious. Indeed, in a purely Chinese state it was well nigh impossible, and so the first Daoist elevation to state religion occurred under a foreign dynasty of Hunnish origin, the Toba-Wei, who conquered north China in 386.

The Toba were relatively small in number and inexperienced in the running of a vast empire, and so needed native institutions and officials to run the country for them, using the so-called indirect rule solution which was also adopted by colonial powers in other periods and parts of the world. Since they distrusted the Confucian establishment, which was sworn to loyalty to the Chinese emperor, they turned to organized religions for administrative support. Both Buddhism and Daoism, at different times, rose to high prominence under Toba rule and became formal state religions, their priests and rituals spreading throughout the country. Following this, Daoism was also venerated as state religion under the Tang dynasty (618–907), whose rulers claimed descent from Laozi and used the religion to enhance political and social harmony.

The Theocracy

The first Daoist rise to state religion is known as the "Daoist theocracy." It began with Kou Qianzhi (365–448), the well-educated son of a Celestial Masters family, who elected to practice Dao and became a hermit on Mount Song in Henan. There, in 415, he received a first revelation from Lord Lao which the official history of the dynasty describes as follows:

> In the second year of the reign period Shenrui, on the *yimao* day of the tenth month [22 November 415], Kou Qianzhi unexpectedly encountered a great divinity, riding on a cloud and mounted upon a dragon. Accompanied by an entourage of hundreds of numinous spirits, he was waited upon by immortals and jade maidens. The entire host assembled on the top of the mountain.

> Lord Lao then spoke to Kou: "A few years ago, in the *xinhai* year [411], the god of Mount Song, chief of the palace of the assembled immortals, submitted a memorial to the celestial officials [to recommend you].
>
> "This is why I have come to see you today. I now bestow upon you the position of Celestial Master and herewith transmit to you the 'Precepts of the New Code, to Be Recited after [the tune] *In the Clouds'* in twenty scrolls. . . . Go, then, and proclaim my new code and with its help purify and rectify the Daoist teaching, abolishing the perverted ideas of the Three Zhangs [traditional Celestial Masters].
>
> "Rice levies and taxes in coin or the techniques of harmonizing the male and female energies—how can the great Dao in its purity and emptiness ever make use of such things? Begin, therefore, by setting up specific formal procedures, then supplement them with methods of diet and physical refinement. " (*Weishu*, ch. 114)

Kou, therefore, was empowered to take the place of the Zhang lineage as Celestial Master and abolish some of their characteristic practices such as the "five pecks of rice" tax and the sexual initiation rituals. Instead, he was to set up a system of religious activity based on longevity techniques and bolstered by a set of thirty-six community rules, handed down by the divinity himself. Before he could do this, however, he had to perfect his own Dao and train in various ascetic practices, which he did until a second major revelation in 423 told him that he was ready to begin his big task.

In the following year, 424, Kou took his divine information to court and found the support of the prime minister Cui Hao (381–450). In due course, he became the head of a state-sponsored Daoism, geared to bringing peace and harmony to the northern empire. This involved setting himself up in a palace-cum-monastery in the capital together with followers and administrators said to have numbered 120, and establishing Daoist institutions—temples, priests, moral rules, and rituals (not unlike the organization of the Daoist Association today)—throughout the country. The high point of Kou's power was reached when, in 440, the emperor himself accepted Daoist initiation and claimed to be the new ruler of Great Peace, changing his reign title to "Perfect Lord of Great Peace" (Taiping zhenjun). Kou's influence and that of Cui Hao continued to grow until the former's death in 448. Cui tried to hold it all together but became a bit too overbearing and megalomaniac in the process, and the theocracy ended after his execution in 450, the Toba looking to Buddhism for their administrative requirements.

At the height of Kou's power, all people in the northern empire were subject to Daoist rules as specified in the revealed text, still partially extant in the Daoist canon as the *Laojun yinsong xinke jiejing* (Scripture of Lord Lao's New Code of Precepts Chanted to the *Clouds Melody*), usually simply called the "New Code. " This code specified that people had to be loyal to the ruler, obedient to their parents and elders, and subservient to Dao. To express their proper attitude, they had to observe daily, monthly, and special festival rites throughout the year. Such festivals could last three, five, or seven days and, as in the Celestial Masters of old, involved community assemblies and formal kitchen-feasts. Daily and monthly rites were performed through a series of bows and prostrations as well as by the burning of incense and offering of a prayer or petition. Strictly forbidden were popular practices such as shamanic séances and blood sacrifices, as well as traditional Celestial Masters rites of sexual initiation.

Still, in many ways Kou's theocracy continued the Celestial Masters system. Sickness, for example, was still considered a cause for cosmic concern and was treated through public confession, ritual prostrations, and the sending of petitions. Daoist priests, moreover, still collected taxes, though now for the state rather than for the religion, serving as civil servants and bureaucrats and rendering the religion the key administrative unit in the state. They were held to an even stricter code of conduct and politeness, adapted to a certain degree from Buddhist rules. Abuse and disobedience were punished not only on earth but also by hell fire and rebirth as an animal. Good behavior, on the other hand, especially as exemplified in the recitation and copying of Kou's "New Code," could lead to ascension into heaven and the attainment of a rank among the immortals. The theocracy with its rules and rituals was, then, like the Lingbao school, another way in which Buddhism and Shangqing cosmology were joined with the ideas and practices of the early Celestial Masters into a new system of Daoist worldview and communal organization.

Louguan

After the end of the theocracy in 450, the Toba rulers turned to their Buddhist subjects for administrative help in the empire and created the so-called *sangha*-households. They undertook practices similar to those of the Daoist theocracy but under Buddhist auspices. The followers of Kou Qianzhi, on the other hand, became free-lance Daoists and many of them congregated in a newly established center in the Zhongnan mountains, about forty miles southwest of the capital. Here Yin Tong, an alleged descendant of Yin Xi (the guardian of the pass at Laozi's emigration), had established his ancestral homestead, which he called Louguan, the "Lookout Tower" after Yin Xi's supposed astrological endeavors. He proceeded to establish a formal legend surrounding this place, claiming that the transmission of the *Daode jing* did not actually take place at the Hangu Pass where Laozi and Yin Xi met but rather at Louguan, where Yin Xi took the sage for his greater comfort.

Over time, Louguan grew significantly and rose to prominence, particularly under the leadership of Wang Daoyi (447–510), who apparently also received financial backing from the court or the aristocracy. As a result, Louguan became the first established monastery of Daoism. It served also as a refuge for followers from the south where Daoism was proscribed under the Liang dynasty. At Louguan many new Daoist scriptures were collected and a great impulse developed to create a new, integrated version of the Daoist teaching. This vision of a new Daoism centered around the key belief of the Celestial Masters that Lord Lao was the creator and savior of the universe, and was the source of sacred scriptures, practical teachings, and organizational rules. Lord Lao existed prior to heaven and earth, made order out of chaos, created and formed the world, never tired of descending to reveal scriptures and teach rulers, and brought forth all different Daoist teachings.

One teaching he was associated with particularly in Louguan was an adaptation of the five precepts of Buddhism: prohibiting killing, stealing, lying, sexual misconduct, and intoxication. In a scripture claimed to be Lord Lao's direct revelation, they are listed, explained, and linked with Chinese traditional cosmology. The *Taishang Laojun jiejing* (Scripture of Precepts of the Highest Lord Lao) says,

> Lord Lao said: The five precepts in heaven are represented by the five planets [Jupiter, Venus, Mars, Mercury, and Saturn].

They rule the energies of the five directions, making sure they remain in harmony and maintain their constancy. As soon as the Dao of heaven loses its precepts, there are natural catastrophes.

On earth, they are represented by the five sacred mountains [Mts. Tai, Heng, Hua, Heng, and Song]. They govern the energies of the earth and rule the weather, gathering and dispelling the clouds. As soon as the Dao of earth loses its precepts, the hundred grains can no longer grow.

Among the seasonal patterns, they are represented by the five phases. As soon as the five cycles lose their precepts, fire and water fight each other, and metal and wood do each other harm.

In government, the five precepts are represented by the five emperors. As soon as rulers lose their precepts, dynasties topple and rulers perish.

In human beings, they are represented by the five inner organs. As soon as people lose their precepts, their health and inner nature goes astray. (Kohn, "Five Precepts," 203)

Louguan Daoists thus merged Buddhist thought actively with traditional Chinese thought. They also expressed their beliefs in several other scriptures, including the mystical and philosophical *Xisheng jing* (Scripture of Western Ascension) and the ordination manual *Chuanshou jingjie* (Transmission of Scriptures and Precepts). Their support of the state, moreover, never wavered and they maintained their prominent role at court in the sixth century and greatly supported the rise of the Tang dynasty in the seventh.

At the same time Daoist worship also spread to the wider populace. Evidence for this is found in archaeology, especially the first known Daoist statues that date from this period. They show Lord Lao clad in a thick robe and wearing a formal square headdress, with a straight triangular beard. He holds a fly-whisk in his right hand, while his left holds a tablet and rests on his thigh. Like the Buddha in comparable Buddhist works, he often has two attendants at his sides, each grasping a jade audience tablet. Usually the group is placed on a lotus-type platform, guarded to the right and left by lions, with an incense burner in front. Most often an

inscription is added on the back of the object, but sometimes there are
additional figures, including buddhas and bodhisattvas.

About fifty such statues or steles have been unearthed to date—as compared with several thousand Buddhist works. Objects of ritual worship,
they were usually placed on mountain sides where they could easily
communicate with the otherworld. Inscriptions typically contain prayers
for the dead, hoping that they avoid the three bad forms of rebirth (as
animal, ghost, or hell dweller) and instead come to life in the heavens.
They also include prayers for the happiness and prosperity of living family members, the imperial family and political peace, and the liberation
of all beings. For example, a stele sponsored by a certain Yao Boduo (dat.
496) says,

> May the governors and rulers
> And all the officers who keep the earth in order
> Guide the people with bright virtue. . . .
> May the good teaching be spread widely,
> And the people follow it in happiness
> Looking up with hope. . . .
> May they have their wishes realized
> And their lives extended!

The Debates

The political dimension of Daoism found further expression in a set of
debates with Buddhists. Representatives of the two religions met in a
formal court setting and presented the strong points of their own teaching—in regards to the well-being of the state—and criticized the shortcomings of their opponents'. These debates occurred mainly in the sixth
century, and their main goal was to find an integrative teaching and civil
organization that would help prepare the ground for the country's military and political reunification. The northern rulers were especially keen
on becoming emperors of all China and thus searched actively for political doctrines to help them achieve their goal. They organized two major
sets of debates, one in 520 under the Toba-Wei, the other in 570 under
the Northern Zhou.

In 520, the two sides argued the seniority of their respective teachings,
focusing on the problem of dating. If Laozi went west to convert the barbarians and become the Buddha, the argument went, he must have left

China earlier than the recorded birth of the Buddha in India. To begin, the Daoists claimed that Laozi was born in 605 B.C.E. and converted the barbarians in 519 B. C. E. , thus proving that Buddhism was a second-hand form of Daoism, created to control the barbarians. Its presence in China could do nothing but harm. The Buddhists countered this allegation by dating the birth of the Buddha back to 1029 B.C.E., finding evidence in an ancient Zhou record of certain phenomena in the western sky that could be interpreted as indicating the birth of a great sage. This dating was again bettered by the Daoists in the *Kaitian jing* (Scripture on Opening the Cosmos), but the Buddhists succeeded in showing that this was a forgery and not a revealed text, and thus emerged victorious from this phase of the debate, gaining great influence at court.

The debate of 570 occurred over a number of separate occasions and was sparked by a memorial by Wei Yuansong, a renegade Buddhist monk. In 567 he had risen to propose a new Buddhist orthodoxy with the people as the flock, the *sangha* as administrators, and the emperor as sacred Buddhist ruler. Because this meant the dissolution of an independent Buddhist organization and the return of all clerics to the laity, Buddhist leaders argued heatedly against it. Emperor Wu of the Northern Zhou, however, liked the idea and honored Wei Yuansong with a formal title. The Daoists similarly presented their creed as a unifying state doctrine in a memorial which continued the ideas used in the theocracy and made some impression on the emperor.

Not willing to decide without his aristocrats' approval, he convened an assembly in 569 to debate the pros and cons of the propositions, but no definite decision was reached. Several more assemblies ended similarly undecided, so that the emperor ordered reports compiled evaluating the teachings. Among these are the *Erjiao lun* (The Two Teachings) by the monk Dao'an, and the *Xiaodao lun* (Laughing at the Dao) by the ex-Daoist Zhen Luan, both dated to 570. The former ignores Daoism completely, presenting instead a combination of Confucian and Buddhist teachings as the best teaching for the state. The latter contains a wealth of information on sixth-century cosmology and practice, typically presenting first a Daoist argument against Buddhism, then refuting it by referring to authoritative scriptures or historical precedents. A typical argument, geared toward the political value of the teachings, would look as follows:

Buddhist Demon Worship Disturbs the Political Order

The *Huahu jing* (Scripture of Conversion of the Barbarians) says: "Buddhism first arose in the barbarian countries. Because the western region belongs to the phase metal, people there are harsh and lack proper rites. Later, the people of the Country of the Gods [China] imitated their observances and established Buddhism. . . They adorned scriptures and carved images, deluding kings and ministers alike. Thus, all over the empire floods and droughts, rebellions and insurrections began to succeed each other. In less than ten years [after the introduction of Buddhism], disasters and strange phenomena came to be common occurrences." . . . .

I laugh at this and say: ... Before the time of Emperor Ming of the Han [r. 58–76 C. E.], when Buddhism was not yet practiced, the Dao and the primordial energy flourished greatly. Why, then, is it that in those times wars and insurrections occurred frequently, that floods and droughts succeeded each other? Blood rained from the sky, mountains tumbled, and famines and disasters succeeded each other. Above all, the tyrants Jie and Zhou punished men by tying them alive to the iron pillar. It has now been five hundred years since the reign of Emperor Ming and the introduction of Buddhism. In this time, have there been any ominous disasters or cruel governments worse than before? (sect. 21; Kohn, *Laughing at the Tao*, 110, 112)

Despite such impassioned arguments in favor of Buddhism, Emperor Wu continued to hang on to his dream of a Daoist-based orthodoxy and set up the Tongdao guan (Monastery for Penetrating Dao) as an official Daoist research institution. Directed by prominent Louguan masters, its members compiled several important Daoist works: the *Wushang biyao* (Secret Essentials of the Most High, dat. 574), the first Daoist encyclopedia containing an integrated vision of the world according to Dao; and the *Xuandu jingmu* (Scripture Catalog of Mystery Metropolis), a canonical collection of scriptures. Despite these efforts, Emperor Wu's vision remained unfulfilled, and unification was achieved from the south and under Buddhist auspices in the Sui dynasty. Nevertheless, the issues raised in the debates remained, and Daoism rose to political prominence again under the Tang (618–907).

The Tang Dynasty

Even before the Tang ascent, millenarian prophecies about a man named Li (the family name of the Tang rulers as well as of Laozi) as the promised Lord of Great Peace greatly aided their campaign. They were also helped by Daoist institutions, such as Louguan which was promptly honored with state support and the new name Monastery of the Ancestral Sage (Zongsheng guan). The ancestral sage was Laozi (Li Er), whom the Tang rulers claimed as their original ancestor. Lord Lao was already known as the helper of humanity, and he now came even closer to the people by serving as the ruler's ancestor and taking an active interest in the fate of the country. He appeared in numerous miracles throughout the dynasty, beginning in 620 with a manifestation on Mount Yangjiao to the commoner Ji Shanxing, which inspired the new Tang ruler to increase his efforts at pacification. The story describes Lord Lao:

> His beard and hair were white and hoary, he was clad in plain, undyed garments and had a black cap on his head. The horse's mane, tail, and hooves were all red. Two lads of about thirteen or fourteen with turbaned heads, red boots, and green clothes were attending him on the right and left, one holding a cloth, the other holding a red whisk.

> The Lord addressed Shanxing saying: "Go and tell the emperor of the Great Tang on my behalf: 'You have now attained the sagely principle, and the gods of soil and grain will support you for a long time to come. At this point it is best that you erect a Palace of Peaceful Transformation to the east of the city wall of Chang'an and install a statue of Dao therein. This will surely grant Great Peace to the empire.'"

> Once these words were concluded, they all lifted up in the air and vanished. (*Youlong zhuan*, ch. 5)

Next, at his birthplace in Bozhou, now a religious center of national importance, Lord Lao made a withered cypress burst into bloom again, and in numerous other locations he caused the discovery of wondrous inscribed stones of old (like the ancient "River Chart"), divine statues, and miraculous images on the walls of cliffs or temples.

The rulers, in turn, gave extensive privileges to Daoists, lavished great gifts on monasteries and temples, established a Daoist track of the imperial bureaucracy, sponsored Daoist compilations, honored Lord Lao with the new title Xuanyuan huangdi or "Sovereign Emperor of Mysterious Origin", and generally elevated the religion. In the eighth century, Emperor Xuanzong (r. 712–755) was a great supporter of Daoism and especially of Laozi, whom he revered as the key to successful government and whose statues he ordered placed in state-sponsored temples of every district in the empire. To this effect he issued an edict in 741, which runs:

> Those who wish to safeguard humankind revere the great Dao. Those who have successfully kept the mandate [of Heaven] have always relied on their illustrious predecessors. They have venerated especially the Great Sage, Emperor of the Mysterious Origin [Laozi]. His way shines forth from the Great Ultimate. He arose before the origin of creation, widely spread the true teaching and everywhere supported transformations.
>
> . . . From the beginning of our rule to the present time, he has time and again conferred good fortune upon us and frequently graced us with the miraculous appearance of his true image. Purity in heaven, peace on earth, abundance in people's lives, proper cycles of nature, and the submission of all foreign barbarians have been responses of the Sacred Ancestor and the great Dao. (*Cefu yuangui* 54. 4b–5a)

Emperor Xuanzong also had the two main ancestral temples of the dynasty in the capitals Chang'an (west) and Luoyang (east) converted into Daoist temples, major institutions of Daoist learning and training centers for Daoist bureaucrats. As a result, Daoism flourished and membership increased greatly. Several imperial princesses underwent ordination as Daoist priestesses in elaborate ceremonies, offering staggering amounts of silk, gold, and valuables. While supporting the religious organization, Tang rulers also established a system of official control. Ordinations had to be formally permitted by the state, all Daoists had to carry official ordination certificates—as travel permits and for exemption from tax and labor—and, for the first time, official legal codes governed the behavior of recluses and punished both violations of civil law and infractions of religious precepts.

Court Liturgy

Adopted as members of the imperial administration, Tang Daoists also performed elaborate seasonal rituals, rites of repentance, and ceremonies on behalf of the state, as described especially in works by Zhang Wanfu (fl. 700–742), a notable ritual master of the period. Under Emperor Xuanzong, moreover, Daoist ritual forms were adopted into the court liturgy. This began in 741 when a statue of Lord Lao was miraculously discovered and the emperor decreed that all districs had to erect a temple to Lord Lao to house its replica. Alongside the deity, a statue of the emperor himself was to be placed and worshiped with Daoist rites. In 743, all ordained Daoists became nominally members of the imperial family and their administration was relocated in the Court of the Imperial Clan. Many Daoist temples were accordingly renamed from *guan* (monastery) to *gong* (palace). In addition, court ceremonies were reshaped according to a Daoist model. Ritual garb was changed in style from formal court dress to simpler religious robes, the official prayer board was replaced by paper, and various Daoist forms of music and dance became part of the official ceremonies.

Daoist poets and choreographers came into the limelight, and other artists, too, began to work more with Daoist themes and melodies. The emperor himself wrote a ceremonial dance, known as the "Dance of the Purple Culmen," giving high priority to Daoist themes. A famous Daoist poet was Wu Yun (ca. 700–778) from Shaanxi who was ordained as a Shangqing priest, was summoned frequently to court, received an appointment to the prestigious Hanlin Academy and wrote both Daoist philosophy and ritual poetry. Among his songs, there are especcially the cycles to the melodies "Pacing the Void" and "Saunters in Sylphdom. " To give one example:

> The host of immortals looks up to the cosmic rule;
> In dignified carriages they rise to pay homage to the divine ancestor.
> Golden stars, they illuminate each other brilliantly;
> Winding along slowly, they ascend to the great void.
> The mysterious seven stars of the Dipper have flown high already.
> With fiery refinement, they arise in the Red Palace of the south.
> Overflowing happiness fills the heavenly lands;

> Overarching harmony permeates the royal rule.
> The spirits of the eight trigrams shine on floating energies.
> The lords of the ten directions dance on auspicious winds.
> Through them I scale to the very source of yang,
> Coming, as I am, from the merit of deep yin.
> Freely I wander above great morning light,
> Penetrating with true sight all and everywhere!
> (cf. Schafer, "Pacing the Void," 393-94)

Many other renowned Tang poets took inspiration from Daoism, including Li Bo (701–762), Du Fu (712–770), and Gu Kuang (735–814). They employed Daoist imagery in describing common themes, expressed Daoist ecstatic visions and excursions in flowery verse, provided literary descriptions of Daoist pilgrimages, and sang the joys and losses of passionate encounters with divine partners. Daoism, in both its cultural and ritual expressions, was at the core of Tang court and literary activities, and the religion flourished.

Further Readings

Barrett, T. H. 1996. *Taoism Under the T'ang: Religion and Empire During the Golden Age of Chinese History*. London: Wellsweep Press.

Bilsky, Lester J. 1975. *The State Religion of Ancient China*. 2 vols. Taipei: Chinese Folklore Association.

Cahill, Suzanne. 1993. *Transcendence and Divine Passion: The Queen Mother of the West in Medieval China*. Stanford: Stanford University Press.

Kamitsuka, Yoshiko. 1998. "Lao-tzu in Six Dynasties Sculpture. " In *Lao-tzu and the Tao-te-ching*, edited by Livia Kohn and Michael LaFargue, 63–85. Albany: State University of New York Press.

Kirkland, J. Russell. 1997. "Dimensions of Tang Taoism: The State of the Field at the End of the Millennium." *T'ang Studies* 15-16.

Mather, Richard B. 1979. "K'ou Ch'ien-chih and the Taoist Theocracy at the Northern Wei Court 425-451. " In *Facets of Taoism*, edited by Holmes Welch and Anna Seidel, 103–22. New Haven, Conn. : Yale University Press.

Seidel, Anna. 1983. "Imperial Treasures and Taoist Sacraments: Taoist Roots in the Apocrypha. " In *Tantric and Taoist Studies*, edited by Michel Strickmann, 291–371. Brussels: Institut Belge des Hautes Etudes Chinoises.

Original Sources in Translation

Benn, Charles D. 1991. *The Cavern Mystery Transmission: A Taoist Ordination Rite of A. D. 711*. Honolulu: University of Hawaii Press.

Kohn, Livia. 1991. *Taoist Mystical Philosophy: The Scripture of Western Ascension*. Albany: State University of New York Press.

Kohn, Livia. 1994. "The Five Precepts of the Venerable Lord." *Monumenta Serica* 42: 171–215

Kohn, Livia. 1995. *Laughing at the Tao: Debates among Buddhists and Taoists in Medieval China*. Princeton: Princeton University Press.

Schafer, Edward H. 1981. "Wu Yün's 'Cantos on Pacing the Void'." *Harvard Journal of Asiatic Studies* 41: 377–415.

Schafer, Edward H. 1983. "Wu Yün's 'Stanzas on Saunters in Sylphdom'." *Monumenta Serica* 35: 1–37.

Part Three

Spiritual Practices

CHAPTER SEVEN

RITUAL AND MEDITATION

Daoism developed numerous different spiritual practices in its history, many of which we have already noted. There are the meditation of tranquility and nonaction of the *Daode jing*, the self-forgetful absorption and mental freedom of the *Zhuangzi*, the ascetic discipline and longevity techniques of the *fangshi*, the spells, talismans, communal ceremonies, and healing rites of the Celestial Masters, the visualization of gods and ecstatic excursions of aristocratic seekers, and the formal rituals of the organized Daoist groups. All these various activities serve to establish contact between the human and divine realms, to enable and ease the transformation of the individual or community into a being of Dao. They can, in our terms, be classified under the two categories of ritual and meditation, but it should be understood that this is not a differentiation recognized in ancient China or by practicing Daoists. Every meditation exercise has to be preceded and accompanied by certain ritual actions— purifications, prostrations, burning of incense—and a ritual is only as efficacious as the meditative powers and efforts of its officiating priest. Still, to better understand the structure of Daoist practice, we shall briefly define "ritual" and "meditation" from the Western perspective.

The phenomenon of ritual is difficult to assess, and there are many different theories surrounding it, as outlined by Catherine Bell in *Ritual Theory, Ritual Practice* (1992). Still, ritual is most commonly understood as establishing a bridge between this world and the divine, or as formalizing the transition from one social, seasonal, personal, or spiritual state to another. As Victor Turner points out in *The Ritual Process* (1969), rites often take place to mark an in-between state, the so-called liminal state (after the Latin word for "threshold"). This liminal state is characterized by a basic ambiguity—no longer being one thing and not yet another— and an accompanying sense of insecurity and vulnerability. In some ways, being in a liminal situation is like being back in a primal state before one was shaped into a specific person, without status, property, rights, and duties.

As a result, people at the center of a ritual often behave in a humble, shy way, allowing themselves to be taken care of and moved about rather than controlling and managing the situation. In order to enter the liminal state, one has to step away from one's previous status; this, known as "separation," often occurs in a preparatory stage of the ritual and is accompanied by measures of purification and detachment. After the ritual is concluded, one leaves the liminal phase and fully enters one's new position and status. This is called "reaggregation" and often ritually expressed by the donning of new garb, the sharing of merits, and various thanksgiving ceremonies. Clear examples of the ritual process in civil societies are weddings, funerals, and coming-of-age ceremonies; in a religious context, it is best documented in ordinations into the priesthood, as we will see below.

The other major form of spiritual practice is meditation. It is defined as the conscious attempt at establishing a certain state of mind, be it tranquility, openness, or a certain vision. Modern analyses of meditation, as exemplified in *Meditation: Classic and Contemporary Perspectives*, edited by Deane N. Shapiro and Roger N. Walsh (1984), follow the ancient Buddhist model, which divides it into two major types called concentration or cessation (*samathâ*) and wisdom or insight (*vipasyâna*). The idea is that the mind first has to be focused and one-pointed, for which usually a single object of concentration is used—a sound, an image, or the breath. Only when properly calmed can the mind be directed outward and trained to dispassionately accept all it encounters, gaining insight by observing reality from a perspective of detachment and wisdom.

The result is a mind free from dualistic divisions such as joy and anger, likes and dislikes, right and wrong, a mind increasingly beyond worldly patterns and psychological obstructions that can then enter higher states, such as the pure Dao or Buddhist nirvana. In addition, a third type of meditation is recognized today: the practice of visualization. As studied by Mike and Nancy Samuels in *Seeing with the Mind's Eye: The History, Technique, and Uses of Visualization* (1975), its practice ranges from traditional artists' visions through Christian contemplation practice to modern-day sports coaching and psychotherapy. It is a powerful way of reshaping the mind—after it has been calmed—toward a new identity and vision of the world. Daoist meditation practice involves all three of these techniques.

The full formulation of both the ritual and meditative Daoist system occurred first in the Tang dynasty. It followed the unification of the country in the sixth century, which in turn was echoed by the unification of religious doctrine, through the Tiantai synthesis in Buddhism and the Three Caverns hierarchy in Daoism. Both systems included all known teachings of their respective religions, joining them in an integrated, hierarchical pattern that allowed disciples to move through the ranks or choose a particular level for their practice.

The Three Caverns

The Three Caverns (*sandong*) system of integrating Daoist teachings goes back to a bibliographic classification by the fifth-century master Lu Xiujing, and was based on the Buddhist notion of the Three Vehicles (*triyâna*) or paths to attainment: listening (*srâvaka*), cultivating oneself (*pratyekabuddha*), and striving for universal salvation (*bodhisattva*). In Lu's version of the system, the Lingbao school with its strong communal focus was placed at the top, with Shangqing ranking second, and a school called the Three Sovereigns (Sanhuang) placed third. This school, which did not survive beyond the mid-seventh century, focused on political divination and proper rulership with the help of talismans and cosmic correspondences. The Celestial Masters were placed at the bottom and thus at the foundation of the entire pyramid—not counted as one of the Three Caverns, yet essential to them all.

In the sixth century, Daoists adopted this scheme, but switched the placement of the Lingbao and Shangqing schools to place the latter at the top. Daoist texts, then, were arranged into three main categories, each school associated with a special "Cavern" and a "Supplement." The latter contained technical and hagiographic materials and served as a home for texts of non-mainstream schools. The overall system, still used in the Daoist canon today, is as follows:

Cavern	School	Supplement
Perfection (Dongzhen)	Shangqing	GreatMystery (Taixuan)
Mystery (Dongxuan)	Lingbao	Great Peace (Taiping)
Spirit (Dongshen)	Sanhuang	Great Clarity (Taiqing)
		OrthodoxUnity (Zhengyi)

Within each Cavern and Supplement, texts were further itemized into twelve classes (adopted from the Buddhist canon) and arranged according to content and format:

1. Fundamental Texts	7. Rituals and Observances
2. Divine Talismans	8. Techniques and Methods
3. Secret Instructions	9. Various Arts
4. Numinous Charts	10. Records and Biographies
5. Genealogies and Registers	11. Eulogies and Encomia
6. Precepts and Regulations	12. Lists and Memoranda

The gods of the Three Caverns, moreover, were joined together into one group known as the Three Purities (Sanqing), or the Daoist trinity. Named after the three major heavens of the early medieval system, they had the Heavenly Worthy of Primordial Beginning (representing Shangqing) at the center, the Lord of the Dao (Lingbao) to his left, and Lord Lao (adopted from both Sanhuang and the Celestial Masters) to his right. The three deities further matched the Three Treasures (*sanbao*) of the religion, another concept adopted from Buddhism, i.e., *buddha* (enlightenment), *dharma* (teaching), and *sangha* (community of followers). In Daoism, they are the Dao, the scriptures, and the teachers. The gods of the trinity represent the Three Treasures in the sense that the Heavenly Worthy is the creative power at the root of all existence, the Lord of Dao is the revealer of scriptures and presenter of revelations, and Lord Lao is the practical teacher, who provides instructions in various techniques and communicates most closely with humanity.

The three gods, now all given the polite title "Heavenly Worthy," are described in the literature as being originally one, while in their differentiation they represent different aspects of Dao in its various manifestations. They first appear in statues in the sixth century, the making of which is described in a ritual text of the early seventh:

> Whenever one makes a sacred image, one must follow the scriptures in fashioning its proper characteristics. . . . The gods' formal garb and thrones must conform to the divine law. The Heavenly Worthies, therefore, should wear capes of nine-colored loose gauze or five-colored cloudy mist over long robes of yellow variegated brocade with mountain-and-river patterns. Their gold or jade headdresses should have tassels and pendants to the right and left and be inlaid in multiple colors.

Their capes must never be executed in monochrome purple, cinnabar, blue, or turquoise, nor must they be depicted with loose hair, long ears, or a horn. On the other hand, they may wear headdresses showing hibiscus flowers, flying clouds, primordial beginning, or the like, but must never have flat head gear, showing the two forces [yin and yang], or anything made from deer skin.

The two perfected assistants on their left and right should be shown presenting offerings, holding scriptures, grasping audience tablets, or with fragrant flowers in their hands. They should be referential and majestic, their hands and feet not too far extended, their garments not hanging oddly to one side. The Heavenly Worthies themselves should sit upright, their fingers entwined in the [sacred sign of] Great Nonbeing, never holding even a scepter or a deer-tail whisk. Their hands are simply empty, and that is all. (*Fengdao kejie*, ch. 2)

These elaborate statues of the gods adorned many Daoist temples and monasteries in the middle ages and can still be seen in sanctuaries today. They represent the totality of the Daoist teaching, symbolizing in one artistic group the integration of all different schools and lineages.

Ordinations

In ritual practice, the system of the Three Caverns led to the establishment of a formal ordination hierarchy, which is first described in the *Fengdao kejie* (Rules and Precepts for Worshiping the Dao) of about the year 620. It consisted of a total of seven ranks:

School	Rank
Zhengyi (Celestial Masters)	Register Disciple
Taixuan (Great Mystery)	Disciple of Good Faith
Dongyuan (Cavern Abyss)	Disciple of Cavern Abyss
Laozi (Daode jing)	Disciple of Eminent Mystery
Sanhuang (Three Sovereigns)	Disciple of Cavern Spirit
Lingbao (Numinous Treasure)	Preceptor of Highest Mystery
Shangqing (Highest Clarity)	Preceptor of Highest Perfection

The first three ranks were those of lay masters, while the last three were monastic, and the middle rank (Disciple of Eminent Mystery) signified a transitional stage that could be held either by a householder or a recluse.

Ordinations into these ranks began very early, with children being initiated first into the Celestial Masters level and receiving registers of protective generals. After that, each level required extended periods of training, the guidance of an ordination master, and several sponsors from the community. Once an official date was set, the candidate went into seclusion to purify himself or herself for a set period, then appeared at a specially constructed three-tiered altar platform. This was usually set up in the courtyard of a major teaching monastery to which the officiating master, in an invitation ceremony, had called down the various gods of the Dao. Then, as the *Fengdao kejie* says:

> At the beginning of the ceremony, ordinands line up at the bottom of the [altar] stairs. Facing west, they bid farewell to their parents and give thanks to their ancestors, bowing twelve times. Then they turn to face north and bow to the emperor four times. The reason for this is that, once they have donned the ritual vestments of the Heavenly Worthies, they will never again bow to parents or worldly rulers. Therefore, when anyone joins the Daoist community, he or she must first bid farewell and give thanks. (ch. 6)

Here we can see clearly the initial stage of a typical rite of passage, the "separation," when the ordinand formally leaves his or her old life behind and gets ready to take the irreversible step into the otherworldly community of Dao. After that, the liminal phase begins with the ordinands bowing and surrendering to Dao:

> The ordinands then stand erect with their hands folded over their chests. Still facing north, they surrender themselves three times to the Three Treasures, bowing three times to each. They say:
>
> With all my heart I surrender my body
> to the Great Dao of the Highest Nonultimate.
> With all my heart I surrender my spirit
> to the Venerable Scriptures in Thirty-Six Sections.
> With all my heart I surrender my life
> to the Great Preceptors of the Mysterious Center.
> (Fengdao kejie, ch. 6)

After this basic form of surrender, ordinands were equipped with the insignia of their new status: religious names as well as the titles, robes, and headdresses appropriate for their new rank. To show their new affiliation, they would tie their hair into a topknot, unlike Buddhists who shaved theirs. Also unlike Buddhism, where nuns had to observe many more rules than monks and were given a lower status, women in Daoism were treated equally. They underwent the same ceremonies and wore the same garb as men, distinguished only by their elaborate headdress, the so-called female hat (*nüguan*), a term also used for "Daoist priestess."

In exchange for their new status, ordinands then made a solemn pledge to follow the Dao and do everything to uphold it. This pledge involved the presentation of lavish gifts of gold, silk, and precious objects to the master and the institution, as well as the formal oath to follow the rules and work toward the goals of the organization. Higher ranks had as many as 300 precepts, focusing on social behavior, interaction with community members, and forms of cosmic consciousness, but most ranks involved the observation of ten precepts first formulated by the Lingbao school. These ten consist of five prohibitions, imitating the five precepts of Buddhism, and five resolutions that reflect Daoist priorities. They are:

1. Do not kill, but be always considerate to all living beings.
2. Do not commit immoral deeds or think depraved thoughts.
3. Do not steal or receive unrighteous goods.
4. Do not lie or misrepresent good and evil.
5. Do not intoxicate yourself, but be always mindful of pure conduct.
6. I will maintain harmony with my ancestors and kin and never do anything that harms my family.
7. When I see someone do good, I will support him with joy and happiness in my heart.
8. When I see someone unfortunate, I will help him with my strength to recover good fortune.
9. When someone comes to do me harm, I will not harbor thoughts of revenge.
10. As long as all beings have not attained Dao, I will not expect to do so myself. (*Dingzhi jing; Shijie jing; Fengdao kejie*, ch. 6)

The taking of the precepts typically came with the formal transmission of a set of written documents (scriptures, talismans, registers), which the new Daoists had to hand-copy soon after the ceremony. They would use the copy for their study, recitation, and ritual work, while the original would be kept in a safe place and eventually be buried with them. The ceremonial exchange of precepts and scriptures formally authorized them as fully ordained masters and officially sealed their expertise in the Daoist methods — ritual and meditation techniques necessary to properly activate the power of the texts. As part of their training, ordinands learned to read between the lines, make sense of subtle hints and phrases, and decide which meditation and incantation to use for which scriptural or talismanic activation. Now that they were sworn in, they were formally acknowledged to have the expertise and powers of their rank. The ceremony typically concluded with another round of formal obeisances to the masters and the Heavenly Worthies, and a communal chanting of the ode in honor of the precepts.

While all this occurred in the liminal stage of the ritual, the final part or "reaggregation" in Daoist ordination followed shortly after, when the new Daoist donned their proper robes and prepared a thanksgiving offering. Again the *Fengdao kejie* as found in a Dunhuang manuscript:

> Three days after receiving the divine law, newly ordained Daoists should choose an appropriate time and prepare an offering as a present to the great sages, masters, and worthies of the various heavens. This is to thank them for their enfolding grace without which the ordination could not have taken place. (S. 809)

Daoist Rites

Daoist rites grew from traditional Chinese ritual, which divides into the three basic forms: sacrifice (*si*), purification (*zhai*), and thanksgiving or offering (*jiao*). In ancient China, as in Confucian and popular rites today, the central part of the ceremony was the sacrifice, the presentation of ritual objects such as wine, tea, rice, sweets, and animal carcasses to the gods and ancestors. This was commonly followed by a communal feast, when the various foods offered were shared by the congregation. Purification meant a set of preparatory measures undertaken before conducting or joining the sacrifice. This commonly involved the abstention from wine, meat, sex, and contact with blood, and included taking baths and donning new and formal robes. The third and concluding part of the ceremony, offering, was a kind of merit-assuring rite after the successful sacrifice, with the goal of inducing the gods to give their blessings to humanity. All these rituals were, moreover, accompanied by specific spells, prayers, and incantations.

Daoist ritual displayed a significant difference from Confucianism and popular religion in that it placed less emphasis on the sacrifice of objects than on the presentation of written documents such as talismans, seals, announcements, petitions, memorials, and mandates. In that it adopted the court ritual of ancient China, which governed the formal interaction of the emperor with his ministers and local representatives. Officials at audiences held special tablets and seals of personal identification and presented their reports and wishes in formally written announcements, petitions, and memorials. From the early Celestial Masters onward, Daoist ritual can, therefore, be understood as the adaptation of traditional Chinese court ritual to the interaction with the divine, now interpreted as the pure forces of Dao and addressed in formal audiences. It still involved purification, but its central focus shifted from the sacrifice to the petition. The killing of animals and blood sacrifices of popular cults were no longer pursued.

In the Lingbao school of the fifth century, a further dimension of ritual was added: the purification (*zhai*) as interpreted and used by Buddhists. All Buddhist followers had to observe the five precepts against killing, stealing, lying, sexual misconduct, and intoxication in their everyday life. In addition they were also encouraged to join the monasteries for specific "purification days," ranging from three to ten per month. On those days, people would take additional precepts, participate in monastic meditations, listen to monks' lectures, and have the opportunity to confess their sins. The practice goes back to the early Buddhist monastic community, which chanted the 250 monks' rules of the *Pratimoksa* and confessed their sins twice monthly, at every new and full moon. In medieval China, these Buddhist purifications were adapted by the laity and turned into highly popular occasions, used not only for merit-making but also as opportunities for social interaction.

The Lingbao school, and through it medieval Daoism, adopted this form of purification, and merged it with the established forms of Celestial Masters rites to created the *zhai* as a new communal ritual. This was a major public and rather spectacular event, best called a "festival of purgation." It involved participants chanting, praying, confessing their sins, presenting offerings and petitions to the gods, and generally coming to-

gether in communal assemblies. Formal confession of sins had already
been undertaken by the Celestial Masters, but it was now made part of a
public spectacle, especially in a festival known as the Mud and Soot Purgation (*tutan zhai*). This rite was believed to alleviate the karma accumu-
lated from the past and help the sinner and his ancestors attain immortal
status, still envisioned as a bureaucratic transfer of registration files. A
typical prayer during such a rite goes as follows:

> For three days and three nights, through all the six [double-
> hour] periods,
> We carry out repentance for our pardon.
> May our millions of forebears and ancestors, all our fathers,
> mothers, uncles, brothers,
> Whether dead already or to die in future, down to ourselves,
> participating here—
> May we all be free from all the evil for *kalpas* still to come!
> For millions of generations, we have committed sins and
> accumulated burdens.
> Reverently we now trust in the rite of this Purgation.
> May our family be complete and ordered!
> May we be bathed and cleansed to purity!
> (*Wushang biyao*, ch. 50)

It was also believed that large-scale ceremonies on behalf of the state and
the community, for example, the Yellow Register Purgation (*huanglu
zhai*), would create cosmic harmony with the larger universe and ease
political and social tensions. Festivals of purgation were then held at
regular intervals, at the Three Primes (the festivals of the Celestial Masters), the Eight Nodes (the beginnings and high points of the seasons),
and at other major annual junctions, as well as on occasions important to
religious or state institutions. The priests who conducted these festivals
had to be formally ordained and were equipped with the most exquisite
robes and implements. They exerted authority as celestial officials, recon-
firming the inherent nature of Daoist ritual as a formal audience with the
gods.

Meditation

Each stage of the ordination hierarchy also came with a different set of
meditation practices. While Daoists on the level of Zhengyi (Celestial

Masters) would know how to engage the protector generals of their registers, Laozi followers would practice tranquility and recite the *Daode jing*, engaging in a visualization of Lord Lao and certain celestial guardians such as the gods of the Northern Dipper. Members of the top rank of Highest Clarity, finally, learned extensive visualization techniques as well as methods of traveling ecstatically to the stars. Instructions for these are even included in their set of 300 precepts, showing the close connection between meditative techniques, ritual, and the ordination system. For example, two of their precepts are:

> May I wander to the Palace of Floating Light in the Great Brahma Heaven, to pay my respects to the Celestial Kings and listen to the heavenly chanting of the wondrous odes of the Empyrean.

> May I wander to the Cleansing Pools in the various heavens, to serenely sit on top of their lotus blossoms, whose fragrance is as pure as spontaneity itself and floats freely throughout the heavens. May the hundreds and thousands of heavenly pools be like a single place to me. May all and everyone be happy and pure through them. (*Dajie wen*, pt. 3)

In preparation for these rather advanced and ritualized meditations, Daoist training also included the practice of longevity techniques, concentration, and insight. Longevity techniques were the most basic, used to make the body fit and healthy and establish it as the proper residence for the gods.

To begin, all diseases had to be eliminated and physical activities of all sorts had to be harmonized. To attain this, different practitioners undertook different measures. Some came to stay in a monastery, while others wandered to sacred mountains; some worked with gymnastics and breathing exercises, while others used diet and reduced their normal food intake to take in pure substances, herbs, and medicines; yet others drank "talisman water," while some absorbed the pure essences of the sun and the moon. In all cases, the goal was to harmonize the different energies of the body, stimulate digestion and blood circulation, make breathing conscious and deep, and generally establish a state of strong health that would allow practitioners to maintain the same bodily posture for an extended period and to live more on *qi* than on food and drink. Thereby, the pure seed of immortality, the inborn "Dao-nature" (*daoxing*), was strengthened and a more spiritual training could commence.

With a body firm and supple, the spiritual training could commence. It followed the classical model of concentration and insight, adapted into Daoism from Tiantai Buddhism, as codified Zhiyi (538-598), and transformed to suit Daoist needs. Concentration was usually practiced by focusing on the breath, either as it entered and left the nostrils or as it expanded and collapsed the abdomen. Its stages are outlined by the seventh-century Daoist, physician, and alchemist Sun Simiao (601-693) in his work *Cunshen lianqi ming* (On the Visualization of Spirit) and the Refinement of *Qi*). He describes concentration's stages as "five phases of the mind" and says:

> 1. The mind experiences much agitation and little tranquility. One's thinking is conditioned by a myriad of different projections, accepting this and rejecting that without any constancy whatsoever. Dreads and worries, plans and calculations keep racing on inside like mad horses. This is the normal mind.

> 2. The mind experiences a little tranquility and much agitation. One curbs agitation and enters concentration, yet the mind at once is scattered again. It is very hard to control and subdue, to stop its agitation and entanglement. This is the beginning of progress toward the Dao.

> 3. The mind experiences half agitation and half tranquility. The tranquil state of mind is somewhat like a unified mind already, but it is not maintained for long. Tranquility and distraction are about equal, but as one makes the mind care about its own agitation and entanglement, it gradually gets used to tranquility.

> 4. The mind experiences plenty of tranquility and only occasional agitation. One becomes gradually versed in controlling the mind, thus any agitation that arises is checked at once. The mind is fully one-pointed, and when one-pointedness is lost it is immediately recovered.

> 5. The mind is turned entirely toward purity and tranquility. Whether involved in affairs or at leisure, there is no agitation at all. From an efficiently controlled mind, firmness and solidity of concentration develop.

Once this strong stability of mind, and absorption in the object of meditation, is reached, practitioners can begin to practice insight, called "observation" (*guan*) in Daoism. Here they learn to see the world with the new
eyes of Dao, letting their Dao-nature shine forth instead of depending on
personal evaluations and egoistic desires. It begins with a critical examination of the practitioner's own psychological constitution, described as
consisting of spirit (*shen*) and bodily form (*xing*). Both were originally
pure cosmic forces, spoiled and distorted by the egoistic, personal forces
of the mind (*xin*) and personal body (*shen*). These limited agents have
captured the original inner purity — sometimes described as the primordial *qi* — and wasted it on engagements with the senses and in passions
and desires. To control this involvement and recover the purity of spirit
and physical body, adepts — in an adaptation of Buddhist worldview —
are guided to realize the changing nature of all (impermanence) and the
non-identity of themselves (no-self). This is explained in *Zuowang lun*
(Discourse on Sitting in Oblivion) by the eighth-century Daoist and
Shangqing patriarch Sima Chengzhen (647–735), a prolific writer and
renowned master who was greatly honored at court:

> Someone who is horrified by death should think of his body as
> the lodge of the spirit. Then, as the body becomes old and sick,
> as breath and strength decline day by day, it will just be like a
> house with rotting walls. Once it becomes uninhabitable, it is
> best abandoned and replaced by another residence. The death
> of the personal body and the departure of the spirit are a mere
> change of location. However, when one hankers after life and
> loathes death, resisting the natural transformations, spirit con-
> sciousness will be confused and led into error. (sect. 5; Kohn,
> *Seven Steps*, 102)

Reaching a state of detachment and new understanding, adepts are freed
from passions and desires and can move on to realize that they themselves are nothing but manifestations of cosmic energy, of Dao, in a particular form and setting. They recover the purity of the spirit and allow it
to radiate freely in all their actions, achieving a new and wider identity
as part of the universe at large. This eventually leads to the ability to
leave one's ordinary self and earthly body behind and ecstatically travel
to the heavens and communicate with the gods. Sun Simiao describes it:

> Going beyond all beings in one's body, one whirls out of nor-
> mal relations and comes to reside next to the Jade Emperor of
> the Great Dao in the Numinous Realm. Here the wise and

sagely gather, at the farthest shore and in perfect truth. In creative change, in numinous pervasion, all beings are reached. Only one who has attained this level of cultivation has truly reached the source of Dao. Here the myriad paths come to an end. This is called the final ultimate. (*Cunshen lianqi ming*)

This meditative attainment in turn activates the higher levels of ritual power. Through it, personal transformation is expanded and transformed into social harmony and the spreading of universal goodness to all.

Twofold Mystery

The concentration and insight parts of Daoist meditation arose especially in the Tang dynasty under the influence of Buddhism. They were theoretically explained in a philosophical school known as "Twofold Mystery" (Chongxuan), a good example of literati Daoism represented by ordained practitioners. It is expressed mostly in commentaries to the ancient classics, such as Cheng Xuanying's exegesis of the *Daode jing* and the *Zhuangzi* and Li Rong's reading of the *Daode jing* and the *Xisheng jing*, and was codified in the late Tang by the court Daoist and ritual master Du Guangting (850–933).

Du Guangting lived during a time of great change and transformation. Seeing Daoism decline and transform, he compiled many works to preserve its medieval system. He wrote major ritual compendia which came to serve as the basis for many later liturgies, hagiographies specifically also of women Daoists, and geographical works that described sacred Daoist mountains and grotto heavens. Also among his works were accounts of miracles that involved more and more ordinary people and not just aristocrats, discussions of the changing role of Daoism in the politics of his day, and commentaries to classical scriptures, such as the *Daode jing*. In one collection of commentaries, he systematized earlier lineages and also outlined the tradition of Twofold Mystery.

While the codification of the school only came about several hundred years after its flourishing, most of its texts were lost in the Daoist canon. Fortunately many were recovered as manuscripts from a place called Dunhuang, a major religious center located in the far west of China at the fork of the northern and southern branches of the Silk Road. Here, hundreds of caves were cut into the sandstone and decked out amply with art and filled with statues. These so-called Mogao caves were closed around 1008 when Muslim invaders threatened the area, and were only reopened in 1900. In one cave, a stash of old manuscripts was discovered, consisting of hundreds of texts, mostly Buddhist but also containing a significant number of Daoist and popular works.

As is made clear in these manuscripts, the expression "twofold mystery" goes back to the line "mysterious and again mysterious" in the first chapter of the *Daode jing*. It is here read to indicate the mystical goal of profundity, silence, and freedom from all obstructions, in the sense of "to make more and more mysterious" through the oblivion of all in "twofold forgetfulness." That is to say, practitioners in their meditative efforts should first give up all ordinary thinking and desires in favor of a perception of emptiness and nonbeing. Then they may move on to abandon this new level and liberate themselves also from emptiness, thus reaching the freedom of celestial ecstasy. Transforming consciousness into nonconsciousness, they attain the highest level of neither consciousness nor nonconsciousness.

This formulation of Twofold Mystery adopts the Buddhist logic of the four propositions as presented in the Mâdhyamika or Sanlun (Three Treatises) school. They were formulated in China by the Buddhist thinker Jizang (549–623), who suggests that practitioners should move along the following four levels:

> affirmation of being
> affirmation of nonbeing
> affirmation of both, being and nonbeing
> negation of both, being and nonbeing.

This means that adepts begin with the worldly assumption that everything exists and transcend this to realize that in underlying reality all is empty. Next, they find that this "emptiness" in itself is nothing but another viewpoint and go beyond it, discarding even nonbeing to realize that all is both being and nonbeing at the same time. From there they attain the highest state and realize that things ultimately neither exist nor not exist. Neither ordinary truth nor absolute truth are in themselves satisfying but have to be overcome and engaged as being either simultaneously present and absent, or neither present nor absent.

As Cheng Xuanying says in his commentary to the *Daode jing*:

> On the outside the sage will not have any mental states that
> would be desirable, on the inside he will not have a mind that
> could do any desiring. Mind and mental states are both forgot-
> ten, thus the mind as such has become no-mind. Where there
> were mental states and illusions before, later there is only the
> emptiness of mind. Yet even though the mind as such is no-
> mind, it shines actually forth in numinous radiance. . . .

> A practitioner must first discard all desires, then proceed to
> discard the level of no-desires. Only then he can truly accom-
> plish double discarding, twofold realization, and wondrously
> merge with the Dao of Middle Oneness. Beings and ego looked
> upon in equalized fashion, mental states and wisdom both for-
> gotten—when someone makes such a state his principle of
> government, then everything will be well-ordered. (ch. 3)

The Twofold Mystery vision, therefore, focuses on the formulation of the
mental states and processes associated with different levels of Daoist
meditation, explaining them in a highly philosophical discourse and
linking them with the ancient classics and with principles of good government and cosmic harmony. It reflects earlier tendencies of Daoist
thought within a new, meditative and Buddhist-inspired context.

The Variety of Practices

The multiplicity of spiritual practices in Daoism often leaves the observer
stunned, since it is hard to know where to begin and what to pursue. In
this, Daoism is very different from Zen Buddhism, for example, where
apparently one straightforward method is taught to all. However, the
contrast is not quite accurate. First, Zen Buddhism is only one school of
Buddhism, while in Daoism we are looking at the entirety of the tradition, which integrated many different schools into one organized system.
Studying Buddhist practices as a whole, one would also have to consider
different forms of concentration and insight, as well as a multitude of
visualizations, recitations, and other techniques.

Second, even in Zen Buddhism there is tremendous variety, and individual masters decide which *kôan* to give to which disciple at what time,
matching the training not only to their personal preferences but also to
the specific situation and mental condition of the disciple. This flexibility

of application is also very much true for Daoism, only here it is so much more obvious since there are so many different practices to be used.

The basic understanding of spiritual practice in Daoism is that it differs from person to person, and the great variety of techniques is not there to create confusion but to allow the detailed tailoring of spiritual activities to the individual's specific needs. As a result, someone may spend much time on certain longevity techniques, do only elementary meditation, and practice some basic rituals. Another may undertake only a few health practices, offer some more advanced rites, and exert all his effort on attaining mystical states through intense meditation.

The tradition's flexibility offers a wide variety of combinations, and also makes it possible to engage non-Daoists in spiritual practices. That is to say, while communal or public rituals should only be performed by properly ordained masters, most other practices can be beneficial to anyone, and indeed Chinese of all periods have helped themselves freely to Daoist techniques to improve their health, good fortune, and wisdom.

Still, not all spiritual techniques are adapted with equal ease. The hardest is probably ritual, which requires a belief in Daoist deities and a commitment to the Daoist tradition. Yet, even here we do not only have the great affairs run by specialized priests—ordinary followers were (and are) encouraged to set up a sacred space for daily prayers in their own homes. In the middle ages, they would have a chamber of tranquility or oratory (*jingshi*), either a separate hut or a room inside the house, about nine feet square and insulated from the hubbub of ordinary activities.

Inside, only four things were allowed: an incense burner, an incense lamp, a prayer bench or cushion, and a brush or writing knife plus paper or bamboo slips. Before entering practitioners had to wash one's hands, comb one's hair, and put on a clean robe and cap. They entered with the right foot first while holding a ritual audience tablet with both hands. Kneeling on the prayer bench or cuchion, Daoists would then swallow the saliva, and regulate their breathing, close their eyes and visualize guardian deities and other relevant gods. Once the divinities were present, they burned incense and recited a prayer, leaving again after having sent off the gods and recited appropriate incantations. Not everybody, of course, could afford a separate room, and so many people had (and have) their own little altar for daily prayers set up somewhere in the home. The simply ceremonies offered there would maintain spiritual awareness throughout ordinary life.

Meditation and longevity techniques are somewhat easier to adapt to more common usage. For both, a trained master is helpful, and if intense practice is desired a stay in a Daoist institution might be desirable. Again, while advanced practices such as ecstatic excursions or the abstention from all food might be reserved for specialized Daoists, other techniques were considered helpful for ordinary people also and were used more generally.

Concentration and wisdom, for example, were applied equally by Buddhists, Daoists, and increasingly also Confucians in their practice of "quiet-sitting" (jingzuo), undertaken in kneeling posture and with a focus on the breath as it moved the abdomen. They were generally appreciated as means for people to have more control over their minds and be more at ease with life's difficulties. They were especially sought after by medieval literati who wished to activate the teachings of the sages, such as Laozi and Zhuangzi, for themselves and learn to develop a higher purity of mind. Some of them, moreover, became dedicated to the Daoist path and learned to attain high, mystical states, learning from and contributing to the tradition without ever taking ordination or getting much involved in ritual.

Longevity techniques, of course, are the most widespread and best known among Daoist techniques. In fact, they are not originally Daoist but go back to a separate tradition in Chinese culture. They have been used widely by many Chinese for various reasons—health, sexual vigor, anti-aging—and without any particular Daoist beliefs, community affiliation, or other contact. In Daoism they were spiritually developed, expanded, and codified, but never to the point of exclusivity. The mere practice of longevity techniques, therefore, is not a criterion for judging someone's status as Daoist, and it is perfectly acceptable and common to see non-Daoists—ordinary people, physicians, Confucian officials, and Buddhist monks—engage in them. A good analogy might be the workouts people do in modern health clubs, which they join independently of their profession or religious conviction. At the same time, just as certain modern organizations take work-outs very seriously and even see them in a spiritual light, so Daoists place a strong emphasis on longevity techniques and find them essential to spiritual progress. In all cases, the variety of practices encourages individual choice and renders the tradition open to interaction with other aspects and representatives of Chinese culture.

Further Readings

Benn, Charles. 2000. "Daoist Ordination and *Zhai* Rituals." In *Daoism Handbook*, edited by Livia Kohn, 309-38. Leiden: E. Brill.

Donner, Neal, and Daniel B. Stevenson. 1993. *The Great Calming and Contemplation: A Study and Annotated Translation of the First Chapter of Chih-i's Mo-ho chih-kuan*. Honolulu: University of Hawaii Press.

Kohn, Livia, ed. 1989. *Taoist Meditation and Longevity Techniques*. Ann Arbor: University of Michigan, Center for Chinese Studies.

Ofuchi Ninji. 1979. "The Formation of the Taoist Canon." In *Facets of Taoism*, edited by Holmes Welch and Anna Seidel, 253-68. New Haven, Conn.: Yale University Press.

Robinet, Isabelle. 1977. *Les commentaires du Tao to king jusqu'au VIIe siècle*. Paris: Presses Universitaires de France.

Schafer, Edward H. 1977. *Pacing the Void*. Berkeley: University of California Press.

Schipper, Kristofer. 1985a. "Taoist Ordination Ranks in the Tunhuang Manuscripts." In *Religion und Philosophie in Ostasien:*, edited by G. Naundorf et al., 127-48. Würzburg: Königshausen and Neumann.

Original Sources in Translation

Benn, Charles D. 1991. *The Cavern Mystery Transmission: A Taoist Ordination Rite of A.D. 711*. Honolulu: University of Hawaii Press.

Bokenkamp, Stephen R. 1996. "The Purification Ritual of the Luminous Perfected." In *Religions of China in Practice*, edited by Donald S. Lopez, Jr., 268-77. Princeton: Princeton University Press.

Kohn, Livia. 1987. *Seven Steps to the Tao: Sima Chengzhen's Zuowanglun*. St. Augustin/Nettetal: Monumenta Serica Monograph XX.

Kohn, Livia. 1993. *The Taoist Experience*. Albany: State University of New York Press. Chs. 3, 9, 11, 14, 39, 31, 43, 45.

Lu Kuan-yü. 1964. *The Secrets of Chinese Meditation*. London: Rider. Chs. 1-4.

Reiter, Florian C. 1998. *The Aspirations and Standards of Taoist Priests in the Early T'ang Period*. Wiesbaden: Harrassowitz.

CHAPTER EIGHT

SPELLS, TALISMANS, AND INNER ALCHEMY

Following the Daoist heyday of the Tang, in the Song dynasty (960–1260) both basic types of spiritual practices, ritual and meditation, developed further to include new forms. Most important were extended ritual practices involving spells and talismans, and the new way to personal immortality through inner alchemy.

The religious and social environment of the Song dynasty was very different from that of the middle ages, and it can even be considered the beginning of Chinese modernity. The change was mainly due to economic developments, notably the building of better roads and a whole new canal system. These increased commerce and opened up the southern part of the country, allowing it to integrate more with the northern part. The merchant class came to prosper and replace the Tang aristocracy in the economic field, just as a new, scholarly trained and officially examined group of bureaucrats took over their roles in the imperial administration.

The growth of the merchant class had three major effects on the religious scene. First, there was a great increase in lay organizations and lay-sponsored temples and practices—ordinary people joined together to worship one or the other deity and perform rites and cultivation practices together, sometimes in private homes, sometimes in special community halls. Second, there emerged a much larger market for practical religious aids to daily life, from talismans for building homes and spells for granting a safe passage to exorcisms for healing, funeral rites (*liandu*) and salvific services for the dead (*pudu*). Third, as more and more ordinary people became religiously engaged, they required more direct contact with gods, spirits, and ancestors. As a result trance techniques increased manifold, either through spirit mediums or by automatic writing with the help of the planchette, a kind of ouija board.

Another major economic change had to do with the invention of printing, first undertaken in the ninth century in a Buddhist environment to facilitate the copying of sutras, which was considered a highly meritorious activity, especially in increased quantities. Printing greatly facilitated mass communication since posters with announcements could be easily placed in villages and city wards where local scholars could read them to the people. It also assisted commerce because instead of carrying large amounts of hard currency in gold and silver, merchants could now take a letter of credit issued by their firm which would be honored by a partner company in another part of the country. This was the beginning of paper currency, which soon overtook the hard and heavy coins, and also of banks, which increasingly replaced the direct partnerships between merchant houses.

In religion, this led to two developments. One was the conveyance of paper bills of so-called spirit money to the ancestors, either by placing them into tombs (instead of the hard coins and cowry shells of old) or by burning them at altars and in temples, a practice still common today. The other was a new belief in a "Celestial Treasury," where divine administrators issued a certain amount of credit to everyone at birth (primordial *qi* now seen as a sum of money) which then had to be repaid over one's lifetime in good deeds and through the burning of spirit money. Anyone who committed bad deeds or who otherwise wasted their credit had to suffer in the prisons of hell.

In terms of culture, several new phenomena appear in the Tang-Song transition, possibly reflecting an increased influence of Central Asian culture on Chinese. For example, it became common to sit on chairs instead of on the fragrant mats (like Japanese *tatami*) that had been common in the Tang. First there were benches with no backrests, then chairs, and eventually chairs with armrests and cushions. Matching these were high tables and more solid earthen or stone floors — it is, after all, hard to place chairs on a soft, cushiony mat. Shoes, previously slippers taken off before entering a dwelling, now became more boot-like and were worn also in the house, protecting the feet from the cold stone floors. At the same time, ceilings became higher and roofs more elaborate, especially in the Southern Song (12th c.). The first two-storied houses for commoners — unlike the military "towers" of old — also were built around this time.

Another set of cultural changes involved women, who had been almost liberated in the Tang and were often depicted wearing low-cut gowns.

They had been highly esteemed in many areas of society and culture, served as equals to men in Daoist rank and competence, and had generally been able to pursue their interests with vigor. Now footbinding was invented, the cruel crippling of girls' feet from an early age that completely hampered all freedom of movement and expression. Over the next hundred years and well into the twentieth century, it became so fashionable that hardly any woman had natural feet. At the same time women's gowns became high-necked and restrictive, and medicine changed to rely more extensively on pulse diagnosis because doctors were often not allowed to see or touch more than a female patient's wrist. One other cultural change in the tenth century was the growing predominance of landscape painting, with its depiction of swirling clouds, twisted trees, lofty mountains, and minuscule human figures, replacing the still lifes and portraits of the Tang.

In Daoism, the more merchant-oriented culture of the Song found expression in the increased application of popular rites and spells for good fortune, supported both by the importation of Buddhist tantric practices and the growth of new schools. For more specialized Daoist practitioners, the dynasty saw the evolution of inner alchemy, a complex system that integrated health techniques, meditations, and visualizations with the ideas of transformation expressed in operative alchemy and the *Yijing*. Numerous new texts were written and collections of Daoist materials undertaken, setting the stage for the modern development of the religion.

Tantric Buddhism

Tantra is originally an Indian phenomenon and involves esoteric and magical practices. It is based on the idea that there is a cosmic force, often described as essentially female and known as *shakti*, which pervades everything and must be aroused to allow for perfection, attainment, and salvation. To activate this force one has to undergo specific initiatory rites, learn methods transmitted orally and in secret, and practice various formal techniques. The latter include sacred spells (*mantra*), divine incantations (*dhârani*), secret hand gestures (*mudrâ*), and the visualization of cosmic diagrams (*yantra*) and cosmic charts of gods and worlds (*mandala*).

It is believed further that these techniques will endow the adept with powers over all sorts of supernatural beings and protect him from demons, misfortunes, diseases, and disasters. Many supernatural beings involved in tantric practice are martial in their look and demeanor, often nasty demons of old are believed to have been converted to the tantric path and are now aggressive protectors of the faithful. They are notably described as diamond kings (*vajra*), strongmen (*vîra*), demon kings, and spirit soldiers. Activating these divine figures will provide empowerment and cosmic protection and often lead to an ability to heal. From its Indian origins, this form of religious practice made its way into Buddhism where a tantric or esoteric school was created, probably around the sixth century. Soon after, it was transmitted to Tibet, where it merged with the indigenous Bon cult and became first dominant and the later national religion.

The first tantric texts arrived in China in 645 with Xuanzang, the fearless monk and pilgrim who spent fourteen years traveling across the Himalayas and all over India. Representatives of the tantric school first appeared in 706, notably Vajrabodhi (671–741) and Amoghavajra (705–775). They were made welcome at the Chinese court, where they taught several gifted Chinese disciples, who in turn trained Japanese pilgrims. Most famous among them was Kûkai (Kôbô daishi), who brought tantra to Japan in 806 where it became known as the Shingon (True Word) school of Buddhism. In China, tantra as a school was closely dependent on the court and did not survive the persecution of 845. Only more independent schools were left unscathed, such as Pure Land and Chan (Zen). It did, however, exert a vast and pervasive influence on Chinese religion, and its gods, rites, and practices came to play an important role in both Daoism and popular religion.

There is hardly any item in the above list of tantric characteristics that cannot be traditionally found also in Daoism. Daoists had their own underlying cosmic force of *qi*, they had sacred spells (*zhou*) and talismans (*fu*) to exorcise demons and protect good fortune, divine incantations (Brahma sounds) believed to lie at the root of all creation, secret hand gestures (*zhangjue*) that were part of healing through the activation of acupuncture points, and diagrams and charts (*tu*) containing depictions of the cosmos that provided spiritual insights and magical powers. They also had their own vast pantheon of supernatural beings to protect adepts from demons and disasters. Many gods, moreover, were quite martial, including the generals of the early Celestial Masters, the demon kings of Shangqing, and the infantry and cavalry spirit armies, that usually accompanied gods at revelations and on miraculous rescue missions.

However, under the influence of tantric texts and practices, these various Daoist techniques were elevated in status and began to appear in the canonical scriptures and essential rites of new schools. As part of this process, the various spells, talismans, and diagrams—as well as the ritual procedures linked with them—were not only standardized but became much more elaborate, increasing in number and developing into sophisticated works of art. Many times, tantric forms were taken over as they were, so that some Daoist spells appeared almost entirely in pseudo-Sanskrit, some diagrams looked like mandalas, and many hand gestures closely imitated Buddhist *mudrâs* while yet connecting back to originally Daoist ideas of healing and cosmic correspondences. A vast new pantheon grew that included both benevolent and martial deities: a group of savior figures based on the idea of the bodhisattva; the famous Ten Worthies Who Save From Suffering (Jiuku tianzun), an adaptation of the buddhas of the ten directions; the ten kings of hell, developed from the rulers of originally eighteen hells; a set of four martial gods adapted from tantric *vajras*; and numerous other guardians and protectors.

A good example of a tantric-inspired Daoist text is the *Huming jing* (Scripture for the Protection of Life), which was revealed in the early Song and rose to popularity in the twelfth century. It is a short, rhythmical incantation that comes with a set of twenty-four talismans. Its purpose is to invoke a number of celestial powers for personal fortune and protection. It begins by placing the devotee into a larger cosmic context:

> Sovereign heaven raises me,
> Sovereign earth supports me,
> Sun and moon glow for me,
> Stars and planets shine on me.

After invoking further deities of the larger cosmos—stars, celestial bureaucrats, deities of time and space—it focuses on immediate human wishes and concludes with a strong appeal to the divinities to remain at the seeker's side and grant him entry into the ledgers of the immortals. It ends with the standard formula of the Celestial Masters for the activation of divine protection:

> Whatever I seek shall be attained!
> Whatever I turn to shall find success!
> Whatever I do shall be in harmony!

Whatever I wish shall come to pass! . . .
Numinous lads and spirit maidens,
Demon destroyers and diamond kings!
All three thousand six hundred of you,
Always remain by my side!
Raising banners, holding talismans,
You go everywhere with me!
As the Highest Lord protects the capital,
So Heaven gives me good fortune.
Entered in the golden register and jade ledgers,
And equipped with the twenty-four talismans,
May I match the cycle [calendar] of the stars!
Swiftly, swiftly, in accordance with the statutes and
ordinances!

New Schools

The increased emphasis on personal and practical protection also appeared as the focus of several new schools which arose to replace the
medieval ordination system of the Three Caverns. Through the social
disorder and political instability at the end of the Tang, court subsidies
for religious institutions had ceased so that temples declined, patriarchal
lineages ceased, and techniques and doctrines were suspended. Individual practitioners of Daoist training no longer had specific key places to
go to or officially recognized masters to follow. They were on their own,
wandering from one sacred mountain to the next, connecting with isolated hermits, perchance finding a stash of old texts, or discovering certain efficacious techniques by trial and error. Occasionally they even se-
cured the support of a local ruler—who was usually more interested in
alchemical ways of making gold than in spiritual pursuits—and proceeded to reconstruct one or another temple center of old.

These practitioners had no financial cushion to fall back on, and thus had
to find ways of serving communities for a fee so they could continue
their quest. As a result—and coinciding fortuitously with the needs of
the growing merchant class—Daoists, in competition with wandering
Buddhists, tantric ritualists, and local shamans, began to offer practical
rites of healing, exorcism, and protection. They issued spells and talismans for concrete goals, and undertook funerals and communication
with ancestors to set people's minds at rest. Daoists of this type became

very common in the Song and were known as ritual masters (*fashi*). They were at the roots of the new schools that soon developed.

One such school is called Heavenly Heart (Tianxin). It can be traced back to a ritual master and shamanic healer by the name of Tan Zixiao (fl. 935) who was active in Fujian in southeast China. While wandering through sacred areas he received a revelation regarding a new dimension of heaven that contained all the necessary powers. This was the Bureau for Exorcising Deviant Forces (Quxie yuan), ruled by the Northern Emperor (Beidi) and administered by his three powerful assistants: the martial gods Black Killer (Heisha, a tantric god), Dark Warrior (Xuanwu, a Daoist celestial constellation), and Heavenly Protector (Tianpeng, a new figure). Tan Zixiao left without creating a formal lineage but his teachings were picked up by Rao Dongtian, another wandering Daoist of the south, who claimed to have come across a collection of sacred talismanic texts in a cavern on Mount Huagai in 994. At first he was unable to decipher them, but he received spiritual help from the three martial gods and developed the school's practices to include rites of the Celestial Masters, ecstatic excursions of Shangqing, and various local traditions of healing and exorcism. The school did not flourish, except locally, until it was formally codified by Rao's descendant Yuan Miaozong in 1116, under Emperor Huizong.

Three things in this first new school of the Song typify Daoism of the time: the founding by a ritual master with strong local ties and powers of healing and exorcism; the discovery of a new celestial realm or department with appropriate deities, talismans, and ritual practices; and the subsequent codification under Emperor Huizong. Huizong (r. 1101–1125) was the last ruler of the Northern Song and a great supporter of Daoism. He sponsored and collected Daoist art and himself engaged both in Daoist painting and the exegesis of Daoist scriptures, notably the *Daode jing*, which was highly venerated by the Song rulers in general. Huizong also organized Daoist rites for state protection and good fortune, and inspired many Daoists to come forward and present their views and texts. In 1114, he initiated the compilation of a Daoist canon to replace a lost collection originally compiled in 1023, of which today only the encyclopedia *Yunji qiqian* (Seven Tablets in a Cloudy Satchel) remains. Unfortunately his reign ended tragically with the invasion of his capital by Central Asian forces, and his Daoist collections were mostly lost.

Huizong was also at the center of another Daoist school of the time, known as Divine Empyrean (Shenxiao) after the central compass point and highest heavenly sphere. It was developed by Lin Lingsu (1076–1120) in 1112 as a special revelation to the emperor, who was identified as the elder son of the Jade Emperor, the Great Emperor of Long Life (Changsheng dadi). This god was believed to be a harbinger of a new age in the world who would bring salvation to humanity and create peace on earth. The system employed talismans, diagrams, sacred lamps, seals, and pennants in elaborate rituals. It followed the cosmology of Lingbao, whose central text, the *Duren jing*, it adopted and expanded from one to sixty-one scrolls by adding its own revealed scripture to it. But the school also integrated the pantheon of Shangqing, whose perfected beings were at the root of many lesser, associated revelations. It was later codified by Wang Wenqing (1093–1153), defined as a continuation of the Shangqing tradition, and involved many forms of visualization.

Not to be outdone, after the end of Huizong's reign and the move of the capital to Hangzhou in the south, the Lingbao school rose in prominence and developed in three new branches. First, there was a recovery of Lingbao diagrams and rituals on Mount Longhu (Jiangxi), the headquarters of the Celestial Masters, carried on mainly by the ritual master and successful rainmaker Liu Yongguang (1134–1206). He did not limit himself to Lingbao, and also integrated Celestial Master rites and a new form of Song ritual, the so-called thunder rites, into the system.

Thunder rites (*leifa*) were a popular form of exorcism and protection that invoked the deities of the new celestial Department of Thunder (Leibu), an agency administered by numerous officials that governed sickness and good fortune and had a direct and efficacious impact on human events. Thunder here stands for the entire complex of thunderstorms, including lightning and the cosmic forces associated with them. Trees struck by lightning, for example, were thought to carry the immediate powers of thunder and were preferred in the making of wooden talismans. Thunder officials were known by name and highly venerated, and the petitions and memorials to them were essential in ritual practice at the time. A contemporary religious memorial describes the new system:

> Illustrious Heaven has done the following—constructed the Thunder Wall and laid out the Thunder Prison [hell], founded the Thunder Offices and assigned the Thunder Administration, propagated the Thunder Civil Norms and issued the Thunder

> Punishments, enlisted the Thunder Deities and commanded the Thunder Troops, deployed the Thunder Magic and wielded the Thunder Instruments — through managing the levers of reward and punishment, and controlling the powers of generation and destruction.

> Through these [institutions] Heaven can seal off mountains and break through caverns, decapitate the demonic and behead the malicious of the dark Yin realm [of the dead] while also destroying the lethal and exterminating the deviant, attacking the wicked and extirpating the vicious in the bright Yang realm [of the living]. (*Leifu zoushi*; Skar, "Administering Thunder," 192)

A second branch of Lingbao was developed by Ning Benli (1101–1181), a southern seeker who traveled to various sacred mountains before settling on Mount Tiantai (Zhejiang). The mountain had been a major religious center since the early middle ages and also the home of the integrative Buddhist school of the same name. He codified the Lingbao rites (then known as Tiantai Lingbao) following the old masters, but he also joined them with new forms of ceremonial practices, notably the elaborate rituals used in Divine Empyrean. His work *Shangqing Lingbao dafa* (Great Rites of Highest Clarity and Numinous Treasure) in sixty-six chapters is a major compendium of the time, and provides much useful information on the ritual forms practiced then.

In contrast to this work, the third branch of Lingbao was formulated in a text of exactly the same title (in forty-four chapters) by Jin Yunzhong (fl. 1224), another southern Daoist. Jin harshly criticized the Tiantai form of Lingbao as being too elaborate and overwhelming, indiscriminate, and reckless. In its place, he proposed a return to the pure, simple, original Lingbao rites of old. He made the *Duren jing* the center of his system, drastically reduced the number of talismans, and focused on fewer, but more efficacious deities. All three forms of Lingbao ritual have influenced later compilations and are, in various combinations, still practiced in China and Taiwan today.

Inner Alchemy

These various new schools were not, however, limited to the spread of incantations, rites, and talismans for popular blessings—they were also devoted to specialized practice through which dedicated Daoists could attain the lofty goal of immortality. For this, in addition to rites and talismans, they practiced inner alchemy (*neidan*), a complex system of techniques that integrated meditative longevity techniques, operative alchemy, and the symbolism of the *Yijing*. Its goal was the attainment of immortality as a form of ecstatic otherworld existence through a series of energetic mutations within the body, which would transform it into a spiritual entity known as the immortal embryo.

Inner alchemy can be traced back to the Tang dynasty but came to flourish in the Song, especially in south China, where it was most closely associated with a school that came to be known as the Southern School (Nanzong). This school followed an earlier tradition known as the Zhong-Lü school after the two immortals Zhongli Quan and Lü Dongbin, and was developed by Zhang Boduan (d. 1082) and Bai Yuchan (1194–1227?).

Zhang Boduan was a government official in Sichuan who received a revelation and turned to inner alchemical practice. He became famous for a collection of alchemical poems called *Wuzhen pian* (Awakening to Perfection/Understanding Reality). Bai Yuchan was an accomplished thunder master from Fujian who, in 1218, received a revelation from the Heavenly Worthy of Universal Transformation (Puhua tianzun), a key deity in the Department of Thunder. He wrote a number of texts that are today contained both in the Daoist canon and in various Song collections on inner alchemy. They include an inner-alchemical interpretation of the *Daode jing* in which he reinterprets ideas of nonaction, no-affairs, and naturalness in terms of the recovery of one's inherent *qi* and spirit, and seeing the state of oneness with Dao in the attainment of the golden elixir.

Despite the variety of schools and traditions, inner alchemical practice can be generalized as a process in three phases, or transformations: from essence or vitality (*jing*) to energy (*qi*), from energy to spirit (*shen*), and from spirit to emptiness (Dao). As the *Zhonghe ji* (On Balance and Harmony) says:

> Making one's essence complete, one can preserve the body. To do so, first keep the body at ease, and make sure there are no desires. Thereby essence can be made complete.
>
> Making one's energy complete, one can nurture the mind. To do so, first keep the mind pure, and make sure there are no thoughts. Thereby energy can be made complete.
>
> Making one's spirit complete, one can recover emptiness. To do so, first keep the will sincere, and make sure body and mind are united. Thereby spirit can be returned to emptiness. . . . To attain immortality, there is nothing else but the refinement of these three treasures: essence, energy, spirit. (*Zhonghe ji*)

Thus the very first step, as in earlier Daoist meditation, is the practice of longevity techniques to make the body strong and stable, followed by the practice of concentration to make the mind tranquil and stable. Then one starts by focusing on essence, the rather gross and materially tangible form of *qi* that develops in the human body as it interacts with the world and appears most obviously as sexual energy — semen in men and menstrual blood in women. Essence is not there at all times but is produced from internal *qi*. Its original form resides in the Ocean of Energy (*qihai*) in the lower cinnabar field in men, while in women it is found in the Cavern of Energy (*qixue*) in the solar plexus or chest area. From here, if left to its natural devices, this *qi* transmutes into essence on a regular basis, in men whenever sexual stimulation occurs, in women with the menstrual cycle. This in turn leads to a discharge of the valuable internal *qi* and to loss of vitality. The aim of this first stage of inner alchemical practice, then, is to restore essence back to its original form as *qi*-energy and to prevent its future disintegration.

To do this, one must avoid the downward movement of essence. For men this means that they should get aroused almost to the point of ejaculation, then mentally concentrate on making the semen flow upward and along spine into the head. This is called "reverting the semen to nourish the brain." Once a man has reached proficiency in the practice and will no longer ejaculate, texts say that he has "subdued the white tiger." Men then proceed to circulate the reverted energy (parallel to the reverted cinnabar in alchemy) along the meridians that follow the spine and run down the front of the body (the governing and conception vessels), in a cycle known as the "microcosmic orbit" (*xiao zhoutian*). Eventually the *qi* will form a divine "pearl of dew" in the abdominal cinnabar field. This is a first coagulation of stronger and purer *qi* that lays the foundation for the next level.

In women the first stage of reverting essence back to energy begins with daily breast massages (moving the hands in various ways and directions), a change in diet to lighter foods, and a series of meditations in which the red menstrual blood is visualized rising upward and transforming into clear-colored *qi*. After several months of practice menstruation will cease, an effect called "decapitating the red dragon." This serves to stabilize the *qi*, which will then come to nurture the "pearl of dew." The pearl is naturally present in women from birth, but if left untended it will dissipate with every menstrual cycle. The beginning of inner alchemical practice is, therefore, the reversal of this natural tendency.

The second stage sees the transformation from this newly found, pure *qi*-energy into spirit. Now the "pearl of dew" is developed into the "golden flower" with the help of transmuted energy. To do this, yin and yang are identified as different energies in the body and described with different metaphors, depending on the level of purity attained. Typically there are the following:

yang = heart = fire = trigram *li* = pure lead = dragon = red bird;

yin = kidneys = water = trigram *kan* = pure mercury = tiger =white tiger.

The texts describing these advanced practices tend to be rather obscure and highly metaphoric. For example, the *Huandan ge zhu* (Annotated Songs on Reverting Cinnabar) says:

> *The red bird is harmonized and nurtured; it brings forth the golden flower.*
>
> The red bird is the phase fire. Among directions it corresponds to the south and to the position *bingding*. In the sky it is the planet Mars; on earth it is fire; in human beings it is the heart. . . . It greatly encompasses heaven and earth, minutely reaches into the smallest nook and cranny. Control it and it will obey, let it go free and it will run wild. In the scriptures it is called the bright fire. . . .
>
> To harmonize it, isolate pure water from the Jade Spring Palace in the upper cinnabar field [in the head]. Join this with the fire of the heart and refine it until it enters the lower cinnabar field [in the abdomen]. Secure it behind the Jade Prison Pass. Once

> locked in, treat it further with yin alchemy. Naturally a new
> spirit soul and a separate sun and moon are brought forth. Af-
> ter nourishing them for a long time, their color will turn bril-
> liant. They combine to form a new entity, called the Golden
> Flower. (Verse 4)

At each stage of the transmutation process, the energies are given a different name and different metaphors are employed. Eventually adepts
learn to not only mix them in the abdomen but to revolve them through
an inner-body cycle that includes not only the spine and breastbone but
leads all the way to the feet and is known as the macrocosmic orbit (*da
zhoutian*). Gradually they are refined to a point where they become as
pure as the celestials and form the "golden flower," the first trace of the
immortal embryo in the lower cinnabar field. The process is complex and
time-consuming, and must be timed in exact correspondence with the
cosmic patterns of yin and yang. As the *Huandan ge zhu* says:

> At midnight call forth the tiger; in the early morning summon the
> dragon.

> This has to do with time calculation. Midnight and tiger belong
> to yin. Yin in turn belongs to the female, and the female has the
> disposition of water. Thus it is associated with the north and
> the position *rengui*. This is the position of water. . . . The
> dragon belongs to the phase wood. Wood is associated with
> the east. It is the position of fire. (Verse 7)

Once the embryo is present, adepts switch their practice to employ a
method called "embryo respiration" to nourish it for ten months. This is
an inner form of breathing, combined with the meditative circulation of
qi, which allows the embryo to grow and makes the adept increasingly
independent of outer nourishment and air. Unlike the first phase, which
was easier for men, the process at this stage is easier for women because
they are naturally endowed with the faculty to grow an embryo. After
ten months, the embryo is complete.

Adepts then proceed to the third stage. The as yet semi-material body of
the embryo is now transformed into the pure spirit body of the immortals, a body of pure YANG, of cosmic LIFE, not of life as opposed to
death or yang as opposed to yin. To attain its full realization the embryo
has to undergo several phases. First it is nourished to completion and

begins to have an independent existence. Then it is carefully nurtured for three more years to grow further and learn to move about on its own. At this level it joins the adept and as one they exit the body along the spine and through the top of head, a point known as the Heavenly Gate. In a third phase, the adept through the immortal child learns to blend his existence with emptiness and dissolve into Dao. This third part is ideally accomplished in nine years of meditation. Finally, the adept becomes an immortal spirit of pure YANG and he or she merges completely with Dao.

The Yijing

The *Yijing* or "Book of Changes" is of key importance in the understanding of inner alchemy, because two of its trigrams, *kan* and *li* (symbols of water and fire, respectively), represent the heightened level of energy as cosmic water and fire, and because the timing of the alchemical process is often described with a series of its hexagrams.

The *Yijing* was allegedly compiled by Confucius around 500 B.C.E., and was originally the official manual of divination in the Zhou dynasty. It is a fortune-telling book that helps people determine the inherent tendencies in the course of Heaven and thus aids them in making good decisions. It does not simply examine natural patterns, as did the bird auguries in ancient Rome, nor does it entice "yes-no" responses from a specific set-up such as the cracks made in tortoise shells and cattle bones in Shang-dynasty oracle bones. Instead, it gives advice based on a rather sophisticated perspective on the general trends of fortune. As a result, the *Yijing* was adopted by the Chinese upper classes to provide personal readings for their official careers and family concerns. It has remained an important classic and received numerous commentaries and interpretations. In recent years, it has also made inroads in the West, where translations have multiplied. People today explore it for spiritual advice, use it for divination, and have trust in its workings.

The system of the *Yijing* is based on the two cosmic forces yin and yang, which are symbolized by written lines: an unbroken line indicates yang, while a broken line shows yin. The two lines, like the binary pattern at the base of computing, are then combined two by two into four symbols:

double yang, yang over yin, double yin, and yin over yang. In addition, the lines are also combined into eight symbols of three lines each, known as trigrams and linked symbolically with cosmic objects. The Eight Trigrams (*bagua*) are as follows:

heaven (*qian*, creative)	☰	earth (*kun*, receptive)	☷
fire (*li*, clinging)	☲	water (*kan*, abysmal)	☵
wind (*sun*, gentle)	☴	lake (*dui*, joyous)	☱
thunder (*zhen*, arousing)	☳	mountain (*gen*, still)	☶

Beyond this, two trigrams each were combined into figures consisting of six lines, the so-called hexagrams. Eight trigrams combined with each other resulted in a total of sixty-four hexagrams, the fundamental fortune-telling corpus of the *Yijing*. Each hexagram comes with an explanation of the image, a judgment, an explanation of the judgment, and a fortune for each individual line. For example, Hexagram no. 5, *xu* ("waiting") consists of the trigrams *kan* and *qian* or water over heaven. Its image explanation runs:

> Clouds rise up to the heaven, the image of waiting. Thus the superior man eats and drinks, is joyous and of good cheer.

This presents the current situation in its essence. Then the text provides a "judgment" which gives advice:

> Waiting. If you are sincere, you have light and success. Perseverance brings good fortune; it furthers one to cross the great water. (Wilhelm, *I Ching*, 24–25)

As this shows, the text gives general advice, often couched in rather ambiguous and vague terms. It reflects the reality of Zhou-dynasty life, where family relations were important, travel and communication were hard, the key relationship was with the lord or great man, and inner sincerity was valued highly. It is accessible today through commentaries, both traditional and modern, and often has to be read with a good dose of intuition and personal feeling.

There are two methods of obtaining a hexagram-fortune from the *Yijing*, both leading to an answer for a specific question one has in mind. The first, more traditional method is also a great deal more complicated. It involves the use of fifty milfoil stalks (long stems of a plant). First, one stalk is put aside, then the remaining forty-nine are divided into two piles. Four stalks are then counted off between each finger until there remain either one, two, three, or none. These remaining numbers are interpreted according to yin and yang—1 = strong yang, 2 = strong yin; 3 = weak yang, 0 = weak yin—and the resulting line is written down, adding a little cross on the side if the line is strong. This is repeated five more times to obtain six lines total. The lines are written down from the bottom to the top. The resulting hexagram can then be looked up in the book. Every line that has a cross next to it, moreover, can be changed into its opposite, again beginning from the bottom and working upward. In this way further hexagrams are obtained which can be looked up and will indicate the later development of one's fortune.

The second method to obtain a hexagram is a great deal easier and more popular today. It involves three identical coins, in which head is designated yang and tail means yin. Yang, moreover, counts 3, while yin counts 2. Throwing the three coins at any one time will result in the total number of either 6, 7, 8, or 9. These translate into lines: 9 = strong yang, 6 = strong yin, 7 = weak yang, and 8 = weak yin. Again, the line is written down, the throwing of coins repeated, and the hexagram obtained.

The fortune-telling powers of the *Yijing* have been popular for many centuries, and numerous Song dynasty literati also used the text for this purpose. However, in inner alchemy this aspect is secondary, and the *Yijing* is used mainly to symbolize energetic transmutations and timing. For example, the pure *qi* of the heart and kidneys (yang and yin), once transformed, becomes the *qi* of cosmic fire and water, then described as the trigrams *li* and *kan*. These show one yin surrounded by two yang, and one yang surrounded by two yin, respectively. The understanding is that the inner line is part of a higher purity and has to be isolated to revert to the pure state of Heaven and Earth, symbolized by the trigrams *qian* and *kun*. This, in turn, is achieved in practice by refining the energies further in the body, hoping to attain a level of cosmic creation that will then allow the attainment of immortality.

Then again, *Yijing* hexagrams are used to symbolize the waxing and waning of yin and yang through the year and the seasons:

Here a series of twelve hexagrams are used, beginning with the hexagram *fu*, which consists of five yin lines and one yang line, and moving through an increase first of yang, then of yin to the hexagram *kun*, which consists of all yin lines. Each hexagram stands for a particular phase in the energetic transmutation and growth of the embryo, allowing a subtle timing and cosmic patterning of the inner alchemical process.

Further Readings

Boltz, Judith M. 1987. *A Survey of Taoist Literature: Tenth to Seventeenth Centuries*. Berkeley: University of California, China Research Monograph 32.

Davis, Edward L. 2001. *Society and the Supernatural in Song China*. Honolulu: University of Hawaii Press.

Ebrey, Patricia. 2000. "Taoism and Art at the Court of Song Huizong." In *Daoism and the Arts of China*, edited by Stephen Little and Shawn Eichman, 95–111. Berkeley: University of California Press.

Gernet, Jacques. 1962. *Daily Life in China at the Eve of the Mongol Invasion*. Stanford: Stanford University Press.

Orzech, Charles D. 1989. "Seeing Chen-yen Buddhism." *History of Religions* 29.2: 87–114.

Skar, Lowell. 1997. "Administering Thunder: A Thirteenth-Century Memorial Deliberating the Thunder Rites." *Cahiers d'Extrême-Asie* 9: 159–202.

Strickmann, Michel. 1996. *Mantras et mandarins: Le bouddhisme tantrique en Chine*. Paris: Gallimard.

Strickmann, Michel. 2002. *Magical Medicine*. Stanford: Stanford University Press

Original Sources in Translation

Cleary, Thomas. 1987. *Understanding Reality: A Taoist Alchemical Classic by Chang Po-tuan*. Honolulu: University of Hawaii Press.

Kohn, Livia. 1993. *The Taoist Experience*. Albany: State University of New York Press. Chs. 16, 30, 36, 42.

Wile, Douglas. 1992. *Art of the Bedchamber: The Chinese Sexology Classics Including Women's Solo Meditation Texts*. Albany: State University of New York Press.

Wilhelm, Richard. 1950. *The I Ching or Book of Changes*. Princeton: Princeton University Press.

CHAPTER NINE

MONASTIC DISCIPLINE

Monasticism is a form of spiritual practice, where a group of like-minded seekers join together in an organized community to pursue self-cultivation. It is known mainly in Hinduism, Buddhism, and Christianity, where it arose in response to different ideals—ascetic discipline to achieve liberation, meditative insight to reach enlightenment, and freedom from social tasks in favor of the pursuit of the love of Christ—but was manifest in highly similar organizations. As is made clear in *Monastic Life in the Christian and Hindu Traditions* (1990), monasticism typically arises from a hermit tradition—wandering ascetics in India, desert fathers in the West—and develops through increasing numbers of hermits flocking to specific centers. This then necessitates the establishment of a set of buildings (sanctuary, community hall, dormitory, refectory, kitchen), an internal hierarchy (abbot, prior, cellarer, infirmarian), a system of sponsorship or other economic resources (tenant holdings, mills, breweries), and a catalog of behavioral rules. All of these are still the major characteristics of monastic life to the present day.

Monks and nuns give up all connections to their previous lives and contact with the outside world. They physically separate themselves by donning special garb, changing their bodily appearance, and taking on new names. They vow to live in poverty, chastity (celibacy), and obedience, and often follow rules of anonymity, equality, humility, simplicity, silence, and altruism. Their minds are set completely on an otherwordly goal, and they disregard discomfort and lack of rank, dedicating themselves fully to their task of cultivation. They place themselves outside of society, yet they have not yet attained the otherworldly state they seek. Thus they can be described as being in a position of prolonged liminality or "communitas" as described by Victor Turner in his *The Ritual Process* (1969)—without firm status and obligations in the world, yet not completely free from it either.

Daoist monasticism has its roots in a combination of the collective practices of the Celestial Masters joined with the hermit asceticism of the medieval self-cultivation groups. It developed fully under Buddhist influence in the sixth century, when the first renunciants (*chujia*) are mentioned and major institutions were founded. Specific rules and imperial sponsorship for monasteries began to flourish only in the Tang, when Daoism was favored at court and many flocked to the religion. On the whole, medieval Daoist monasteries were quite similar to their Buddhist counterparts, but official celibacy among Daoists was only required in the early Song, when monks and nuns had to be properly registered. The main form of Daoist monasticism, which still survives today, arose only in the twelfth century with the Quanzhen school.

The Quanzhen School

The school of Quanzhen (Complete Perfection, Complete Reality) goes back to the twelfth century and its founder Wang Chongyang (1112–1170). He was born among local gentry in northwest China (Shaanxi), received a classical education, and spent most of his life as an official in the military administration of the Central Asian dynasty of the Jurchen-Jin. The Jurchen had conquered north China in 1125, causing Huizong's court to move south to Hangzhou and thus precipitating the beginning of the Southern Song. In 1159, at age forty-eight, Wang retired from office and withdrew to the Zhongnan mountains near modern Xi'an, where he built a thatched hut and began to lead the life of an eccentric hermit, appearing increasingly mad. Then he had a revelatory experience:

> While he was drinking and eating meat in the town of Ganhe, two men dressed in woolen cloaks came into the tavern. They seemed to have identical manners and qualities about them. Wang was captivated by them and, following them to a quiet place, proceeded to bow and pay respects to them. They looked at him and said: "This man may become a disciple." So they taught him by oral instruction.

> Following this, Wang became even more mad and composed a verse:

> Only when forty-eight did I meet them

Now I have oral teachings and finally I'm getting somewhere.

> In the following year, he met with them again . . . and received
> five songs. . . . After that, he sent away his wife and married
> his daughter off to fully dedicate himself to his calling.
> (*Quanzhen jiaozu bei*; Tsui, *Taoist Tradition*, 19–20)

Wang was made privy to religious Daoist secrets and became the confi-
dante of the two mysterious strangers, who were later identified as the
two alchemical masters and immortals Zhongli Quan and Lü Dongbin.
Wang intensified his dedication and asceticism, losing his sanity to the
point where he dug himself a grave called "the tomb of the living dead."
In 1167, he burned his hut to the ground while dancing around it and
moved to Shandong in eastern China, where he preached his visions and
began to win followers. He founded five religious communities, all located in northern Shandong, and continued to spread his teaching until
his death in 1170.

His work was continued by seven disciples, six men and one woman,
known collectively as the Seven Perfected (*qizhen*). After observing the
standard three-year mourning period for their master, they went separate ways to spread his teaching in different parts of north China, each
founding various communities that developed into separate branches or
lineages (*pai*). The most important among these disciples is Qiu Chuji
(1148–1227), better known as Master Changchun, the founder of the leading Longmen lineage (named after a mountain range in Shaanxi where
he spread the teaching).

As patriarch of the school, he was summoned to see Chinggis Khan in
his Central Asian headquarters in 1219. Since the Mongols by this time
were well on their way to conquering China (and to ruling as the Yuan
dynasty) and were likely to endanger the lives of many people, Qiu
could not refuse the summons. Despite his advanced age of 72 years, he
undertook the strenuous, three-year journey in the company of eighteen
leading disciples. This was documented by his disciple and patriarchal
successor Li Zhichang in a text known as the "Journey to the West" (*Xiyou ji*), translated into English as "The Travels of an Alchemist." Qiu
seems to have established good communication with the Khan, although
he could not give him the secret of immortality. As he was leaving, the
Khan appointed him the leader of all religions of China and exempted
his followers from taxes and labor. This, in one stroke, made the Com-

plete Perfection school the most powerful and popular religious group in north China and contributed greatly to its prominence which continues to this day.

Another prominent member of the Seven Perfected was Wang Chuyi (1142-1217), who started out as an ordained Daoist and converted to the new system. He came to the attention of the court and, in the 1180s, was invited variously to explain the teachings to the emperor and preside over court-sponsored Daoist ceremonies. His other call to fame is his end—a well-witnessed ascent to immortality by complete dissolution. While officiating at a Daoist ceremony, he was sending off a "pure poem" prayer to Lord Lao in the holy fire when the deity appeared in a vision, hovering on a five-colored luminous haze above the altar. Wang bowed in recognition of the vision and continued with the burning of the prayer.

> Then the crowd saw the figure of a boy, little more than a foot high, of strange countenance and marvelous attire, rising from Wang's incense burner and greet the Highest Lord as if he was following a summons. When the burning of the poem was complete, there was no trace of Wang. (*Tixuan zhenren xianyi lu*)

The only female member of the original group of disciples was Sun Bu'er (1119-1182), the wife of the Perfected Ma Yu (1123-1183). She was born into a powerful local family and received a literary education, then married and raised a family. In 1167, Wang Chongyang came to their Shandong home and both she and her husband converted to his organization, becoming active disciples. Eventually Sun Bu'er separated from her husband, who went off to found his own communities, and grew to be leader of the local Complete Perfection association. She went on to attain the highest ritual rank with the right to teach and ordain other followers. Her cult grew over the following dynasties, and she served especially as an inspiration to women seekers.

After the first generation of disciples, Quanzhen had spread widely in north China and was the officially recognized religious organization of the country. People came to it in great numbers, and the school greatly helped the people during the difficult years of the Mongol conquest, but its newly elevated status also had its drawbacks. For one, many people joined it not for spiritual or religious reasons but because it granted safety from marauding armies, exemption from taxes and labor, and increased social influence. For another, certain members began to abuse the school's power, militantly occupying Buddhist monasteries and temples, replacing their statues with Daoist images, and mistreating Buddhist practitioners and their sanctuaries. Buddhists protested against this treatment at court and several hearings ensued, dealing not only with the charges of abuse but also questioning the general validity of the two teachings.

These hearings were not unlike the court debates under the Toba-Wei in the sixth century. The Mongol rulers themselves were inclined toward tantric Buddhism and, favoring Tibetan masters, tended to listen to the Buddhist side. As a result, Daoism—not just Complete Perfection, but in all its forms—was prohibited and persecuted in 1281. Many scriptures, with the exceptions of the *Daode jing* and a few texts associated with Lord Lao, were burned at the time, and many sanctuaries were restored to or handed over to the Buddhists. Although the Daoist canon collected under the Mongols did not survive—it had been created to replace the one sponsored by Huizong—these events otherwise do not seem to have had a lasting ill effect on either Daoism or Complete Perfection. Records indicate that by the late 1280s a major building effort was already underway in Daoist holy places, and soon Daoist leaders were back in the good graces of the rulers.

Monastic Life

The dominant form of Complete Perfection Daoism is the monastic life, which goes back to Wang Chongyang's own hermit asceticism. In the early years of the school, followers were encouraged to leave society, become celibate, and dedicate themselves fully to Dao. To do so, they were instructed to built themselves thatched huts on lonely mountain sides and pursue spiritual techniques. Over time, these huts grew into larger religious communities, which eventually, following traditional Chinese palace and temple architecture, consisted of a series of sanctuaries and halls, divided by courtyards and laid out along a central north-south axis. This was surrounded on both sides by other buildings such as meditation cells, ancestral shrines, dormitories, kitchens, workshops, and the like (see Fig. 3).

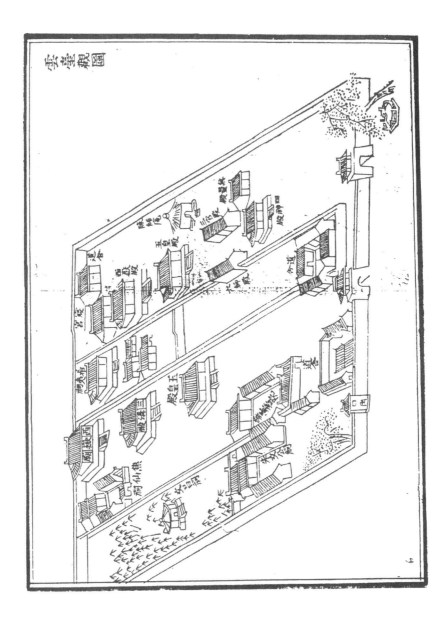

Fig. 3. The layout of a Daoist monastery. Source: *Huayin xianzhi.*

The arrangement of buildings, as well as their names, mirror Chan Buddhist institutions and reflect a thinking that associates the monastery with the human body: the central axis with the main buildings is the torso, the upper support divisions are its arms and hands, and the lower support sections serve as its legs and feet. A good example today is found in the Baiyun guan (White Cloud Monastery) in Beijing, the school's central temple and the headquarters of the Chinese Daoist Association.

Complete Perfection followers live in monasteries most of the time, but the ancient hermit tradition is still alive in that they are encouraged to spend some time wandering around the countryside. This, again, matches a Chan Buddhist practice, where novices have to spend time on the road, being *yunshui* or "wandering clouds." Wang Chongyang himself describes the practice in his *Lijiao shiwu lun* (Fifteen Articles on Establishing the Teaching).

> *Wandering Like the Clouds*
> There are two different ways of wandering. The first is to relish the spectacular scenery of mountains and rivers and enjoy the colorful bloom of flowers and trees. Someone who wanders like this . . . gets confused in his mind and weak in his energy. Such a one vainly wanders like the clouds.
>
> The second way of wandering is to pursue inner nature and destiny and search for mystery and wonder. One who wanders like this climbs into high mountains over dangerous passes and visits enlightened teachers without tiring. He crosses distant streams with turbulent waters and inquires for the Dao without slackening.
>
> Then, even a single saying received in the right spirit may open up complete understanding. The great realization of life and death dawns within and you become a master of Complete Perfection. As such, you truly wander like the clouds. (Kohn, *Taoist Experience*, 87)

This wandering is, therefore, not of the "free and easy" kind but represents another form of spiritual practice, regulated in some detail. A seventeenth-century manual on Complete Perfection, the *Guiju xuzhi* (Rules to Know) describes the necessary implements:

> All wandering monks of Complete Perfection should have the
> following Seven Treasures with them:
> 1. a rush mat, to keep free from demons on the outside;
> 2. a quilted robe, to cover heart and inner nature;
> 3. a single calabash, to contain the food and drink of the wise;
> 4. a palm-leaf hat, to keep off wind and rain, frost and snow;
> 5. a palm-leaf fan, to brush off dust from things;
> 6. a pure satchel, to carry and hold the sacred scriptures;
> 7. a flat staff, to point to the great Dao, pure wind, and bright moon.

A similarly simple, ascetic lifestyle is also the norm within the monastery. It is ruled by a strict hierarchy, with the abbot at the head, the prior as the key manager of personnel (assisted by an overseer and several scribes), the provost as main administrator (assisted by a superintendent, treasurer, cellarer, as well as several vergers and cooks), and the meditation master in charge of spiritual practice (assisted by an ordination master, manager of offerings, and several overseers).

The time schedule is very rigid: a typical day begins at 3:00 A.M. and ends at 9:00 P.M. It consists of several periods of seated meditation, worship, meals, and work, including—again as in Chan Buddhism—work in the gardens and the fields. Everybody is kept busy at all times, and all movements throughout the day are exactly prescribed and have to be executed with utmost control. Usually meditation, sleep periods, and meals are times of complete silence, and even at other times words are to be used with care and circumspection. Daoists, moreover, observe the natural cycles of the seasons and often eschew the use of artificial lights, so that their winter days are a great deal shorter than those in summer, allowing for more extensive rest in the darker phases of the year.

Spiritual Attainment

The essential goal of the monastic life in Complete Perfection Daoism is to allow practitioners to pursue immortality with the greatest support and the least distraction. It begins with a strong emphasis on simplicity, morality, and stability of mind. As the *Yeyue guanji* (Record of Looking at the Wild Moon) says:

> The teaching of Complete Perfection aims at training its followers to endure hard labor and be diligent in working in the

fields. Thus food and lodging are not given to them unless they earn it. Unadorned and coarsely clad, the monastics are free from worries and jealousies. What others find unendurable, they calmly deal with. They attain full control over themselves and strive to recover their true inner [Dao] nature. They do not give a thought to matters of life, death, or fate. (Tsui, *Taoist Tradition*, 13)

Monastics should, therefore, be hardworking and disciplined, never shying away from low, menial tasks such as tilling the fields or collecting firewood, and always maintaining a low ego and sincere mind. In addition, they must be truthful in their interactions with others, be they fellow monks or outsiders, should keep themselves and their living space spotlessly clean, and must avoid all laziness, pride, arrogance, and anger. While this matches requirements in the Hindu, Buddhist, or Christian traditions, Daoist monks and nuns are not dead to ordinary society but still under the obligation to serve their families and the ruler of the country. As the ten precepts of Complete Perfection have it:

1. Do not be disloyal or unfilial, without benevolence or good faith. Always exhaust your allegiance to your lord and family, be sincere in your relation to the myriad beings.

2. Do not secretly steal things or harbor hidden plots, harm others in order to profit yourself. Always practice hidden virtue and widely help the host of living beings.

3. Do not kill or harm anything that lives in order to satisfy your own appetites. Always behave with compassion to all, even the multitude of insects and worms.

4. Do not be lascivious or defile yourself, debasing the numinous *qi*. Always maintain chastity and be without shortcomings or blame.

5. Do not defeat others to gain yourself or leave your kith and kin. Always use Dao to help others and support the nine clans living in harmony.

6. Do not slander or defame the wise and virtuous or boast of your own skill to elevate yourself. Always praise the beauty and goodness of others and never fight about your own merit and ability.

7. Do not drink liquor beyond measure or eat meat in violation of the prohibitions. Always maintain a harmonious energy and peaceful nature, and do your duty in purity and emptiness.

8. Do not be greedy and acquisitive without ever being satisfied, accumulating wealth without ever being generous. Always practice moderation in all things and show sympathy for the poor and destitute.

9. Do not have any relations with the unwise or live among the unclean and defiled. Always rise to overcome yourself and live in purity and emptiness.

10. Do not speak lightly or make fun of serious matters, be agitated in language, or abuse perfection. Always maintain seriousness and speak humble words, making the Dao and its virtue your main duty. (*Chuzhen jie*)

On the basis of this strict discipline and strong morality, practitioners then engage in spiritual training, described as the dual cultivation of "inner nature" and "destiny" (*xingming shuangxiu*). Inner nature refers to the psychological dimensions of the practice, while destiny indicates the more physical aspect of one's being. Both have to be developed equally, until a level is reached that is often described in terms of "purity and tranquility" (*qingjing*). It indicates a state where the mind has been freed from desires and is completely absorbed in the inner workings of Dao. Through this practice, a first recovery of spirit is achieved, necessary for the attainment of immortality. A key text on this is the *Qingjing jing* (Scripture of Purity and Tranquility, also known as Scripture of Clarity and Stillness), a short collection of verses chanted daily in Complete Perfection monasteries. It says,

> The human spirit is fond of purity, but the mind disturbs it.
> The human mind is fond of tranquility, but desires meddle with it.
> Get rid of desires, and the mind will be tranquil.
> Cleanse your mind, and the spirit will be pure.
> Naturally the six desires [of the senses] won't arise,
> The three poisons are destroyed.
> Whoever cannot do this:
> You have not yet cleansed your mind,
> and your desires are not yet driven out.
> Those who have abandoned their desires:
> Observe your mind by introspection,

And see there is no mind.
Then observe your body from without,
And see there is no body.
Then observe others by glancing out afar
And see there are no beings.
Once you have realized these three,
You observe perfect emptiness!

Eventually practitioners move on to engage in inner alchemical training, working to create an internal elixir and an immortal embryo through the transmutation and refinement of body energies. They then learn to identify themselves with this immortal embryo and become cosmic people with a higher consciousness and a new level of energy. Spending their lives alternating between high celestial states and monastic work, they eventually go beyond all sentient existence, find their true subtle bodies, leave the world behind in their minds, give up the physical body, and ascend to the immortals as pure spirits. As Wang Chongyang describes it in a poem:

I shall explain carefully the way to cultivation:
Enlightenment will come only to a tranquil heart.
When nothing arises in the eye, the dragon will gladly stay;
When the nostrils remain open, the tiger will happily dwell.
When the tongue retreats from tasting, the spirit in the
heart will be glad;
When the ears stop listening to sounds, the water in the
kidneys will be clear.
North and south intermingle in harmony and unite into one;
East and west unite in intercourse and all demon parasites
will be destroyed.
Wood and metal rely on this and come to rest;
The infant and the virgin follow the lord's talisman.
Then the golden elixir forms,
And one can leave the body through the head —
Moving straight into the heavens as five beams of light.
(*Quanzhen ji*; Tsui, *Taoist Tradition*, 33)

The Pantheon

Although the monasteries of Complete Perfection were geared primarily toward providing optimal conditions for immortality training, they also had a devotional and ritual component. Monks and nuns honored the gods in daily services and celebrated their feast days with formal offerings (*jiao*) that could last for several days. Also, there were numerous lay followers who worshiped its divinities and interacted with them, increasingly through séances and spirit-writing.

The Complete Perfection pantheon is exceptionally large, integrating not only its own key deities but also official gods of the Song and Yuan dynasties and popular deities. Its key gods appear in three groups: the Five Patriarchs, the Seven Perfected, and the Eight Immortals. The Five Patriarchs are the divine leaders of the religion, responsible for its initial revelations. They include Lord Lao, the Imperial Lord of Eastern Florescence (Donghua dijun), the two alchemist-immortals Zhongli Quan and Lü Dongbin (also members of the Eight Immortals), and the founder Wang Chongyang. The Seven Perfected are the seven main disciples of the founder, mentioned earlier; Qiu Chuji is most important but the others six also receive veneration, especially the lady master Sun Bu'er.

The Eight Immortals are a group of seven men and one woman who are said to have attained immortality, inspired by each other, and who continued to serve humanity by appearing in séances and inspirations. As a group, they appeared first in theater plays of the thirteenth century, portrayed as an eccentric and happy lot who respond to pleas in emergencies and grant favors and protection. They remain highly popular today, as symbols of long life and happiness, and they appear on congratulation cards for various happy occasions and in shops and restaurants as signs of good luck and enjoyment. They play an active part in Chinese folk culture and have been featured time and again in comic books and popular movies.

Each immortal has his or her story and characteristic sign. The first among them is Zhongli Quan, also known as Han Zhongli, a general of the Han dynasty whose troops were completely vanquished in Central Asia. Desperate, he fled to a remote village where he encountered a Daoist immortal and learned to ascend to heaven, helping others from his new position despite his failure in his official duties. He is usually depicted as a large, stately man with a round pot-belly.

The second immortal is Zhang Guolao, an old man with a long white beard, who smiles a great deal and usually travels across the country riding backwards on a white donkey. He has powers over life and death. When he arrives in a town and does not need his donkey for a while, he blows his *qi* on the animal and shrinks it to pocket-size; when he wishes to travel onward, he blows it up again to regular dimensions.

Lü Dongbin is the third and most popular immortal of the group. He appears frequently in spirit-writing sessions and serves as the patriarch of many Daoist groups and techniques. Depicted as a Confucian gentleman with aristocratic features and a sword, Lü is best known for the story of the "Yellow Millet Dream."

> Lü dreamt that he went up to the capital as a candidate of the imperial examination and passed it at the top of the list. Starting his career as a junior secretary to one of the Boards, he rapidly rose in rank to positions at the Censorate and the Hanlin Academy. Eventually he became a Privy Councilor, after he had occupied, in the course of his unbroken success, all the most sought-after and important official posts.

> Twice he was married, he further dreamt, and both wives belonged to families of wealth and position. Children were born to him. His sons soon took themselves wives, and his daughters left the paternal roof for their husbands' homes. All these events happened before he even reached the age of forty.

> Next he found himself Prime Minister for a period of ten years, wielding immense power. This corrupted him. Then suddenly, without warning, he was accused of a grave crime. His home and all his possessions were confiscated, his wife and children separated. He himself, a solitary outcast, was wandering toward his place of banishment beyond the mountains. He found his horse brought to a standstill in snowstorm and was no longer able to continue the journey. (*Zengxiang liexian zhuan*)

Then Lü wakes up, finding that while he went through an entire official career and family life, his millet has not even cooked yet. He realizes that life is but a fleeting dream and decides to leave the world to become an immortal, following Zhongli Quan for his training. The latter then puts him through ten tests, in which his selfless nature and sincere dedication to Dao are examined. For example, once he comes home to find his family dead; without great wailing and sorrow, he proceeds to arrange the burial, understanding that life is unstable and death but another transformation. Another time, he encounters a hungry tiger ready to pounce on a flock of sheep; disregarding his personal safety he throws himself in the tiger's path. Passing all ten texts, he is eventually accepted as

Zhongli's disciple and becomes a leading immortal, not only among the eight but for the faithful in general, who find him supportive and ever ready to provide oracles and supernatural advice.

The next immortal of the group is Li Tieguai or Ironcrutch Li, another popular figure, who also has power over life and death. The story here is that he was an expert in ecstatic excursions and once decided to go up into the heavens, leaving his corpse-like body behind for an entire week. To make sure nothing happened to it, he ordered a disciple to keep watch, but the boy got called away. Assuming that his master would not return anyway, he cremated the body. When Li returned, he found his own body gone and entered that of a recently dead man who happened to be an old, crippled beggar. To help himself get around, he then used an iron crutch, thus his name. Despite his transformation, he lost none of his vigor or magical powers.

The remaining four immortals are lesser figures. They include Cao Guo-qiu, a member of the Song imperial family who was disgusted by the evil ways of the world and decided to become a hermit. He was trained by Lü Dongbin and is depicted as an aristocrat with a scroll. Next is Han Xiangzi, a naturally gifted magician and music master who plays the flute and can make flowers bloom. Then there is Lan Caihe, who has powers over the body and is not subject to heat and cold. He, too, enjoys flowers, and is usually depicted carrying a basket of them. Finally, there is He Xiangu, the only woman in the group, who as a young girl received a dream revelation from the immortals and decided to leave the world. Overall, the group stands for the possibility of attaining a happy life and making the best of difficult situations—be it military defeat, examination failure, or even the loss of one's body. They show that the world is full of miracles and wonders and that one should never lose hope or stop smiling at life.

Additional figures commonly found in Complete Perfection temples include the Three Purities as representatives of the various Daoist schools, and the gods of the Northern Dipper as key functionaries of fate and good fortune. They usually appear with an extensive entourage of celestial helpers and assistants, golden lads and jade maidens, dragons and phoenixes. In addition, monasteries often honor popular Chinese deities, such as the Emperor of Heaven, the God of Earth, the Patriarch of Fire, and the Jade Emperor; astral deities like Doumu (Mother of the Dipper); martial gods such as Xuanwu (Dark Warrior); cosmic powers such as the

Gods of the Four Directions; popular heroes like Guandi (god of wealth); as well as various Confucian saints and meritorious ancestors.

An example of an early depiction of the Complete Perfection pantheon is found in the Yongle gong (Palace of Eternal Joy), a temple located in Ruicheng (Shanxi) that was first completed in 1252. It consists of three halls — to the Three Purities, Patriarch Lü, and Wang Chongyang — each illustrated with extensive murals. The first one alone shows 290 deities on a total wall space of 94 meters. The figures include all major deities of the school, depicted in elaborate garb and arranged in a formal procession of celestials. They are well preserved and offer a unique opportunity to examine Complete Perfection worship in its early phases.

Devotional activities to the gods in temples such as the Yongle gong usually take the form of audience rites with the gods. These are not only geared toward gaining divine protection, but also help the development of a proper mind of humility and devotion. As the *Guiju xuzhi* says:

> Audience services of Complete Perfection serve to show veneration and serious respect through majestic rites on the outside, while on the inside they develop the mystical mind and sincere devotion. To perform them properly, concentrate your spirit and focus on the inner vision of the gods; stand upright and face straight toward the altar.

> Perform three bows of increasing devotion. First, bend down slightly in simple salute, then again bend your body forward to look like a half moon. Third, prostrate yourself fully, so that your five limbs [arms, legs, head] touch the floor. Retain this position and do not get up until you feel the *qi* complete within. Then rise in body, but keep your spirit pure and humble. Pay obeisance like this several times.

Further Readings

Katz, Paul R. 2000. *Images of the Immortal: The Cult of Lü Dongbin at the Palace of Eternal Joy.* Honolulu: University of Hawaii Press.

Kohn, Livia. 2001. "Daoist Monastic Discipline: Hygiene, Banquets, and Greetings in Medieval China." *T'oung Pao* 87: 153-93.

Lai, T. C. 1972. *The Eight Immortals.* Hong Kong: Swinden Book Co.

Steinhardt, Nancy S. 2000. "Taoist Architecture." In *Taoism and the Arts of China*, edited by Stephen Little and Shawn Eichman, 57–76. Berkeley: University of California Press.

Tsui, Bartholomew P. M. 1991. *Taoist Tradition and Change. The Story of the Complete Perfection Sect in Hong Kong.* Hong Kong: Christian Study Centre on Chinese Religion and Culture.

Yoshioka, Yoshitoyo. 1979. "Taoist Monastic Life." In *Facets of Taoism*, edited by Holmes Welch and Anna Seidel, 220–52. New Haven, Conn.: Yale University Press.

Original Sources in Translation

Kohn, Livia. 1993. *The Taoist Experience.* Albany: State University of New York Press. Chs. 12, 23, 46.

Waley, Arthur. 1931. *The Travels of an Alchemist.* London: George Routledge & Sons.

Wong, Eva. 1992. *Cultivating Stillness: A Taoist Manual for Transforming Body and Mind.* Boston: Shambhala.

Yetts, Percifal. 1916. "The Eight Immortals." *Journal of the Royal Asiatic Society* 1916, 773–807.

Part Four

Modernity

CHAPTER TEN

CHANGES IN THE MING AND QING

Modern Daoism began in the indigenous Ming dynasty (1368–1644) and evolved under foreign Qing or Manchu rule (1644–1911) to acquire the form it has today. The two dynasties were similar in many ways. Both continued the Mongol practice of having their capital in Beijing (except for a short period in the early Ming, when Nanjing was capital) and established central agencies to rule all different aspects of the country. Especially religious movements, with their potential threat of rebellion, were kept under strict control. For Daoism this meant that all groups and lineages had to align themselves with one of the two accepted organizations, the Celestial Masters or Complete Perfection. At the same time, rulers sought to standardize the religions' practices and sponsored large projects, such as the publication of religious scriptures (e.g., the Daoist canon) and the establishment of major religious centers (e.g., on Mount Wudang).

These standardizing and unifying efforts resulted in a new level of religious integration among the upper classes, who eagerly embraced the movement of "unifying the three teachings" (*sanjiao heyi*) of Confucianism, Daoism, and Buddhism. This had first begun in the Song but became the dominant form of religious thought under the later dynasties, when Daoist inner alchemical practices were actively joined with Chan forms of meditation and Confucian visions of realizing virtue. Many thinkers of the time came from a Confucian background, then turned to study Buddhism or Daoism, or both. They, in turn, created religious worldviews that have been described as syncretistic and often cannot be clearly assigned to a single tradition. In addition, a number of new deities arose. Many had been popular gods limited to certain localities or specializations who then grew to national status and became important enough to be integrated into the official and/or Daoist pantheons.

The most profound changes, however, occurred on the popular level, and many of them remain in place today. Commerce was flourishing and the control of thought and writing that was exerted over the upper classes had little affect on the common people. They formed local groups, many of which engaged in direct communication with the spirits, either by automatic speech or through spirit-writing. The latter employed the planchette, a tray of sand in which a medium in trance would write characters dictated by the gods. Various deities were channeled, but most common was — and remains today — the immortal Lü Dongbin. Among the materials received in this manner are, first of all, instructions on the organization and formation of sects and cults, which were often obeyed to the letter. Longer channeled works include so-called precious scrolls describing the life and deeds of specific deities and the proper methods for their veneration, and morality books on the effects and karmic consequences of various good and bad deeds. Spirits also revealed instructions on longevity practices, martial arts (Gongfu, Taiji quan), and inner alchemy. This often generated secret groups that would follow a particular regimen and learn to become immortal and invincible upon the god's command.

Another innovation on the popular level was the growth of a body of vernacular fiction, including a number of novels with strong religious themes, which recount the adventures of gods, saints, and immortals. Here, again, martial arts play an important role, heroes being equipped with supernatural swords, staffs, and lances, and the knowledge of just how to use their own and their opponent's qi to stage the most audacious and impressively victorious fight. A well-known example, based on a Buddhist tale, is the "Journey to the West" (*Xiyou ji*, or "Monkey"), in which the monkey god Sun Wukong accompanies the pilgrim Xuanzang to India on his quest for Buddhist scriptures and fights all kinds of battles on the road. Various matching tales exist also in Daoism, although few have been translated to date.

Court Policies

The first ruler of the Ming dynasty, Emperor Taizu (r. 1368–1399), was highly suspicious of all independent organizations and decreed many administrative measures to control the various religions of the country. Most of these remained in place until the founding of the Republic of

China in 1911. To begin, he set up a new administration system, making all religious affairs subject to approval and control by the Ministry of Rites. Within this institution, all Daoist affairs were supervised by the Bureau of Daoist Registration, which had branch offices in each province (Bureaus of Daoist Institutions), each prefecture (Bureaus of Daoist Supervision), and each district (Bureaus of Daoist Assemblies). In this way, even the most remote Daoist activity occurring in the empire could be monitored and controlled by an arm of the central government.

Among other things, these offices were responsible for issuing and monitoring ordination certificates. These were official passports for monks and nuns that every sect member received at ordination and had to carry at all times to show his or her tax-exempt status, and as a permit to travel across country. Such certificates had been first established under the Tang, but had quickly been abused through theft, bribery, and forgery. In the Ming dynasty, however, the system was instituted with renewed vigor and kept under strict government control. Only specially designated monasteries were allowed to hold ordinations, ceremonies were limited to once in three, five, or even ten years, and the number of monks and nuns was restricted to serve the government's needs.

Furthermore, men could only undergo ordination between the ages of fourteen and twenty (so they would not join to evade draft and taxes), while women were not permitted to become nuns while still of child-bearing age. Soldiers and artisans were excluded categorically. Those who made it into the ordination system not only had to carry their certificate at all times but were also subject to the so-called All-Knowing Register, an official list that contained the names of all Daoists who had ever spent any time in a monastery. This list was used to trace the whereabouts and movements of every religious practitioner. Private temples, owned and sponsored by local aristocrats, were severely curtailed and had to have an official stamp of approval from the government before they could house any religious practitioners. The overall effect of these measures was twofold: it reduced enthusiasm for the religious path among the population, and it effected a high level of standardization among institutions and practitioners.

But the central government was not only restrictive — it also opened up new venues for Daoists. One of these, at the central court, was the Office of Divine Music, a department under the direct command of the emperor that served to provide music and dance for court rituals. Here religious practitioners could meet with the emperor in person and participate actively in the formation of some of the most sacred rites of the dynasty. Another positive venue was the appointment of the Celestial Master to the central government with an office and staff of his own. This, depending on the inclination of individual rulers, could mean considerable political influence and power at court.

In art, the Ming emperors sponsored many Daoist-inspired and ritual works; also, several new schools of Daoist painting developed, showing the gods in their full splendor. Nonreligious painters, too, took up Daoist themes, paiting gods, immortals, heavens, and rituals, and left behind a rich heritage of visual documentation of the religion. In yet another area, the early Ming emperors, and especially the third, known as Chengzu or the Yongle Emperor (r. 1403–1425), also greatly supported Daoism by expanding the Daoist sanctuaries and training facilities on Mount Wudang (Hubei), and by granting strong sponsorship to the martial Daoist deity Xuanwu (Dark Warrior). This deity in turn advanced to become a key protector of the dynasty. Most importantly, however, the Yongle Emperor also provided the means and facilities for the compilation of a major canon, appointing as the main editors the Celestial Master, Zhang Yuqing (1364–1427), and the chief of the sanctuaries on Mount Wudang, Ren Ziyuan (fl. 1400–1422). This canon (*Daozang*) remains our main source of Daoist texts today. It was printed first in 1445 and contains about 1,500 texts from all different schools and ages. Toward the end of the dynasty, in 1607, it was expanded in a "Supplementary Daoist Canon" (*Xu Daozang*), and further developed in two later collections: the "Repository of the Daoist Canon" (*Daozang jiyao*; dat. ca. 1820) and the "Essential Blossoms of the Daoist Canon" (*Daozang jinghua*; dat. 1920). Again, the measures of the court, even in their supportive mode, served to increase the standardization and centralization of the religion, curbing or at least controlling local and independent growth and discouraging the emergence of new sects and inspirations.

New Forms of Inner Alchemy

In this general atmosphere of government control and the standardization of teachings, Daoists developed new forms of thought that integrated current ideas of Confucianism and Buddhism. At the same time, Confucian intellectuals, following the same trend, actively engaged in inner alchemy and used its vocabulary to explain their vision of the progress toward universal virtue and oneness with Heaven and Earth. A typical way of joining the three teachings, then, was to see Confucianism as maintaining society through its emphasis on moral values, Chan Buddhism as concentrating on the cultivation of inner nature through meditation, and Daoism as encouraging bodily transformation through the enhancement of inner nature and destiny.

In mainstream Ming thought, moreover, several Daoist concepts became prominent. They include the vision of Dao as the pure underlying essence of the universe as expressed in the *Daode jing*, the refinement of the inner elixir and its proper timing, the original power of *qi* and its cultivation by inner circulation, the regulation of breath as a means to concentration and good health, embryo breathing as a form of gaining inner subtlety, and the use of the trigrams and hexagrams of the *Yijing* to mark progress.

Confucian thinkers such as Wang Dao (1487–1547), Zhan Ruoshui (1466–1560), Wang Yangming (1517–1579), and Lin Zhaoen (1517–1598) would use these concepts, often in conjunction with Chan Buddhist meditation practice and Daoist ways of breath control. With their help these thinkers explained the inner development of subtler states of mind, which led them to the realization of "innate knowledge" (*liangzhi*) — seen as a function of *qi* — and the true self. This in turn was found essential for the unfolding of the bright virtue, connecting everyone both to the original cosmos and to the world at large. This was the goal of Neo-Confucian realization. According to this view, everyone is inherently part of the larger universe and connected with it through principle (*li*) and *qi*-energy. These abstract/mental and concrete/physical aspects of existence can be (and have been) related to Buddhist notions of Buddhanature and karmic retribution, as well as to Daoist ideas of inner nature and destiny. Both aspects have to be cultivated equally for the ideal state to arise, a state that in the three teachings is called, respectively, oneness with Heaven and Earth, nirvana, and immortality. Now we find this ideal state increasingly seen as being a combination of them all.

Within Daoism there were also several new systems of inner alchemy, among which the *Jinhua zongzhi* (Secret of the Golden Flower) is best known in the West. Originally received as a spirit-writing document, it was used by various lineages and became a major work of Complete Perfection. Its teachings are said to go back to the immortal Xu Xun, a third-century figure venerated as the founder of a fourteenth-century Daoist school famous for its Confucian tendencies and known as the Jingming zhongxiao dao or "Way of Pure Brightness, Loyalty, and Filial Piety." Xu Xun decided to reveal the scripture and to this end sent Lü Dongbin and two of the Seven Perfected to transmit it to humanity. It focuses primarily on the radiant inner light known as the "Golden Flower," which is the essential *qi* of the One at the root of creation. To cultivate this light, one must recognize and gather it, then make it circulate through one's body so that it can create the golden elixir which will grow into the immortal embryo. With the help of this spirit being, the practitioner can then leave his or her body and participate in the essential mode of the cosmos. Throughout the process a strong concentration of mind is essential. One must also avoid distractions and preoccupations with demons while increasing strength and mental openness. Eventually, one begins to feel light and free, open to the emptiness and infinity of Dao, and there is a complete change in both mind and body. As the text describes it:

> If, when there is quiet, the spirit has continuously and uninterruptedly a sense of great joy as if intoxicated or freshly bathed, this is a sign that the light-principle is harmonious in the whole body. Then the Golden Flower begins to bud. When, furthermore, all openings are quiet, and the silver moon stands in the middle of heaven, and one has the feeling that this earth is a world of light and brightness, this is a sign that the body of the heart is opened to purity. Then the Golden Flower is opening.
>
> Furthermore, the whole body comes to feel strong and firm, so that it fears neither storm nor frost. Things that displease ordinary people are met and cannot cloud the brightness of the spirit seed. Yellow gold fills the house; the steps are of white jade. Rotten and stinking things on earth are touched by one breath of the true energy and come back to life. Red blood becomes milk; the fragile body of the flesh is pure gold and diamonds. Then the Golden Flower is crystallized. (*Jinhua zongzhi*; Wilhelm, *Golden Flower*, 49)

These changes affect every part of the practitioner's life, so that he or she can continue in ordinary activities and manage them increasingly with inner spontaneity and intuition, a sense of detachment and marvelous Dao-based perception. Unlike earlier forms of inner alchemy, the teaching here is not directed primarily at monks and nuns, but geared toward attainment for lay practitioners and increased beauty and efficacy of daily living.

A similar practical attitude is also found in another inner alchemical text, the *Xingming fajue mingzhi* (Instruction on the Methods of Inner Nature and Destiny) by Zhao Bizhen (b. 1860) of the late Qing dynasty. Here, the human body is described as the alchemical stove and furnace, and an orbit is created through its various gates, cavities, and passages. Inner, sexual energies of yin and yang are aroused, then guided to mingle and merge with each other in a rhythm ruled by conscious breathing.

As a result, a pure generative force is isolated and located in the lower cinnabar field, which in turn becomes a burning crucible. Refined in this fiery pit, the transmuted force is next moved up into the middle cinnabar field near the solar plexus. Increased refinement and heating further purify the force and it rises up into the upper cinnabar field in the head. The body now consists of three active cauldrons or gates: the lower or primary, the middle or central, and the upper or precious. In the circulation of rarified energies among these three, the spirit light or Golden Flower develops in a state of complete tranquility and serenity. The text says:

> As energies are circulated through the three gates, all psychic centers are cleared of obstructions so that the vital forces, now developed fully, can move freely about, ascending and descending endlessly. This is how they help in creating the immortal embryo. With time, they will circulate of themselves without the practitioner even being aware of them. This is how the immortal embryo comes about.
>
> After a long time, while this mindless absorption continues, the practitioner should focus his eyes on the lower cinnabar field. After ten months, the vital forces will become so subtle that only a feeble vibration is felt in the navel area, which otherwise seems to be completely empty. One year later, even this vibration will cease. At this stage, one should not take salt when eating or drinking. Now only spirit remains, serene and radiant, which is the true embryonic respiration. Outer breathing will appear to stop and the pulses will beat no more. There is state of deep serenity.
>
> After staying still for a long time, the heart, spirit, and thought will again begin to vibrate, causing the breath to feel like an ant crawling within. This is the immortal embryo which . . . now begins to stir. (*Xingming fajue mingzhi*; Lu, *Taoist Yoga*, 149-50)

This immortal embryo then grows and develops, and practitioners increasingly identify with it. Doing so, they lose their sense of personal and bodily identity and are sublimated ever further until they become a cosmic, indestructible diamond body. Like the earlier "Secret of the Golden Flower," this work too addresses ordinary people, has less esoteric terminology, and places great emphasis on bodily transformation—all characteristics shared by Qigong, the twentieth-century adaptation of inner alchemical practice.

New Gods

As Daoists focused more on the needs and activities of ordinary people during the Ming and Qing dynasties, they also adopted a number of local and popular deities into their pantheon, which expanded further and came to be depicted most commonly as a processon of celestial deities (see Fig. 4). The most important among the new gods is the Dark Warrior (Xuanwu), also known as the Perfect Warrior (Zhenwu). Originally a constellation in the northern sky, he appears first in the Han dynasty as the mythical animal of the north, depicted as an intertwined turtle and snake, both yin animals and thus representative of the north. The turtle is also an ancient Chinese symbol of the universe and an image of the sky dome, while the snake is an emblem of earth that, as it winds around the turtle, shows the intertwining of heaven and earth in the process of continuous creation. Taken together, the Dark Warrior and its representation show yin at its maximum strength, indicating the continuous creation taking place at the hibernating, latent stage of the universe.

Beginning with the Song dynasty, the Dark Warrior was worshiped at court and by the aristocracy, and even appeared to Emperor Huizong in a vision as a mighty and fully armed warrior with stern face and loose hair. Both the Yuan and Ming dynasties associated him with political power and venerated him in officially sponsored sanctuaries. Under the early Ming, the Yongle Emperor greatly expanded the god's center on Mount Wudang in Hubei. The deity was duly supported by both leading Daoist schools, Complete Perfection and Celestial Masters, and grew in popularity. He appeared also in popular literature and as the central subject of the vernacular novel *Beiyou ji* (Journey to the North).

Another popular deity adopted into Daoism at this time was the city god (Chenghuang), a popular continuation of the earth gods of old. The city

Fig. 4. The gods of the Dipper in celestial procession. Source: *Doumu jing*.

god was a divine office, filled upon popular demand by the ancestral spirit of a local benefactor, who served both as the divine protector for the area and as the people's mediator to the celestial administration, notably the Department of Destiny. Different in each city, the god had enormous powers over people's lives and fates and enjoyed great popularity. The institution was adopted into Daoism through the creation of a celestial archetype, a single central City God who resided in the heavens of the Dao and received his powers from Lord Lao directly. The Daoist *Chenghuang xiaozai jifu jing* (Scripture of the City God Dispelling Disasters and Accumulating Happiness, dat. 1376) describes this deity as follows:

> This God:
> Heaven and earth store his essence,
> Mountains and rivers support his power.
> He is majestic and numinous, shines forth in glory,
> Representing the sage Dao, he is lofty and illustrious.
> He shows no favor, no one-sidedness,
> But is public and loyal, upright and straight.
> Whatever one asks of him will come to pass
> Like a shadow inevitably follows a shape.
>
> He has the authority of heaven and orders all on earth,
> Cuts off all evil and dispels all killing.
> He protects the state and guards the country,
> With great merit aids the gods of soil and grain.
> He widely sends his sweet kindness down
> To save all living beings far and wide.
>
> He commands eighteen perfected marshals,
> Has a million divine generals at his call.
> Accumulating merit and doing all good deeds,
> He has the proper rank of City God.
> With an authority foremost in all under heaven,
> He majestically suppresses the myriad forms of evil.
> (Kohn, "City God," 94)

Then again, there is the Celestial Consort (Tianfei or Mazu), the protectress of fishermen originally venerated in Fujian, and one of the most popular deities in south China and Taiwan today. She was honored with a Daoist title and official mission by Lord Lao, empowered to slay demons, dispel disasters, and rescue humans from all kinds of difficulty. In many characteristics she resembles Guanyin, the Buddhist goddess of mercy. According to the *Tianfei jiuku lingyan jing* (Scripture on the Numinous Efficacy of the Celestial Concert in Relieving Distress, dat. 1409), she pledged herself to the service of humankind, taking the following vow:

> From this day forward, whether a traveling merchant or resident shopkeeper seeking assets in doing business, whether farmers in their sowing or artisans in their professions, whether troops in transit engaged in battle arrays, whether there be difficulty in childbirth that is not resolved, whether there be disturbances from public wrongs, whether there be any abusive language that results in grief and injury, or whether there be any malady or affliction to which one is inextricably bound and from which there is no respite—
>
> Should anyone [so mentioned] but reveal reverence and respect in his or her heart and call my name, then I will offer immediate and trustworthy response and cause them to attain whatever it is they wish and to achieve whatever pursuits they have in mind. In my travels throughout the celestial realm, I will always keep watch over humankind, to the extent that whatever is sought on land, in waters, rivers, or at sea—in every location—all shall be granted as wished. (Boltz, "T'ienfei," 224)

Again, like other popular gods adopted into Daoism, the Celestial Consort gives support and reassurance to ordinary people, exerting celestial powers on their behalf, rescuing them from difficulties, and granting their wishes. Daoist gods, rather than representing only the pure power of Dao at creation or sojourning in a far-off heaven, are there for ordinary folk and address commoners more than full-time practitioners.

Other popular deities adopted into the Daoist pantheon at the time include two further goddesses, both well known for helping women in their plight. One is the Goddess of the Morning Clouds (Bixia yuanju), the daughter of the Lord of Mount Tai (Taishan fujun), one of the ancient gods of the dead. The other is the Mother of the Dipper (Doumu), originally a Tantric goddess named Marîcî, daughter of Brahma and personification of light, who rules human destiny and saves people from peril. In addition, there was also the God of Literature (Wenchang), originally a Sichuan hero who became known for his efficacious support of struggling scholars. All these deities have relvant scriptures that were adopted into the Daoist canon.

Spirit-Writing

The increased popularization of Daoism is also evident in the expanded practice of spirit-writing. Although officially prohibited by the government, it was widely practiced because officials as much as commoners used it to divine their futures and the probable outcome of their ventures. Spirit-writing involved the automatic writing of a medium in trance, possessed by the spirit of a deity. It was usually undertaken with the help of a sand tray known as the planchette (*fuji*), and performed during séances held in the communal meeting house or "enlightenment altar" (*juetan*) of a lay worship group, nowadays called a "Daoist altar" (*daotan*).

A meeting involved an officiating priest who conducted the ceremony, a medium or shaman to go into trance and wield the wooden writing stick attached to the planchette, an interpreter to read each character out loud as it appeared in the sand, a scribe who put it into legible Chinese; various helpers to assist in the process, and an audience of believers. Spirit-writing was originally a way of fortune-telling to predict marriage, success, and remedies for ill health, but it developed into a common method of religious devotion accompanied by formal offerings of flowers and incense and the activation of spells and talismans.

Many séances were rather short and messages tended to be sparse, simply providing answers to concrete questions and issuing organizational instructions. But some lasted for extended periods and produced long scriptures—most prominently "precious scrolls" and "morality books." Precious scrolls (*baojuan*) were issued by both popular and unknown deities, and contained information on the organization and life of the otherworld; accounts of the creation, development, and eventual end of the world; hagiographic details on the life and efforts of the transmitting deity; practical materials on chants and talismans; and instructions for healing and efficacious ceremonies. They often centered around a creator goddess known as the Eternal Mother (Wusheng laomu), and combined popular religious beliefs with Daoist and Buddhist tenets.

Another popular form of religious literature at the time was morality books (*shanshu*). They go back originally to the *Ganying pian* (Treatise on Response and Retribution), a Song-dynasty treatise written by the Confucian official Li Zhiji (d. 1182) in an effort to raise the moral standard of the people. The text asserts that good and bad fortune do not befall people by accident but are visited upon them because of the moral quality of their deeds, and it encourages them to accumulate virtue and increase merit. It then presents a long description of the various ways in which people do evil and outlines their punishments:

> For all these crimes, the officials of the Department of Destiny deprive the guilty, in accordance with the lightness or gravity of their offense, of years of life, ranging from twelve years to one hundred days, thus causing them to die an early death. If, however, at death there is still an offense unexpiated, the resulting bad fortune will be transferred to their children and grandchildren.
>
> Moreover, all those who wrongly seize the property of others may have to compensate for it through their wives, children, or other family members, the expiation being in proportion up to a punishment by death.
>
> If the guilt has not been expiated by death, they will suffer various evils, through fire and water, theft and robbery, disease and illness, loss of property and ill repute, to compensate for any unlawful violation of justice. Further, those who unlawfully kill others will in turn have their weapons and arms turned on themselves. They will kill each other. (*Ganying pian*; Suzuki and Carus, *Treatise*, 64)

Stories supplemented to the text invoke the threat of the underworld prisons, a series of ten judicial courts of the otherworld where sinners are punished according to their crimes and then released for an appropriate rebirth. The so-called ten courts of hell go back to Buddhist visions of the afterlife; they were first integrated into Daoism in the middle ages, and have been a part of popular religion since the Song. Drawn by the deeds of his life, the dead person walks down a narrow pathway into the otherworld, soon arriving in a ghost-city with shops, hotels, and restaurants. In the distance, the Gate of Ghosts comes into view, splendid and protected by guards. Behind the gate is the otherwordly residence of the local city god, who keeps the records for the Department of Destiny. As the descendants of the deceased report the death to the city god above, so this underworld office retrieves his files and passes them on to the first court of hell, believed to lie beneath the ocean or deep inside a sacred mountain.

About three days after death, the sinner is examined by this first court, the so-called Terrace of Sins. He faces a judge who looks like a traditional Confucian official, sits behind a high dais, and is assisted by two half-human bailiffs named Horseface and Cowhead. He or she is stripped of any clothing and has to walk before the mirror of destiny, which will show every evil committed—in some cases they may also have to step on a set of scales to have their deeds weighed. The first judge then decides to which hells the sinner will be committed and for how long a period.

The following hells, then, are arranged in a circle, set up exactly like the first, with a judge and bailiffs on duty, but each specializing in different sins and punishments. The second hell, for example, is the prison of hunger and thirst, where people are thrown into boiling water, put into iron clothes, or stretched on racks. It punishes the sins of seduction, stealing, bodily harm, and marrying for gain. The third hell consists of a salt desert, where people are tied up and chained, have their faces cut with knives, and their bodies squeezed with pinchers. Sins punished here include treason, lack of gratitude, and the failure to do one's duty toward one's elders, the state, or at work.

After more of the same in the fifth and sixth hells, a break comes with the seventh, called the Terrace of Repentance. Here the sinner has a last chance to look back home and see the damage he or she has done to family, friends, and business partners. The belief is that however long the punishments may seem to the sinners in hell the process actually takes seven earthly days per hell, so that the deceased has the last home contact after seven weeks, or forty-nine days. At this time, the descendants celebrate a major rite, offering prayers and spirit money for the sake of the deceased.

After this, the dead person may be incarcerated in the eighth and ninth hells to be punished more extensively for sins not yet expiated. Eventually he or she arrives in the last hell, the Palace of Rebirth, where bridges lead to the five forms of rebirth—gods, humans, animals, hungry ghosts, and hell-dwellers—and where all past memories are cleansed. People are equipped with new skins and sent back to try again—or, if atonement and prayers were sufficient, promoted to attain residence in heaven. All this does not affect their powers as ancestral spirits, which are considered a separate aspect of an individual's spirit-being.

Morality books place a heavy emphasis on the hells, describing them in torturous detail and often illustrating them with graphic depictions.

There are numerous texts of this type, channeled by various gods, and inspiring people to act more conscientiously and compassionately in the world. They are still popular today, sometimes consisting of short pamphlets, sometimes forming large tomes with detailed descriptions of heaven and hell and the various deeds that get one there. They are, moreover, often linked with the practice of keeping a "ledger of merit and demerit" (*gongguo ge*), in which practitioners record their deeds on a daily basis, assigning plus or minus points to each to see where they stand in the scheme of cosmic retribution.

Another type of planchette-transmitted literature is found in instructions for martial arts and gymnastic practices, such as Taiji quan. A number of forms and groups originated with such revelations, often inspired by Lü Dongbin. However, some are also inspired by the popular immortal Zhang Sanfeng, a legendary master of the early Ming dynasty. He wandered around famous mountains and eventually settled on Mount Wudang where he inspired the growth of a major school of Daoist martial arts. While his historical circumstances are shrouded in mystery, his spiritual autobiography was transmitted through spirit-writing and is found in the *Zhang Sanfeng quanji* (Complete Collection of Zhang Sanfeng), edited by Li Xiyue (1806–1856).

Aside from spirit-writing, Daoist materials spread among the population through folk novels. They reflect the general tendency of the time to idolize martial arts and fictionalize the lives and deeds of inspiring heroes. Daoist folk novels typically focus on some divine figure and recount his or her adventures, progress in attaining immortality, and efforts for the salvation and benefit of humanity.

Two are best known (and translated), the first being "Creation of the Gods" (*Fengshen yanyi*), by Xu Zhonglin (d. 1566) or Lu Xixing (ca. 1520–1601), a mythological account of the fight of the Zhou against the last tyrant of the Shang. During the battle developments on earth are paralleled by activities in the heavens, with Daoist gods appearing variously to support the fight of the righteous and battle vigorously with all the martial means at their disposal. The other novel is "Seven Daoist Masters" (*Qizhen shizhuan*) written by an anonymous author around the year 1500. It retells the story of Wang Chongyang and the Seven Perfected of Complete Perfection, including their various adventures, complete with magical powers and supernatural connections.

Further Readings

Boltz, Judith M. 1986. "In Homage to T'ien-fei." *Journal of the American Oriental Society* 106: 211–52.

Berling, Judith. 1998. "Taoism in Ming Culture." In *The Cambridge History of China*, vol. 8, pt. 2, edited by F. W. Mote and D. Twitchett, 953–86. Cambridge: Cambridge University Press.

Dean, Kenneth. 1998. *Lord of the Three in One: The Spread of a Cult in Southeast China*. Princeton: Princeton University Press.

DeBruyn, Pierre-Henry. 2000. "Daoism in the Ming (1368-1644)." In *Daoism Handbook*, edited by Livia Kohn, 594-622. Leiden: E.Brill.

Esposito, Monica. 2000. "Daoism in the Qing (1644-1911)." In *Daoism Handbook*, edited by Livia Kohn, 623-58. Leiden: E.Brill.

Eberhard, Wolfram. 1967. *Guilt and Sin in Traditional China*. Berkeley: University of California Press.

Katz, Paul. 1999. "Morality Books and Taiwanese Identity." *Journal of Chinese Religions* 27: 69–92.

Kohn, Livia. 1996. "The Taoist Adoption of the City God." *Ming Qing Yanjiu* 5: 68–106.

Little, Stephen, and Shawn Eichman. 2000. *Daoism and the Arts of China*. Berkeley: University of California Press.

Original Sources in Translation

Kleeman, Terry F. 1994. *A God's Own Tale: The Book of Transformations of Wen-chang, the Divine Lord of Zitong*. Albany: State University of New York Press.

Gu Zhizhong. 1992. *Creation of the Gods*. 2 vols. Beijing: New World Press.

Lu Kuan-yü. 1970. *Taoist Yoga: Alchemy and Immortality*. London: Rider.

Seaman, Gary. 1987. *Journey to the North*. Berkeley: University of California Press.

Suzuki, D. T., and Paul Carus. 1973 [1906]. *Treatise on Response and Retribution*. LaSalle, Ill.: Open Court Publishing.

Wilhelm, Richard. 1962 [1929]. *The Secret of the Golden Flower*. New York: Harcourt, Brace and World.

Wong, Eva. 1990. *Seven Taoist Masters*. Boston: Shambhala.

CHAPTER ELEVEN

DAOISM TODAY

Daoism in China, as much as all other forms of religion there, has suffered greatly in recent years due to civil wars and communist suppression. Denounced as part of a debilitating and destructive traditional culture, it lost ground in the early twentieth century. After the end of World War II, it rebounded in Taiwan and other Chinese communities, but was completely outlawed in mainland China. Numerous lineages were disrupted, organizations disbanded, temples and statues desecrated, and texts and ritual knowledge destroyed. Only since the 1980s has it regained some of its former status, but it is still nowhere near the pervasive religious institution it once was.

Today, Daoism is alive in the two major schools of the Celestial Masters and Complete Perfection. The Celestial Masters school, a lay organization whose methods are transmitted from father to son, is located predominantly in Taiwan (also the home of the current 65th Celestial Master). It focuses on rituals of cosmic harmony, purification, healing, and burial. Two major types of Daoists are involved in the school, known as red-head and black-head because they wear red kerchiefs and black headdress, respectively.

Red-head Daoists tend to be more shamanistic and popular, using magical implements such as the buffalo horn and learning their rites by word of mouth. Their main activities involve ceremonies to grant protection for residences, pregnancies, children, and good fortune, as well as exorcisms to dispel evil spirits, droughts, dangers, and diseases. Black-head Daoists, who tend to be rather disdainful of their "red" colleagues, are more scripturally oriented, and work with written liturgies and use elaborate implements such as formal vestments, sacred staffs, and often an entire orchestra of music. They perform funerary and requiem services for the dead and conduct the festival of renewal for the living.

The Complete Perfection school is still monastic but now much smaller than it used to be. It is dominated by the Longmen (Dragon Gate) branch, with its headquarters in the Baiyun guan (White Cloud Monastery) in Beijing. Its members practice daily rituals together with individual cultivation along the lines of inner alchemy. Daoist forms of cultivation, moreover, have taken on a life of their own and grown outside of institutional frameworks, blossoming in the so-called Qigong movement, a popular adaptation of longevity and Daoist health practices.

For several decades now, aspects of Daoism have also been transmitted to the West. Here they are present predominantly in forms of traditional Chinese self-help, including various healing and longevity techniques. Also increasingly popular is the art of fengshui, the way of siting houses, rooms, and furniture to ensure maximum good fortune, which is not Daoist *per se* but, like longevity techniques, forms an essential part of Daoist practice. In addition, there are a number of ritual masters in the West, and particularly in the United States, who have established community temples that offer prayer services, purifications, and exorcisms to an increasingly international community of followers. Both the Celestial Masters and Complete Perfection forms of Daoism are represented, often carried by masters of rather obscure lineages who create new forms of the religion, adapting to its new cultural environment.

Recent History

For the past two centuries, China has been in a prolonged state of civil unrest and difficulty, interrupted by only short periods of stability and peace. The period began with the intensified activities of Western powers eager to establish more footholds in East Asia, who moved in and annexed or forcefully leased parts of China, notably sea ports along the eastern and southern coastline. By the 1840s, after the Opium War (1839–1842), there were Germans in Qingdao (Shandong), French and British in Shanghai, British in Canton (Guangdong) and Hong Kong, Portuguese in Macao, and a number of smaller protectorates along the coast. For the Chinese this led to loss of status and often unemployment as well as a general atmosphere of insecurity.

This situation resulted in the growth of millenarian movements, some of which rose in rebellion. The most serious of these was the Taiping Rebellion of 1850, led by a Chinese peasant who believed himself to be Jesus's younger brother with a destiny to bring China into the new golden age. It lasted for fourteen years, affected fifteen provinces, and created a death toll of thirty million in a population of about 400 million. Another uprising was the so-called Boxer Rebellion in 1900, when groups of martial arts practitioners protested against the enforced Westernization of their country and marched on Beijing.

By this time the imperial Manchu government of the Qing dynasty was beleaguered by all sides. Chinese intellectuals were increasingly being educated in Japan, which had modernized since 1868, and they demanded new forms of government and a more efficient administration — the people in power knew less of Confucian classics and more about modern technology and management. In 1911, a major revolution broke out, which led to the founding of the Republic of China on 1 January 1912. It was led by the physician and dedicated democrat Sun Yatsen (1866–1925).

However, the unrest was far from over — many local warlords took advantage of the weakness of the new government and foreign powers vied for more profits. After Russia became communist in 1917 it too sent emissaries into China, and soon the Chinese Communist Party was founded and became a force to be reckoned with. In the meantime, the Japanese had their own imperial agenda, occupying Korea and Manchuria and, in 1937, launching a major invasion of China. This involved the country in World War II, which ended in East Asia with the dropping of nuclear bombs on Hiroshima and Nagasaki in August 1945. In China, this gave rise to yet another round of civil war, in which the Communists (CCP), under the leadership of Mao Zedong (1893–1976), battled the Republicans (Kuomintang), led by Chiang Kaishek (1888–1975). It ended in 1949 with the flight of the Republicans to Taiwan and the establishment of the People's Republic of China.

Throughout this period religion had a difficult time. The monastic life was attacked as a form of escape from a country that badly needed workers and soldiers, while popular practices were condemned as superstitious and wasteful. Traditional myths and stories were being debunked, gods toppled, and organizations declined. On the other hand, spirit-writing, and longevity and martial practices continued to flourish, if on a smaller level and often in secrecy.

Communism exacerbated the situation. Its official doctrine followed Karl Marx in seeing religion as an opiate for the people, necessary only while their living conditions were horrendous, which would naturally evaporate once the true realm of freedom under the dictatorship of the proletariat had been realized.

Mao Zedong, however, had no desire to wait for this natural demise of religion, and speeded it along in various ways. Practically every campaign in the country in one way or another affected religion negatively, until very little of the old traditions was left. In 1952, private holdings of land were outlawed and all was collectivized into large communes. Religious organizations, both monastic and secular, were dissolved, monks and nuns returned to the laity, and temples made into schools, assembly halls, garrisons, or storage facilities. In 1958, during the Great Leap Forward, every commune was encouraged to have its own steel mill, and all metal was confiscated to be used for industrial progress; many metal statues and religious artifacts found their way into the furnaces.

Finally, during the Cultural Revolution (1966–1976), young people (the so-called Red Guards) were encouraged to do away with all remnants of traditional and Western culture. Even stone artifacts and many remaining temple buildings were destroyed, desecrated, and defaced. This only ended with the death of Mao Zedong in 1976 and the new leadership of Deng Xiaoping, who in 1978 began the Four Modernizations, opened the country economically and politically, and paved the way for the massive development that has occurred since then. This, too, affected religion, and since 1980 religious organizations and practices, as well as the academic study of religion, have undergone a revival. Only recently another obstacle has arisen with the persecution of the newly grown Falun dafa movement, a Buddho-Daoist synthesis of enlightenment beliefs and Qigong practices. At the same time, traditional religions have continued to flourish in Taiwan and Hong Kong (as well as in Singapore and overseas), undergoing modernizations and adaptations in accordance with the needs of the various communities.

Contemporary Ritual

Medieval Daoist ritual, as discussed earlier, was dominated by the rite of purgation (*zhai*). This was often an extended festival that included the various elements of traditional ancestor worship, court ceremonies, and Daoist liturgies, and involved both the presentation of written memorials and a feast of communal consumption. In the Song dynasty a shift occurred toward the *jiao*-offering, which also included the full range of ritual activities and was celebrated at major occasions such as gods' birthdays and temple festivals. It has since developed into an elaborate event that can last from three to seven days and is seen as central to the renewal of cosmic energies. The Daoist *jiao* today is ideally celebrated once in every sixty-year cycle, and is held jointly by various villages or city wards, involving numerous citizens and attracting much outside attention and support.

The celebration typically begins with a one-month purification period, during which participants are to practice abstinence and purity, including mental cleansing by repenting sins and thinking of the gods. Next the sacred space or altar (*tan*) is prepared, usually a large, multi-level platform in the temple, and the official deities of the temple are temporarily moved from their central thrones. Then, in a rite of formal invitation, the guests of the ceremony are summoned — gods, people, and ancestors. Gods include Daoist celestials (Three Purities, Northern Dipper), popular deities (Guandi, Mazu, Guanyin), and celestial administrators. The people are the members of the community and their relatives, visitors, and passers-by. Ancestors include ghosts and various kinds of spirits, all called together to share the merit and receive the blessings of Dao.

Each group of participants is visualized by the officiating priest as they are called upon and asked to take their seats. The Daoist gods are placed to the north, so they can face south as did the emperor of old. Popular deities are placed to the south; heavenly bureaucrats of yang quality, administering the living, earth, and dragon spirits, are in the east; those of yin quality, ruling the dead, water, and tiger spirits, are in the west. People occupy the southeast, and the various other types of spirits are in the remaining corners.

Three major types of rites are performed. Secret ceremonies are held behind locked doors in the temple to establish a close relationship between humanity and the gods. Semi-public rites of merit and repentance include the reading of relevant texts and the offering of prayers for the forgiveness of sins, healing of diseases, and mending of social disharmonies. Fully public rites are highly dramatic and include the enactment of Daoist myths of creation and renewal. The ritual ends with a large banquet, joined by everyone—friends and foes alike—to celebrate the successful cosmic invigoration of the community.

The other major form of Daoist ritual is a requiem service for the dead. It, too, goes back to the Song dynasty, when funerary rites (*liandu*) and rites of deliverance of the dead or universal salvation (*pudu*) first became part of the Daoist repertoire. It is similarly held in a specially arranged altar area, and typically consists of a two-day sequence of ceremonies. It begins when an announcement is sent to all the major gods ordering them, in a formal mandate, to come and attend the event.

Its central rite is the delivery of the writ of pardon, a written statement of forgiveness of sins and deliverance from all punishments which is sent to the underworld to be officially executed. It is enhanced by three talismans called down from the otherworld to destroy hell, rescue souls, and secure the protection of nine celestial dragons. It is accompanied by a file of rebirth in Heaven that will ensure complete freedom from death. The delivery of the writ of pardon involves the ritual descent of the priest or his divine messenger into the underworld, which is enacted with high drama and skillful acrobatics to the accompaniment of vibrant ritual music.

Other parts of the requiem service involve the chanting of a litany to the Rulers of Darkness, the ten kings of hell. Aided by ten talismans and geared to dispel dangers and diseases, this rite also supports growth, good fortune, and the rebirth of the dead. Further ceremonies in the sequence are the Untying the Knots, which includes the delivery of another mandate for the liberation of souls, and the rite of Filling the Treasury, which ensures that all debts to the celestial treasury have been paid and that the loan of life has been cleared.

Both of these major forms of Daoist ritual, as well as their lesser counterparts, are still actively undertaken in Taiwan, Hong Kong and overseas Chinese communities, and are undergoing a mounting revival on the mainland. They continue to develop in new forms and patterns as the religion grows with the changing times.

Qigong and Taiji quan

Qigong (Ch'i-kung) literally means "energy exercises" and indicates a complex system of meditations and breath control, diets, gymnastics and other longevity techniques (both medical and Daoist), as well as martial arts and healing by the laying-on of hands. As an integrated system it developed in the twentieth century on the basis on inner alchemy—the term was coined in the 1950s—and is used today to heal diseases, increase vitality, aid concentration, and attain supernatural powers. Qigong practices can be divided into two major groups: martial and healing. They involve techniques of both movement and stillness, and can be undertaken for oneself or on behalf of others.

A typical Qigong sequence, like all traditional forms of Daoist meditation, begins with concentration. This is achieved in a standing or seated meditation, during which the practitioners are encouraged to remain unmoving, keep their eyes closed, and let their mind be empty and without thought. A set of breathing exercises follows, sometimes associated with six regulatory sounds (*liuzi jue*) that match and strengthen the inner organs. Following this, practitioners are guided towards a more open awareness, as in insight meditation, during which outer *qi* is guided deep into the lungs and abdomen, while the inner *qi* is felt to increase and strengthen.

There are also sets of exercises traditionally classified as *daoyin* or gymnastics. They consist of stretches and slow, concentrated movements of certain parts of the body, or again entire sequences of movements that involve rotations, bends, twists, and kicks. In all cases, it is important to have an insightful awareness of the *qi*, and to think of it as flowing along with one's intention, breath, and body movements. Often Qigong forms are based on the imitation of certain animals, and carry their names: the Crane Pattern, the Five Animals Pattern, the Snake and Tortoise Pattern, and so on. Then again, they also follow the structure of the cosmos, as for example in the well-known forms of the Five Phases or the Eight-Trigrams. The goal of the practice is to make the *qi* flow smoothly and consciously through the meridians, and thereby secure healing of diseases and an increase in overall vitality. Practitioners universally state that after only a few months of practice they can both feel and see the *qi* as it courses through their meridians and issues from themselves and from others.

Once they have gained a good reserve of *qi* and are strong in their practice, adepts can also use it to engage in advanced, martial training, or to project it into someone else for healing. The latter is known as "external *qi* healing." The practitioner mentally projects his or her inner *qi* outward while extending a hand or foot in the appropriate direction. Recipients often feel a warm, tingling sensation, which helps them get well but can also render them completely limp, so that they cannot stand up to the force of the Qigong master. Thus we encounter impressive performances of a single, often slender master pushing over a line of five or more powerful men with a tiny movement of his hand. In addition, mastery over one's *qi* can also lead to supernatural powers, such as the ability to see through walls, read other people's thoughts, bend metal objects, or secure good fortune.

Qigong integrates ancient longevity techniques and medieval meditation—thus the frequently heard claim that it goes back thousands of years—with Daoist inner alchemy and training in martial arts. It is similar to Taiji quan in the meditative state achieved and in the slow, deliberate body movements used. However, while Qigong is used very specifically to heal certain ailments in the body and is geared toward an empowerment of the individual, Taiji quan aims at the creation of a sense of inner peace and cosmic harmony. As a Qing-dynasty document describes it:

> Taiji is round [like Heaven]. Regardless of whether inner or outer, up or down, left or right, it never leaves this roundness. Taiji is square [like the Earth]. Regardless of whether inner or outer, up or down, it never leaves this squareness. In and out with roundness; advance and retreat with squareness. From squareness to roundness, and back and forth. Squareness is for opening and expanding; roundness is for tightening and contracting. The square and the round are the highest normative standard. Can anything fall outside it? In this way one achieves complete freedom of movement. Higher and deeper, subtler and even more subtle, visible and invisible, brighter and brighter, it goes on forever without end. (Wile, *Tai-chi Classics*, 76)

Taiji quan, therefore, provides an overall coordination of body, breath, and thought, and focuses on soft, round body movements. It helps the individual to find a sense of oneness with the greater universe rather than the attainment of personal, martial, or supernatural powers. It also usually involves a long set of movements, often called by special names such as "grasping the bird's tail," "single whip," "playing the lute," and "embrace tiger, return to mountain." Not only cosmic, however, it also has beneficial health effects, especially on blood pressure, muscle coordination, and the sense of balance, and is very helpful to the elderly.

The Qigong Movement

Unlike the more meditative Taiji quan which goes back several centuries, Qigong first arose in the early twentieth century. A man named Jiang Weiqiao (or Master Yinshi, 1872–1955), in a desperate effort to heal himself of tuberculosis, began to follow the regimen outlined in an inner-alchemical text, practicing meditation, breathing, and slow movements. Soon he began to feel the *qi* move within and experienced it flowing along the spine and torso in the so-called microcosmic orbit. Eventually he became very proficient at the practice and achieved complete recovery.

Later he compiled a treatise on it entitled *Yinshizi jingzuo fa* (Quiet Sitting with Master Yinshi, dat. 1914), describing his techniques in modern biomedical terms rather than those of traditional Daoist cosmology. For example, instead of using the traditional expression "cinnabar field" for the central area of *qi* accumulation, he describes it with the term Center of Gravity (*zhongxin*), and explains the need to keep it solid and strong with modern physics, which teaches that all natural objects and man-made buildings must be well-centered or they will collapse.

Similarly he reinterprets the microcosmic orbit and flow of *qi* around the body by understanding the body in terms of Western natural science. To him, the body is not a replica of the cosmos, energized by the patterns of yin and yang, but rather an integrated physical mechanism that works by continuously circulating substances, such as breath and blood, thereby integrating fresh materials and discarding the old and waste. Moreover, the major vehicle of energy circulation to him is not the *qi* but the blood, which pulsates around the body in accordance with the rhythm of the respiration. This, again in accordance with Western scientific preference, can be measured and quantified: one revolution of the blood, he says, takes 24 seconds, there are 3,600 revolutions in one full day, during which time one breathes more than 20,000 times and inhales about 95 gallons of air (Jiang, *Yinshizi jingzuo fa*, 67–68).

With Jiang Weiqiao's work the stage was set both for Qigong to become focused on healing, and its interpretation in terms of Western biomedicine. Others followed his example, and in the 1950s the first Qigong clinics were opened. Despite the Cultural Revolution, during which Qigong was condemned, there was further experimentation, and different masters began to create new systems and regimens.

In the 1980s, Qigong exploded into a major boom that also spilled over into the West. Innumerable new patterns were created, clinics were founded, books were published, and millions of people began to practice daily. The tendency was to describe Qigong strictly as a medical technique and completely exclude all religious and spiritual connotations. *Qi* itself was defined as an electro-magnetic force; machines were built that could measure *qi* as transmitted by a master and even emit *qi* themselves for automatic healing. The overall goal was bodily health, and the Chinese government supported it because it kept insurance costs down and the populace working. A negative side-effect of this medicalization of Qigong was the utter helplessness of masters and officials when a certain number of people, inspired by the Crane Pattern to let themselves go into a state of automatic movements, were found stuck in the trance, unable to come out. Many were hospitalized and remained in an altered state over prolonged periods. The government discouraged practice of the Crane Pattern.

In the 1990s, the thrust of the Qigong movement changed to recover some of the lost spiritual dimension, but soon went overboard toward the other extreme. Masters began to advertise methods that would lead to marvelous supernatural powers: just imagine you could read your partner's thoughts, look through the person in front of you at his exam paper, magically transport yourself to the beach, or lift heavy objects with no effort at all! It was a great popular success, and many different forms appeared in various parts of the county.

In 1992, a new form of this kind of Qigong based on Buddhist doctrines arose under the name of Falun gong or Falun dafa, "Exercises of the Dharma Wheel." Its founder, Li Hongzhi, claimed to be the reincarnation of a bodhisattva and promised practitioners complete recovery from all illnesses, supernatural powers, and the attainment of cosmic enlightenment. To attain this they first had to have the right karma that would bring them to him. Then he would install a *falun* or dharma wheel in their lower cinnabar field to allow them to undertake advanced practices. This installation is central to the process of Falun dafa; it can be done either through a representative, a book, or a video, but ideally through Li himself, in person. As he says in a lecture:

> We believe in predestined relationship. I can do such a thing for everyone sitting here. Right now we have only more than two thousand people. I can also do it for several thousand or more people, even over ten thousand people. That is to say, you do not need to practice at a low level. Upon purifying your bodies, and moving you up, I will install a complete cultivation practice system in your body. Right away you will practice cultivation at high levels. It will be done, however, only for practitioners who come to genuinely practice cultivation; your simply sitting here does not mean that your are a practitioner. . . . Here we talk about holistically adjusting practitioners' bodies to enable you to practice cultivation. With an ill body you cannot develop cultivation energy at all. Therefore, you should not come to me for curing illnesses, and neither will I do such a thing. The primary purpose of my coming to the public is to guide people to high levels, genuinely guiding people to high levels. (Li, *Zhuan Falun*, 7–8)

The practice is therefore not aimed at healing, although physical health will be an inevitable byproduct. It demands a serious commitment by the practitioner, expressed in the daily practice of five exercises and three moral virtues. The exercises involve a set of arm stretches, a standing meditation, an up-and-down movement of the arms, a guiding of *qi* throughout the body by passing one's hands over it, and a sitting meditation that has to be performed in the full lotus posture. Every so often, hands are circulated over the lower abdomen, symbolizing the movement of the dharma wheel. If done properly, the exercises take about two hours to perform.

Even more important, however, are the three moral virtues *zhen, shan, ren* — truth, goodness, forbearance — which entail being honest in all one's dealings, exerting kindness toward all beings, and not retaliating against any wrongs. Working on these virtues, so the teaching claims, will make practitioners better people, and only if they become better people can the five exercises open up their inner powers and lead them to cosmic enlightenment. This moral dimension of Falun dafa distinguishes it profoundly from all other forms of Qigong, even those that set spiritual goals. It has attracted large numbers of followers, both in China and abroad, and has a high success rate in creating friendlier people, more harmonious social environments, and greater health and vitality.

It has, however, also led to the veneration of Li Hongzhi (who now resides in the United States) by hundreds of thousands of people, which the Chinese government has come to perceive as a threat to inner security and political stability. As a result, since the summer of 1999 Falun dafa has been outlawed and its followers persecuted, often violently and with torture. This is not limited to Falun dafa; all forms of Qigong have become suspect in China, making spiritual activities once again the victim of politics and creating an atmosphere of distrust and fear among Daoist and other religious followers.

Daoism in the United States

The first awareness Americans had of Daoism was philosophically through translations of the *Daode jing*, which began to appear around the year 1900. To many, the text presented an alternative way of looking at the world, a celebration of naturalness and ease as opposed to the harsh realities of technology and competition. It became popular first among fringe groups, but the text grew increasingly mainstream and today is one of the most frequently published works in the country. Daoist practice made its debut in the 1950s with the arrival of Taiji quan. It was first taught mainly to immigrants but, like Zen and meditation, soon became popular within the growing counterculture of the sixties. More organized Daoist lineages and ritual teachings began to appear in the 1980s, and have been growing ever since.

Today we can distinguish three different forms of Daoism in the United States, serving both immigrants and Westerners: ritual lineages, based on original Chinese traditions of the Celestial Masters; self-cultivation schools, both based on established Quanzhen lines and of rather obscure background, practiced in temples and centers; and followers of various related practices of self-improvement—medical, martial, or environmental—usually trained by Chinese masters. This pattern reflects and continues the traditional division of Daoism, apparent since the middle ages, into organized groups, self-cultivation societies, and practitioners of spiritual and longevity techniques.

Among ritual lineages, there is first Hsuan Yuan, originally from Tai-wan, who runs the American Buddhist and Taoist Association (ABTA) in New York City. This is basically a local temple which offers purification ceremonies, prayers, and community festivals. Then there is Liu Ming, originally Charles Belyea, who was adopted into a Daoist family lineage in Taiwan and represents a form of Celestial Masters Daoism in his Or-thodox Daoism of America (ODA), located in Santa Cruz. His commu-nity consists mostly of Westerners and its practices include the study of texts, such as the *Daode jing*, ritual activities along the lines of the Celes-tial Masters, and self-cultivation following traditional meditation and inner alchemy. To him,

> the important part of Daoist education is "*qi* transference" — the traditional initiatory rituals play an important role in de-claring certain intentions, but these intentions must be substan-tiated by conduct and study. The rituals, practice, and study are all one in Daoism. In the end it is the "digestion" of the text transmission that counts. (*Frost Bell*, Summer 2000, 14)

Another, similar ritual temple, also based on a Daoist family lineage, is run by S. K. Lew in Los Angeles, and still another flourishing community has congregated around the Taoist Center in Washington, D.C.

Self-cultivation schools are groups that place much less emphasis on rit-ual practice and do not serve as community centers. Their main focus is the practice of longevity techniques, Qigong, and inner alchemy, with the goal of finding personal realization. They can be divided into those based on established Complete Perfection lineages and those originating from an individual master who created his own system after studying with various teachers.

There are three major institutions of Complete Perfection background: The Fung Loy Kok Temple in Denver is a branch of a Hong Kong or-ganization, whose most prominent and prolific member is Eva Wong. The Xuanji guan (Temple of the Mysterious Pivot) and Taoist Studies Institute in Seattle are run by Harrison Moretz, offering training in a va-riety of practices, including Taiji quan and Qigong. Finally, the Center for Traditional Taoist Studies, originally called the New England Center of Tao, near Boston, was founded by Alexander Anatole. It holds classes in Daoist philosophy and provides training in meditations and Chinese health techniques.

Three other self-cultivation schools are run by individually trained masters. The best-known among them is Mantak Chia, originally of Thailand, who was trained in Hong Kong, Singapore, and Thailand, and subsequently founded of the Healing Tao Center in upstate New York. The Center offers training in complex and advanced systems of inner alchemy. He states the goals of his practice as follows:

> The word *dao* means *the* way, the way of nature and the universe, or the path of natural reality. It also refers to a way in which we can open our minds to learn more about the world, our spiritual paths, and ourselves.
>
> Daoism is a practice of body, mind, and spirit, not just a philosophy of mind. When we have the true sense of the Dao, of the real knowledge and wisdom, we will be able to make the right decisions in our lives. Daoism involves many practical disciplines that can restore our lost youth, energy, and virtues while awakening our deepest spiritual potentials. Daoists regard these practices as a technology that can help us learn universal truths if we are willing to open our minds.
>
> The ancient masters recognized that these potentials can include the possibility of attaining conscious freedom in the after-death state. Through specific exercises, one can avoid suffering the experience of death by expanding the consciousness beyond the physical body before its demise. This makes it possible to determine one's future existence before leaving this life. (Chia and Chia, *Awaken Healing Light*, 1)

Here the goal of Daoist practice is the spiritual expansion of consciousness, not only for leading a better life in the here and now but also to attain immortality upon death. It is a highly personal goal, undertaken with others insofar as we are all spiritually interdependent, but ultimately an individual effort, guided by the master and learned in workshops.

Another prominent Daoist master in the United States who presents a similar program is Ni Hua-ching. Working out of southern California, he presents an extensive philosophy of inner alchemy and detailed methods for the attainment of immortality in numerous books and in workshops held at the Shrine of the Eternal Breath of Tao in Malibu, and the College of Tao in Prado (New Mexico).

In addition, there is an American-run organization that supports Daoist practice both in China and the West, known as the Taoist Restoration Society. Centered in Colorado and led by Brock Silvers, it organizes projects to repair and restore temples on Daoist mountains in China, is concerned about religious freedom of Daoists, and supplies Westerners with guidance for practice and the material implements necessary for Daoist practice.

Beyond these, there are numerous masters of related techniques, such as Taiji quan, Qigong, *daoyin* gymnastics, *anmo* massage, Chinese medicine, martial arts, and fengshui, who claim a more or less close relationship with Daoism and offer ways to self-cultivation and perfection along Daoist lines. Recently fengshui (lit. "wind and water") has become the most popular of these, providing ways to create the most harmonious flow of *qi* and thus the best possible fortune through the siting of houses, altars, and furniture. Fengshui is essential to all forms of Daoist practice, both ritual and cultivation, but it is also part of mainstream Chinese culture and is practiced in popular religion and business for the creation of better luck.

In the United States, the practice of fengshui tends to focus on interior design, teaching people to avoid anything that creates either rushing *qi* (*shaqi*), which takes good fortune away, or *qi* blockages (*siqi*), which obstruct its arrival. Long corridors, staircases facing the door, and windows directly across from doors, for example, are venues of rushing energy, whereas clutter, dirty windows, dark corners, and blocked drain pipes are causes of obstruction. Obstructions are cleared by cleaning and creating more light (e.g., with mirrors), while rushing *qi* is slowed down by adding plants, curtains, or hanging objects (e.g., a crystal). Generally balance is the ideal, and all colors of the five phases and the various aspects of yin and yang (heavy and light, dark and bright, soft and hard) should be represented in every room.

A further common method of analysis is to conceptually divide a living space into eight corners, based on the eight trigrams of the *Yijing*, the so-called *bagua*. To determine the eight corners, one stands in the front door and looks around the house or apartment in a clockwise direction (to the left), beginning with the central area of the wall that contains the front door. The corners then are: career, wisdom, health, wealth, fame, marriage, children, and helpful people. In other words, in any living space, the corner to the far right when standing in the front door or entrance area will be the "marriage corner," the one in the far left will be the

202 / Daoism and Chinese Culture

"wealth corner," and so on. Each corner should be treated with care, kept free of clutter, and contain a suitable positive item such as a bowl of coins in the money corner, a wedding picture or flowers in the marriage corner, etc. This arrangement, so the masters assure us, will create a harmonious flow of *qi* and help with the overall health and good fortune of all inhabitants of the space.

Like fengshui, the various practices associated with Daoism in the United States today tend to focus on personal self-help, on increasing benefits and well-being for their followers. There is little concern with supernatural powers, and the number of seriously dedicated practitioners of immortality is small. While only a few groups can be traced to established lineages or historically known schools of Daoism, the overall scene of the religion in China today and also in the United States is very much like what it has been all along: Daoists organizing themselves in ritual associations, self-cultivation groups, or in lineages of physical cultivation. Again, as was the case in traditional China, so today in China and the United States many people use Daoist methods in their own personal way and to their own concrete advantage, matched by a few full-time practitioners who specialize in certain aspects and follow established traditions but often also combine various teachings to create new forms of worldview and practice. Daoism in its own unique way is very much alive and continues to unfold, ever open to the processes of religious growth and transformation.

Further Readings

Cohen, Kenneth S. 1997. *The Way of Qigong: The Art and Science of Chinese Energy Healing*. New York: Ballantine.

Hardy, Julia. 1998. "Influential Western Interpretations of the *Tao-te-ching*." In *Lao-tzu and the Tao-te-ching*, edited by Livia Kohn and Michael LaFargue, 165–88. Albany: State University of New York Press.

Lagerwey, John. 1987. *Taoist Ritual in Chinese Society and History*. New York: Macmillan.

Saso, Michael. 1972. *Taoism and the Rite of Cosmic Renewal*. Seattle: Washington University Press.

Spear, William. 1995. *Feng Shui Made Easy*. San Francisco: Harper & Row.

Towler, Solala. 1996. *A Gathering of Cranes: Bringing the Tao to the West*. Eugene, Oreg: Abode of the Eternal Tao.

Original Sources in Translation

Cleary, Thomas. 1997. *Opening the Dragon Gate: The Making of a Modern Taoist Wizard*. By Chen Kaiguo and Zheng Shunchao. Tokyo: Tuttle.

Dean, Kenneth. 1996. "Daoist Ritual in Contemporary Southeast China." In *Religions of China in Practice*, edited by Donald S. Lopez, Jr., 306–26. Princeton: Princeton University Press.

Li, Hongzhi. 1999. *Zhuan Falun*. Taipei: Universe Publishing Company.

Lu, Kuan-yü. 1964. *The Secrets of Chinese Meditation*. London: Rider. Chs. 5–6.

Wile, Douglas. 1996. *Lost T'ai-chi Classics from the Late Ch'ing Dynasty*. Albany: State University of New York Press.

Original Sources

Belyea, Charles, and Steven Tainer. 1991. *Dragon's Play: A New Taoist Transmission of the Complete Experience of Human Life*. Berkeley: Great Circle Lifeworks.

Chia, Mantak, and Maneewan Chia. 1993. *Awaken Healing Light of the Tao*. Huntington, NY: Healing Tao Books.

Ni, Hua-ching. 1992. *Internal Alchemy: The Natural Way to Immortality*. Santa Monica: College of Tao and Traditional Chinese Healing

Silvers, Brock. 2001. *A Taoist Manual: An Illustrated Guide to Traditional Taoist Practice*. Boulder, Col.: Sacred Mountain Press.

DAOISM IN OTHER EAST ASIAN COUNTRIES

Although primarily a Chinese religion and intricately tied in with Chinese culture, Daoism has been transmitted to other East Asian countries at several points in its history—both as part of Chinese culture carried by emigrants and through adoption by non-Chinese. The first such export occurred in the Tang dynasty, the heyday of Chinese culture and also of Daoism, when the Chinese empire extended throughout Central and East Asia. It affected mainly Korea and Japan, and probably also Vietnam, which adopted many features of Chinese culture and also of Daoism, but about which historically detailed information is currently scarce. In Korea and Japan, Daoism—just as Buddhism which was transmitted at the same time—was confronted with a full set of indigenous beliefs and practices. Known as shamanism in Korea and as Shintô in Japan, these beliefs focused to a large extent on nature worship and involved shamanic and spiritistic forms of interaction with the divine. They had their own origin myths, sacred places, gods, and rituals, and were also intimately linked with the political system of the country; the ruler was typically a ritual figure, surrounded by shamanic-type helpers.

With the arrival of Chinese culture, the government structures became more complex, and the literary and philosophical horizons broadened to include Chinese themes. In addition, Buddhism and Daoism offered alternative forms of religious life which ended the monopoly of the indigenous systems. Native priests did not, at first, take kindly to this competition, but after a period of contrariness and rivalry the various systems found an arrangement of cohabitation and fruitful coexistence. Typically, Buddhists dominated the religious scene, but they did not suppress the other forms. Rather, they integrated and absorbed them into their own worldview and practices by, for example, appointing their gods and spirits as guardian deities of the dharma, or maintaining a shrine to a mountain god in the compound of a Buddhist temple.

Daoism in this context was transmitted in three different venues and forms. First, it came as part of Chinese culture in general, represented in its emphasis on yin and yang, fortune-telling, the various stories and motifs of immortality, and the *Daode jing*. None of these items—with exception of the last—are specifically Daoist, but scholars of both Korea and Japan have frequently pointed to them as proof for the presence of Daoism.

Second, it came as part of the political system, in Japan influencing the role and understanding of the Tennô (emperor), in Korea leading to the establishment of formal Daoist-based state temples. This type of Daoism was immediately related to its role as state-supporting religion in the Tang dynasty; it involved a certain amount of Daoist cosmology and ordination, and also brought the worship of Daoist gods such as the Queen Mother of the West, the Northern Dipper, and the Lord of Mount Tai. However, this was still far from a full transmission of the religion.

Third, Daoism came with Korean or Japanese Buddhist monks who had traveled to China to learn more about their new religion and visited various sacred mountains and religious centers. Along with sutras and forms of meditation they acquired longevity techniques and various other practices. These techniques, then, did not remain limited to the Buddhist clergy but were adopted by the aristocracy and became part of Korean and Japanese upper-class culture, from where they spread into the wider populace. Many longevity techniques, including diets, breathing, gymnastics, massages, sexual techniques, and meditations, were transmitted in this way. In fact one of the most comprehensive medieval collections of such techniques, with ample citations from Daoist texts, was compiled in Japan: the *Ishimpô* (Essential Medical Methods) by Tamba no Yasuyori, which was presented to court in 984.

Among religious practices, the most important is the so-called Kôshin cult, which goes back to the Daoist belief—already found in the third century C.E.—that there are three corpse-worms in the human body whose main goal is to make the person sick and die. Since they are officials of the celestial administration, however, they cannot just do this on their own but must receive proper orders. They obtain such orders upon filing a report on the person's behavior—the more morally depraved the person is, the sicker they can be made. They file this report once in every sixty-day cycle, on the *kôshin* (*gengshen*) day; hence the cult's name. The actual practice involves purification exercises and a vigil during the eve of the Kôshin day, based on the assumption that the worms, like souls, can only leave the body if and when the person is asleep. It also involves a vegetarian feast, community activities, and prayers to a protective deity who will help believers. The latter is a tantric god known as the Blue-faced Vajrapani (Shômen kongô). Originally a time of confession and repentance, the Kôshin eve became a major social event in medieval Korea and Japan, and to the present day it is celebrated in some Buddhist temples.

Another merging of Daoism and Buddhism in the early period occurred through the adoption of their practices into indigenous forms of nature worship and shamanic mountain cults. Notable in Japan was Shugendô, which integrated the Buddhist goal of enlightenment, Shintô beliefs in sacred mountains, and Daoist magical and ritual practices including spells and incantations, talismans and sacred diagrams, dietary methods and exorcistic rites of empowerment. These practices are still undertaken today and form an important part of Agon-shû, one of the new new religions of Japan (founded in 1984).

The second major wave of Daoist exports into East Asia occurred in the seventeenth century and brought a strong culture of inner alchemy to Korea, and the practice of honoring and following morality books to both Korea and Japan. Partly carried by immigrants, partly encouraged by the adoption of Neo-Confucianism as state doctrine in both countries (under the Chosôn [1392–1910] in Korea and under the Tokugawa [1600–1868] in Japan), many Daoist texts arrived, were studied and interpreted, and became part of a developing tradition of inner alchemy and popular morality. Daoism was a leading way to self-cultivation and personal improvement, and continued in this role to inspire the founding of certain new religions, especially in Korea. These included the Donghak (Eastern Doctrine) religion (now called Chôndo kyo or Teaching of Heavenly Principles), founded by Choi Jaewu in 1860, and the Jûngsan kyo (Teaching of Jûngsan), founded by Kang Ilsun in 1901. Both of these Korean religions make ample use of Daoist talismans and ecstatic excursions, worship gods of the Daoist pantheon, and name immortality as their key spiritual goal.

In Vietnam, too, a new religion called Caodai arose under Daoist influence. Founded in 1921 by Ngo Minh Chien after a revelation from the creator god Caodai—the High Tower and heart of the universe. It integrates all major world religions through the notion of Caodai's dispensation to the Buddha, Laozi, Confucius, Moses, Jesus, Mohammed, and finally Ngo. In practice it combines the virtues and social consciousness of Confucianism, the precepts and vegetarianism of Buddhism, and the rituals and talismans of Daoism, with an organization patterned on the

Catholic church and guided by a central leader known as "pope." Caodai has undergone a varied fate through the twentieth century, and is still active today, especially in southern Vietnam.

Generally, therefore, Daoism in other East Asian countries has tended to be transmitted in venues other than the religion itself, has appeared only in special, selected elements, and has commonly been adopted into indigenous patterns, serving indigenous purposes. A large full-scale transmission of Daoism cannot be found; in Korea and Vietnam there were only a few Daoist temples, run by Chinese or Chinese-trained Daoist priests, and there were none in Japan. Only portions of Daoist beliefs, worldview, practices, and forms of worship were ever actively followed.

However, Daoism, especially with its longevity and talismanic techniques, exerted a pervasive and continuous influence on East Asian cultures. Daoism here cannot be dismissed, yet it is a far cry from the complete Daoist society that can be found among the Yao in southern Yunnan and northern Thailand, an ethnic group that adopted Celestial Masters Daoism as their main organizational and religious system in the twelfth century. All Yao youngsters are initiated around age seven and receive registers of protective generals; all official functions are filled by priests of high ritual standing; all major festivals and events are celebrated with Daoist rites; and all sacred texts and communications with the divine are written in classical Chinese. It is also significantly different from the active Daoist lineages found in the United States, either of Celestial Masters or Complete Perfection background.

Further Readings

Jung, Jae-Seo. 2000. "Daoism in Korea." In *Daoism Handbook*, edited by Livia Kohn, 792–820. Leiden: E. Brill.

Kohn, Livia. 1995. "Taoism in Japan: Positions and Evaluations." *Cahiers d'Extreme-Asie* 8: 389–412.

Lemoine, Jacques, and Chino Chien, eds. 1991. *The Yao of South China*. Paris: Pangu.

Masuo, Shin'ichirô. 2000. "Daoism in Japan." In *Daoism Handbook*, edited by Livia Kohn, 821–42. Leiden: E. Brill.

APPENDIX TWO

DATES OF DAOISM

Year	Chinese History	Daoism	West
BCE			
1766	**Shang Dynasty**		
1122	**Zhou Dynasty**		Iron age (ca. 1200)
			King Solomon (-932)
722	**Springs and Autumns**		Babylonian exile (722)
481	**Warring States**		Persian empire (558–330)
	Confucius (551–479		
	Mozi (c.479-438)		Socrates (-399)
	Yang Zhu (440-360)	*Daode jing* (400–350)	Plato (427–347)
		Historiographer Dan (374)	Aristotle (384–322)
	Mencius (c.371–289)	Zhuangzi (c. 370–290)	Alexander the Great (-323)
	Qu Yuan (340–278)		Rome rising (265)
221	**Qin Dynasty**		
206	**Western Han Dynasty**		
	Chuci (ab. 200)		
	Emperor Wen (179–156)	Mawangdui (168)	Book of Daniel (165)
	Dong Zhongshu (179-103)	*Huainanzi* (145)	Rome conquers Greece (146)
	Emperor Wu (140–86)	*Shiji* (104)	
	Liu Xiang (77–76)	Yan Zun (ca. 83–10 C.E.)	Julius Caesar (-44)
		First *Taiping jing* (31-7)	Augustus (33-14 CE)
6	**Interregnum**		
CE			
23	**Eastern Han Dynasty**		Crucifixion of Jesus (30)
			St. Paul (-64)
			Jewish revolt (70)
		Celestial Masters (142)	
		Taiping revelation (145)	
		Laozi ming (165)	
	Xiang Kai's memorial (166)	*Taiping jing* (166)	
	Ge Xuan (164-244)	Zhang Jue and Taiping (175)	
		Laozi bianhua jing (180)	

		Taiping Rebellion (184)	Zhang Lu under Cao Cao (215)	
220		Three Kingdoms		Mani (216–77)
			Wang Bi (226–49)	Origen (–251)
280		**W. Jin Dynasty**	Wei Huacun (251–334)	
		Xu Xun (239–92)	Guo Xiang (252–312)	
			Ge Hong (287–347)	
			Sanhuang wen (292)	
			Huahu jing (ca. 300)	
317		**E. Jin Dynasty**		
		Wang Xizhi (303–73)	Xu Mai (301–)	Emp. Constantine (312–37)
			Baopuzi (320)	Council of Nicea (325)
		Huiyuan (334-417)	Yang Xi (330–86?)	
			Xu Hui (341–)	
			Xu Huangmi (361–429)	
			Tao Kedou (–362)	
			Shangqing revelations (364–70)	
			Lingbao school (390s)	
389		**N. Wei Dynasty**		
		Sun En rebellion (399)		
		Kumârajîva (344–409)		
		Cui Hao (381–450)	Kou Qianzhi (365–448)	
			Kou revelation (415)	Rome sacked (410)
			Daoist theocracy (424–51)	St. Augustine (354–430)
			Taiping zhenjun (440)	Attila the Hun (–453)
			Louguan (ca. 470)	
			Wang Daoyi (447–510)	
		Debates (520)	Wei Jie (497–569)	St. Patrick (–461)
420		**Liu-Song Dynasty**		
			Lu Xiujing (406–77)	
			Santian neijie jing (420)	
			Lingbao catalog (437)	
479		**S. Qi Dynasty**		Franks turn Christian (493)
502		**Liang Dynasty**		
			Tao Hongjing (456–536)	
			Zhen'gao (500)	
			Daoism proscribed (504)	St. Benedict (480–547)
		Zhiyi (538–598)		Emp. Justinian (527–65)
557		**Chen/N. Zhou Dynasty**		
		Debates (570)	*Wushang biyao* (574)	
		Jizang (549–623)		
589		**Sui Dynasty**		
			Yinyuan jing (ca. 600)	
618		**Tang Dynasty**	Lord Lao miracle (620)	
		Tang Debates (621–622)	*Fengdao kejie* (620)	Muhammed (–635)

	Xuanzang return (645)		Islam in Persia (651)
		Sandong zhunang (680s)	
		Daojiao yishu (680s)	Carolingian emp. (687)
	Amoghavajra (705–75)	Sun Simiao (601–93)	
	Vajrabodhi (671–741)	Zhang Wanfu (fl. 700–742)	
	Tantra in China (706)	Princesses' ordination (711)	Islam in Turkey (717)
	Li Bo (701–62)		
	Du Fu (712–70)		
	Emperor Xuanzong (712–56)	Sima Chengzhen (647–735)	Venerable Bede (–735)
		Daode jing named classic (737)	
		Heavenly Treasure find (741)	
		Daoists as imperial family (743)	Islam in China (750)
		Wu Yun (ca. 700–87)	
	An Lushan rebellion (755)	Gu Kuang (735–814)	
	Tantra to Japan (806)		Charlemagne (800)
		Persecution of religion (845)	
		Du Guangting (850–933)	
	Zu Shu (fl. 889–904)		
907	**Five Dyn./Liao Dynasty**	Tan Zixiao (fl. 935)	
960	**N. Song/Liao Dynasty**		
		Ishimpô (984)	
		Tianxin texts found (994)	Russia Christian (989)
	Dunhuang caves closed (ca. 1008		First Millennium (1000)
		Daoist canon created (1023)	
		Yunji qiqian (1023)	Norman conquest (1066)
		Lin Lingsu (1076–1120)	Orthodox schism (1054)
	Emperor Huizong (1101–25)		First crusade (1096)
		Shenxiao school (1112)	al-Ghazali (–1111)
		Tianxin texts codified (1116)	
1126	**S. Song/Jin Dynasty**	*SOUTH:*	
		Ning Benli (1101–81)	
		Zhang Boduan (–1182)	
		Bai Yuchan (ca. 1194–1227)	
	Chinggis Khan in China (1206)	Jin Yunzhong (fl. 1224)	St. Francis (–1226)
		NORTH:	

		Wang Chongyang (1112–70)	
		Complete Perfection (1167)	
		Sun Bu'er (1119–82)	
		Wang Chuyi (1142–1217)	Maimonides (d. 1204)
		Qiu Chuji (1148–1227)	Papal schism (1207)
		Qiu travels to Khan (1219)	
		Qiu religious leader (1223)	
		Yongle Temple (1252)	Mongols in Baghdad (1252)
1260	**Yuan Dynasty**		
		Liu Yu (1257–1308)	
		Daoism persecuted (1281)	Rumi (d. 1273)
		Zhao Yizhen (–1382)	St. Thomas Aquinas (–1274)
			Dante (–1321)
			Turks in Europe (1326)
			Black Death (1348–50)
1368	**Ming Dynasty**		
	Emperor Taizu (1368–99)	Zhang Yuqing (1364–1427)	
	Yongle Emperor (1403–25)	Daoist canon (1445)	Byzantium ends (1453)
		Wang Dao (1487-1547)	America discovered (1492)
		Zhan Ruoshui (1466–1510)	
	Wang Yangming (1517–79)		Leonardo da Vinci (–1519)
	Lin Zhaoen (1517–98)		Reformation (1520)
			Mexico conquest (1521)
			St. Ignatius (1556)
		Canon supplement (1607)	Shakespeare (–1616)
			Anglican church (1634)
1644	**Qing Dynasty**		English civil war (1642)
			Galileo (–1642)
			Descartes (–1650)
			Cromwell (–1658)
			Louis XIV (1648–1715)
		"Golden Flower" (1775)	American revolution (1776)
		Daode jing trl. (ca. 1800)	French revolution (1789)
		Li Xiyue (1806–56)	
		Daozang jiyao (1820)	British rule India (1818)
	James Legge (1815–1897)		Karl Marx (1818–1983)
	Opium War (1839–1842)		Telegraph (1844)
	Taiping Rebellion (1850–1864)		Indian mutiny (1857)
		Zhao Bizhen (1860–)	

	Sun Yatsen (1866–1925) Boxer Rebellion (1900)	Donghak kyo in Korea (1860) *Daode jing* in U.S. (ca. 1900)	Einstein (1879–1955)
1911	Dunhuang caves opened (1905) **Republic of China**	Jiang Weiqiao (1872–1955)	First automobile (1903)
		Jûngsan kyo in Korea (1901) *Daozang jinghua* (1920)	World War I (1914–1918) Russian revolution (1917)
	Caodai in Vietnam (1921)	Daoist canon reprinted (1923)	
	Mao Zedong (1893–1976) Chiang Kai-Shek (1888–1975)		
1949	Japanese invasion (1937) **People's Republic of China**		WW II (1939–1945)
	Communes (1952)	Taiji quan in U.S. (1950s)	Korean War (1951–1953)
		Qigong clinics (1950s) Li Hongzhi (1952–)	Suez crisis (1956) Cuba crisis (1961)
	Great Leap Forward (1958)	Daoist canon repr.(1962)	President Kennedy (–1963)
	Cultural Revolution (1966–1976) Four Modernizations (1978)		Vietnam War (1965–1976)
	Revival of religion (1980–)	Daoist practice in U.S (1980–) Qigong boom (1980s)	
	Mawangdui excavated (1983)	Supernatural Qigong (1990s)	Soviet empire ends (1990)
	Guodian excavated (1993) Hong Kong returned (1997)	Falun dafa founded (1992) Falun dafa persecuted (1999)	Gulf War (1991) President Clinton (1992-2000)

Glossary/Index